The Story of God's Chosen Family SERIES

The Story of God's Chosen Family

God's Chosen Family as a Nation

Old Testament Study from

Saul to Malachi

Grade 6

Teacher's Manual

Rod and Staff Publishers, Inc.
P.O. Box 3, Hwy. 172, Crockett, Kentucky 41413
Telephone: (606) 522-4348

Acknowledgments

We give thanks first to God for the Holy Scriptures, "which are able to make [our students] wise unto salvation through faith which is in Christ Jesus" (2 Timothy 3:15).

God's Word is the textbook for this course. The goal of this workbook is to instill in our children a deeper appreciation for God and His Word, to broaden their understanding of Bible facts, and to guide them toward competent study and use of the Bible for themselves.

A number of brethren worked together in writing and editing the material for this study guide. Others spent many hours reviewing the material and preparing the manuscript for publication. Brother Lester Miller drew the illustrations, and Sister Barbara Schlabach illustrated the cover.

Most of the maps in this course are based on Mountain High Maps® Copyright© 1993 Digital Wisdom.

"Thou art worthy, O Lord, to receive glory and honour and power: for thou hast created all things, and for thy pleasure they are and were created" (Revelation 4:11).

Copyright, 1999

by

Rod and Staff Publishers, Inc.

P.O. Box 3, Hwy. 172, Crockett, Kentucky 41413

Printed in U.S.A.

ISBN 0-7399-0425-6

Catalog no. 17691

3   4   5   6   7   —   17   16   15   14   13   12   11   10   09   08

Table of Contents

CHAPTER FOUR: David's Family Reigns Over Judah

CHAPTER FIVE: Judah Taken Captive

CHAPTER SIX: The Jews After the Captivity

TEACHER'S INTRODUCTION

Rod and Staff Bible Series Outline

The Story of God's Chosen Family (Grades 5–8)
Grade 5: God Chooses a Family
  (Old Testament—Creation to the prophet Samuel)
Grade 6: God's Chosen Family as a Nation
  (Old Testament—Saul to Malachi)
Grade 7: God Visits His Chosen Family
  (New Testament—the Gospels and Acts)
Grade 8: God's Redeemed Family—the Church
  (New Testament—Romans to Revelation)

The Pupil's Book

Use: Workbook Versus Textbook
The pupil's book may be used as a consumable workbook or as a textbook. It is designed as a workbook, which allows the student to write answers in the book and to keep it after he completes the course. However, since most exercises are numbered or lettered, schools that prefer to reuse the books for several years may ask students to write their answers on paper.

Chapter and Lesson Divisions
The pupil's book is divided into six chapters. Each chapter has four lessons and a review. A supplementary lesson entitled "Life in Bible Times" is placed after each chapter review. A chapter (and its supplementary lesson) is intended to provide work for six weeks. Chapter tests and a final test are available in a separate booklet.

This series (The Story of God's Chosen Family, Grades 5–8) follows a chronological sequence through the Bible. This workbook begins with King Saul and ends with the period between the Old and New Testaments. The four regular lessons in each chapter follow a chronological order. Besides teaching Bible facts, these lessons help students learn to use the Bible. They have the following pattern.
  1. **Lesson Introduction**
  2. **A. Answers From the Bible**—These exercises direct the student to Bible passages for answers. This is the core section of the course and should be completed by all students.
  3. **B. Bible Word Study**—These exercises increase the student's understanding of unfamiliar words.
  4. **C. Thinking About Bible Truths**—These are questions for class discussion or additional assignment. They are often more challenging than the other exercises.
  5. **D. Learning More About the Bible**—These drawings, maps, and background information are to help students better understand Bible facts, customs, and lands.

"Life in Bible Times" Lessons
The lessons between the chapters teach about life in Bible times and give practice with using a concordance, Bible dictionary, or other Bible study help. These lessons are not essential to the chronological Bible study, but they should be completed if time permits. The oral reviews in the Teacher's Manual and the final test include questions from them, but the regular chapter reviews and tests do not.

The Teacher's Book

Oral Review

These questions are for optional use during the class period. They provide a continual review of some main points, lessening the need to review everything before the test. If you wish, you may duplicate the questions and hand them to the students for written work or for personal study.

In This Lesson

Scope

This section gives the Bible chapters or verses on which the lesson is based. Because of limited time and space, the lesson covers only a few key points rather than giving a thorough coverage of the whole Bible scope. Additional facts and themes could be drawn from the scope if time permits.

Main Events

This section provides a brief outline of main events covered in the lesson. The purpose of this course is to increase the student's factual understanding of the Bible. For this reason the course follows a chronological order through the Bible, rather than following themes or character studies. The goal is to have the student gain a working knowledge of Bible accounts, as well as to broaden his understanding of the Bible with maps, charts, sketches, and other supplementary information.

In the "Life in Bible Times" lessons, this section is titled Main Points, since these lessons do not follow the chronological series of events.

Objectives

This section gives a list of important facts or skills that students should learn.

Truths to Instill

Although the main purpose of this course is to teach Bible facts, it also provides an excellent opportunity to instill spiritual truths. Several of the main truths in each lesson are listed for your benefit. The list is not exhaustive, nor should you feel it necessary to cover all the points mentioned. Rather, the list is for your benefit, to provide inspiration and a sense of direction. Teach as the Lord directs, with truths He has instilled in your heart.

Answer Key

A copy of the pupil's page is provided, with the answers given in colored ink. Teachers should use their own judgment when deciding whether an answer is correct. Vague or incomplete answers will not suffice. When exact answers can easily be found in the Bible, do not give credit for guesses based on the student's previous Bible knowledge. In certain cases, however, some variation is permissible.

The pupils are instructed to write complete answers for the questions with long blanks. A complete answer is more than one or two words. However, since schools and pupils vary, you will need to decide exactly what constitutes a complete answer. Perhaps you will want your pupils to write complete sentences for these answers. Be sure your pupils understand what you expect of them. The pupils' wording of these answers will vary. Therefore, unless a longer answer is needed for clarity, the Answer Key gives brief answers. The pupils' answers should include what is given in the Answer Key.

Sometimes the Answer Key gives several options for an answer or has some other directions for the teacher to consider in relation to a question. If this requires too much space to fit in the Pupil reduction, two arrows (>>) direct you to look in the margin for the additional answers or further direction.

Notes

Along the right margins are additional directions and notes that you may find interesting and helpful in teaching. The directions are in italic type, with the first line indented. The notes are preceded by bullets.

Note for Schools Outside the United States

To keep this workbook simple, metric measures have not been included in the lessons. However, the table of measures in the back of the pupil's book gives metric equivalents, and the answer key gives answers in metric units. If you normally use the metric system, tell your students to give all answers involving measure in metric form.

Lesson Plans

Since this course may be used in a wide variety of situations and schedules, no detailed lesson plan is provided for each lesson. However, many schools have Bible classes two or three times a week. You may find the following suggestions helpful.

Two-Day Plan

First Day
—Read or discuss the introduction together.
—Read at least some of the lesson verses in class.
—Assign "Answers From the Bible."

Second Day
—Discuss "Thinking About Bible Truths."
—Discuss "Learning More About the Bible."
—Assign "Bible Word Study" and "Learning More About the Bible." Also assign "Thinking About Bible Truths" if you did not complete this part in class.

Three-Day Plan

First Day
—Read or discuss the introduction together.
—Read some of the lesson verses in class.
—Assign some of "Answers From the Bible."

Second Day
—Read more of the lesson verses in class.
—Assign the rest of "Answers From the Bible."
—Assign "Bible Word Study."

Third Day
—Discuss "Thinking About Bible Truths."
—Discuss "Learning More About the Bible."
—Assign "Learning More About the Bible." Also assign "Thinking About Bible Truths" if you did not complete this part in class.

Time Line: The Human Register

Learning about the Bible stretches a child's concept of time. Suddenly "a long time" as a child sees it becomes longer and longer. Very easily it becomes too long for him to comprehend.

A child needs the help of his parents and teachers to avoid stretching his concept of time to the point where time becomes meaningless, and ancient events separate from the present to drift into the realm of mystery-shrouded legend. A child with this concept of the Bible will see its stories in an unnatural light. Even the miracles recorded in the Bible will lose their significance for him. Anything could happen, the child believes, in a world and age divorced from reality.

One purpose of this Bible course is to counteract such an idea. Children must learn to accept without question that the Creation and other Bible events are historical facts. A supplementary wall chart, The Human Register, has been designed to give substance to a child's concept of time. It should help children comprehend that every person, from the time of Adam to the present, lived on the earth we live on, breathed the air we breathe, drank the water we drink, and was born and died in our real, historical age. The stronger the link between Bible times and our time in a child's understanding, the better he will grasp Bible truths. The Bible will not be like a fairy tale to him. It will be like a true story told to him by his parents or grandparents about things that happened before he was born.

The Human Register may be displayed in an unbroken line along one side of your classroom. Before beginning this course, show and discuss with your students the entire scope of time. This will introduce the Human Register as a framework onto which other Bible facts learned throughout the course may be placed.

The Human Register continues to the present to show students the brevity of the modern age, to be a help in making comparisons, and to give them a realistic grasp of the length of various time periods in the Bible. The life of Noah, for example, was as long as the time from the Vikings' day to the present.

The Human Register uses pictures in an attempt to fix impressions. Symbols such as the bulrushes around Moses, the star of Bethlehem, and the Viking ship mark certain events to make them more readily identifiable.

The dates that appear on the Human Register will not agree with all other Bible chronologies. Certain periods of Bible chronology are unclear, and it does not seem possible to state with certainty exact dates in early history. The focus is not on precise chronology, but on the scope of human history.

After 967 B.C. (the fourth year of Solomon's reign), the dates match those generally accepted in most reference books. The 480 years of 1 Kings 6:1 are used to date the Exodus at 1447 B.C. If the 430 years of Exodus 12:40 include the time of Abraham and Isaac, as well as Jacob's sojourn in Egypt, Abraham's call came in about 1877 B.C. The data given in Genesis 5:1–12:4 and Acts 7:4 give approximate dates of 2304 B.C. for the Flood and 3960 B.C. for the Creation.

Some people prefer Philip Mauro's system for dating the judges and early kings. (See *The Wonders of Bible Chronology*, by Mauro.) According to this view, the 480 years of 1 Kings 6:1 include only the years when God ruled through godly men. An additional 114 years of oppression and usurpation are added to these 480 years, placing the Exodus at about 1561 B.C. and the Creation at about 4074 B.C. This harmonizes well with Acts 13:20 and with the total years for the individual judges. However, this system also raises some questions, especially regarding Jair's judgeship and the 300 years of Judges 11:26, the lack of allowance for gaps or overlaps, and the assumption that Eli became judge immediately after forty years of Philistine oppression. The Human Register follows the more traditional interpretation of 1 Kings 6:1, even though that leaves open the question of Acts 13:20.

Bible Memorization

Bible memorization should have an important place in a Christian school. If everyone knows a passage well, reciting it together can be a pleasant, worshipful exercise. With enough practice, any class can learn to recite Bible verses fluently and clearly. It is unfortunate when students see Bible memorization as drudgery.

Hints for Bible Memorization

1. Teachers can inspire enthusiasm for memorizing by being enthusiastic themselves about learning new verses.
2. Assign a reasonable number of verses for memorization. Students should learn only as many verses as can be effectively drilled in class. Memorizing a few verses well is better than trying to learn a large number without mastering them.
3. Select verses that the students can understand and relate to. Explain each passage as meaningfully as you can.
4. Have short, frequent classes for Bible memorization, possibly as the first thing after the morning devotional or after the lunch break.
5. You may wish to copy the day's assignment onto the chalkboard, writing the passage in lines like the lines of a poem. After the students have read the first lines and recited them with their eyes closed, begin erasing the lines.
6. Group memorization is a great help. It offers variety and serves as an effective stimulant. But individual testing, both oral and written, also has its place.
7. Do not assign Bible memorization as a punishment.
8. Review previously learned verses throughout the school year. During the last few weeks of the year, the entire Bible memory program could be devoted to review.
9. Students may learn to memorize a series of verses by "counting fingers," associating each verse with a finger.
10. If you are teaching more than one grade, you may wish to assign the same memory passage to everyone in the room.

Suggested Memory Passages

The following suggestions may be helpful to you in selecting Bible passages for memorization.

For each chapter in this course, three Scripture passages are given. There are also three thematic selections of verses, arranged according to the theme of the chapter being studied. From these six suggestions, which are of various lengths, choose the one you feel is best suited to your class. Divide your selected passage or theme into five weekly assignments, with modification as needed.

As much as is feasible, the thematic selections have been arranged to avoid awkward transitions of person and tense. If you use these selections, you may find it helpful to type them so that the students have them all together. Typing the verses after the following pattern will make it easier for the students to memorize them line by line.

> Psalm 15:1, 2
> LORD, who shall abide in thy tabernacle?
> who shall dwell in thy holy hill?
> He that walketh uprightly,
>   and worketh righteousness,
>   and speaketh the truth in his heart.

Choose one group of verses for each chapter.

Chapter One—Israel Becomes a Kingdom

Passage Selections
1. Psalm 51
2. Proverbs 3:1–18
3. Psalm 34

Thematic Selections: Words of David
4. (14 verses) Psalm 15:1–5; Psalm 18:1–3; Psalm 23:1–6
5. (18 verses) Psalm 16; Psalm 19:1, 2, 7–11
6. (20 verses) Psalm 27:1; Psalm 61:1–4; Psalm 62:5–8; Psalm 103:1–6, 15–19

Chapter Two—The Northern Tribes Set Up a Separate Kingdom

Passage Selections
1. James 5
2. 1 Kings 18:21–39
3. Ephesians 2

Thematic Selections: God Speaks to Fallen Man
4. (17 verses) 1 Kings 18:22, 23, 26, 30, 38, 39; Isaiah 44:24; Isaiah 45:5, 6; Psalm 107:1–8
5. (17 verses) Psalm 100:3; Psalm 96:3–7; 1 Kings 18:22, 23, 26, 30, 36–40; Isaiah 12:6; Isaiah 52:10
6. (19 verses) 1 Kings 18:17, 18, 21–26, 30–40

Chapter Three—Israel's Downfall

Passage Selections
1. Galatians 5:22–6:10
2. Hebrews 10:19–39
3. Psalm 27

Thematic Selections: God's Works
4. (18 verses) 2 Kings 2:9–14, 23, 24; 2 Kings 5:9, 10, 14, 15; 2 Kings 6:1, 2, 5, 6; Psalm 33: 4, 5
5. (17 verses) Psalm 25:10; 2 Kings 2:19–22; 2 Kings 4:1–7; 2 Kings 6:15–17; Psalm 46:10, 11
6. (19 verses) 2 Kings 2:9, 14, 15; Psalm 40:5; Psalm 86:8; Psalm 92:4, 5; Psalm 111:1–10; 2 Kings 13:20, 21

Chapter Four—David's Family Reigns Over Judah

Passage Selections
1. 1 John 2:1–17
2. Isaiah 55
3. Matthew 13:1–23

Thematic Selections: God Stands With Those Who Serve Him
4. (13 verses) Isaiah 37:21–23, 33–36; Isaiah 26:3, 4; Isaiah 24:23; Isaiah 33:22; Daniel 4:3, 35
5. (15 verses) 2 Kings 22:1, 2; 2 Kings 23:1–7, 21; Leviticus 26:1; Deuteronomy 27:15a; Psalm 97:7; Isaiah 42:17; 1 John 5:21
6. (16 verses) 2 Kings 22:1, 2; 2 Kings 23:1, 2, 6, 12, 14, 19–21; Psalm 44:20, 21; Psalm 97:5–7; 1 John 5:21

Chapter Five—Judah Taken Captive

Passage Selections
1. Lamentations 3:22–41
2. 2 Timothy 2:1–15
3. Daniel 1

Thematic Selections: Examples of Faithfulness
4. (16 verses) Daniel 3:1, 4–6, 8, 9, 12, 13, 16–18, 21, 24, 25, 27, 28
5. (17 verses) Daniel 1:8; Daniel 2:1, 2, 27, 28, 47, 48; Daniel 6:4, 5, 19–23; Daniel 7:2, 13, 14
6. (16 verses) Esther 2:16, 17; Esther 3:8, 9; Esther 4:13–16; Esther 7:1–6, 10; Esther 9:5

Chapter Six—The Jews After the Captivity

Passage Selections
1. Psalm 103
2. Haggai 1:3–13; 2:1–9
3. Revelation 22

Thematic Selections: Repentance and Restoration
4. (10 verses) Ezra 10:1–5, 9–12, 17
5. (15 verses) Ezra 7:6, 8, 10; Ezra 9:1–6; Ezra 10:1, 9–12, 17
6. (17 verses) Nehemiah 4:6–9, 14; Nehemiah 8:2, 5, 6; Nehemiah 9:2; Psalm 119:1–7; 1 John 5:3

Teaching Subjective Thinking Skills

What Is Subjective Thinking?

Two basic kinds of questions are used in teaching. The most common is the objective question, which asks about a fact. This type of question tests recall and research skills, but does not necessarily test understanding. For instance, an objective question might ask how many legions of angels Jesus could have called to help Him. The student can read Matthew 26:53 and answer, "More than twelve legions." However, just because he has given the fact does not guarantee that he understands his answer. He may have no idea what a legion is.

The other type of question is the subjective question, which requires the student to apply facts he has learned and draw conclusions from them. A person who thinks carefully about Matthew 26:53 will realize several things that are not stated. First, he will see that Jesus submitted to the mob in the Garden because He wanted to. He had the ability to overpower them, but He did not use it. Second, Jesus could have refused to go to Calvary. Subjective questions guide the student to make this kind of conclusion.

Subjective thinking should not be allowed to become mere fantasy. It is based on fact and stays within the bounds of logic and reason.

Suppose you are traveling down a highway in a car. As you pass a house, you see a large, angry dog chasing a man down the driveway toward his car. What happened after you were past? The objective answer is that you do not know. However, you do have some facts that help you reach a probable conclusion. The dog was angry. The man was running to get away from him. A car was waiting at the end of the drive. You know that angry dogs can be vicious. Given these facts, which of the following is the most likely conclusion to the incident?

1. The man stops at his car to pat the dog and to praise him for being a good watchdog.
2. The dog chases the man all the way to his car, biting his leg as he frantically tries to open the door.
3. Just as the dog reaches him, the man sprouts wings and soars away to safety.

The first answer is not reasonable, given the facts you know about the situation. The second one is the most likely. The third is fantastic—men do not sprout wings. Subjective reasoning is the process that helps us reach conclusions like this.

Why Do We Need to Teach Subjective Thinking?

Everyone does some subjective thinking. However, some people have not learned to think logically and subjectively at the same time. Because of this, they often jump to wild conclusions. At other times, they reach wrong conclusions because they have not taken time to learn all the related facts. Such people need training in how to use subjective thinking properly.

Other people allow the reasoning process to replace faith. They decide that they will not believe anything that they cannot reason through. Since they cannot understand Bible miracles, they refuse to believe them. This is the opposite extreme from jumping to conclusions, but it is even more serious because it destroys faith in God and His Word. Such people also need training in how to use subjective thinking properly.

We must teach our students to avoid these overreactions. They must learn that faith in God and the Bible is a necessary part of the reasoning process. It is a fact that God is not tied to the same limitations that we are. On the other hand, God overrules natural laws only for special purposes, and His character always limits Him from doing evil.

A person who has learned to think properly knows that what he does today will affect his future. By applying verses such as "Love not the world, neither the things that are in the world," he realizes that television, tobacco smoking, and a host of other modern evils are wrong, even though the Bible does not specifically mention them. Subjective thinking trains a person to look at life realistically, and prepares him to cope with it. As a teacher, you have an obligation to teach your students good thinking skills.

How Can We Teach Subjective Thinking?

This course includes a number of subjective questions. Since subjective thinking may still be difficult for some sixth graders, it is important to take time to introduce these questions. Otherwise, some students may blindly guess at answers without understanding how to reach a reasonable conclusion.

Most subjective questions in this course are multiple-choice exercises. This gives the student a starting point for his evaluation. Teach him to read the question carefully, taking time to understand what it is asking. Then he should evaluate each possible answer, comparing it with the facts that he knows about the situation. If he follows this process, he should usually be able to eliminate the wrong answers.

If he thinks that two answers could be right, he must ask himself, "Which of the two is the better answer?" At this age level, most of the questions have only one correct answer, but some questions require the choice of the best answer. At first some students may not understand how a correct answer can be the wrong one, but explain that no answer is really right if a better answer is available. This is an important skill for every Christian to learn and practice.

It may take some time for your students to develop subjective thinking skills, but do not omit those questions. Instead, discuss them together. Most students can eventually learn the necessary skills.

CHAPTER ONE

Israel Becomes a Kingdom

My soul, wait thou only upon God;
for my expectation is from him.
He only is my rock and my salvation:
he is my defence; I shall not be moved.
In God is my salvation and my glory:
the rock of my strength,
and my refuge, is in God.
Trust in him at all times; ye people,
pour out your heart before him:
God is a refuge for us. Selah.
Psalm 62:5–8

TIME LINE—Chapter One

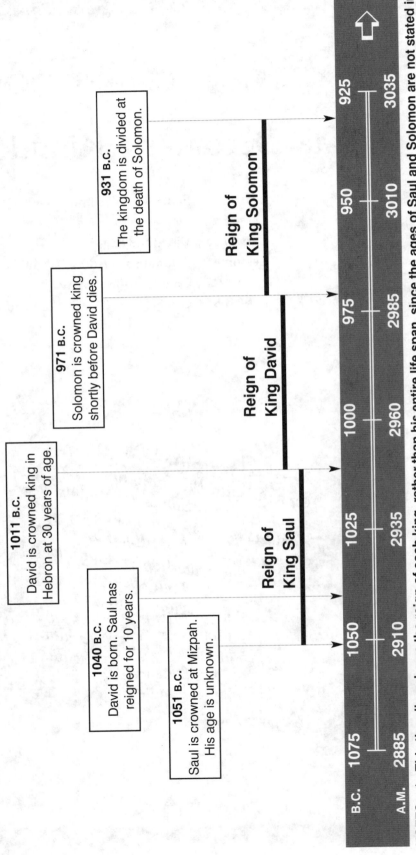

| 1040 B.C.
David is born. Saul has
reigned for 10 years. | 1011 B.C.
David is crowned king in
Hebron at 30 years of age. | 971 B.C.
Solomon is crowned king
shortly before David dies. | 931 B.C.
The kingdom is divided at
the death of Solomon. |

1051 B.C.
Saul is crowned at Mizpah.
His age is unknown.

**Reign of
King Saul**

**Reign of
King David**

**Reign of
King Solomon**

| B.C. | 1075 | 1050 | 1025 | 1000 | 975 | 950 | 925 |
| A.M. | 2885 | 2910 | 2935 | 2960 | 2985 | 3010 | 3035 |

NOTES: * This time line shows the reign of each king, rather than his entire life span, since the ages of Saul and Solomon are not stated in
the Bible. All dates are approximate.

* Each of these three kings reigned for forty years.

9

Lesson 1. Saul—From Humble Son to Proud King

This Bible study book covers the period between Samuel and the New Testament, about one thousand years. During the first part of this period, God's chosen family was ruled by kings. You will meet Israel's first king in this lesson.

Saul was the tallest man in Israel, but at first he did not try to draw attention to himself. In fact, when the Israelites came together to crown him king, Saul was too bashful to appear. The Israelites had to ask God where he was hiding.

After the ceremony, Saul went back home to his farm. Imagine that—a *king* herding oxen! God could use a humble king like that.

Not long after Saul became king, the Ammonites encamped against an Israelite city. The Spirit of God came upon Saul, and with God's help he won a great victory over the Ammonites. Then the Israelites all gathered to strengthen the kingdom and to hold a great feast in Saul's honor.

When Saul was humble, God helped him overpower mighty enemies. But after Saul defeated the Ammonites, he met an enemy he did not conquer. This enemy was pride in his own heart.

Saul became proud and began to do foolish things. He decided to offer a sacrifice to God instead of waiting for Samuel, as Samuel had told him to do. Later he disobeyed God's command and then blamed the people for his sin. He became jealous of David after David received praise for killing Goliath. The more Saul allowed pride to rule him, the more foolish he became.

God sent a message to Saul through the prophet Samuel: "When thou wast *little in thine own sight,* wast thou not made the head of the tribes of Israel? . . . Wherefore then didst thou not obey the voice of the LORD, . . . and didst evil in the sight of the LORD? . . . The LORD hath rent the kingdom of Israel from thee this day, and hath given it to a neighbour of thine, that is better than thou" (1 Samuel 15:17, 19, 28).

God looks for humble men to lead his people.

A. ANSWERS FROM THE BIBLE

Israel's First King

When Samuel was old, he appointed his two sons to judge the Israelites. However, his sons were not honest judges like Samuel. They accepted bribes and overlooked wrongdoing. The Israelites used this as an excuse to ask Samuel to appoint a king over their nation. They no longer wanted God to be their king. They wanted to have an earthly king as the nations around them had.

Samuel was displeased. He asked God what he should do, and God told him to anoint Saul king of Israel. But God also told Samuel to warn the people that having a king would bring them many problems.

✎ *Open your Bible to 1 Samuel and study the verses that go with each section. Fill in the short blanks with single words. Whenever possible, use exact words from the Bible. Write complete answers for the questions with long blanks. For multiple-choice questions, circle the letter of the correct answer.*

1 Samuel 10:17–27

1. Samuel had already privately anointed Saul, but God wanted all Israel to know whom He had chosen to be their first king. First God showed that the king would come from the tribe of _____Benjamin_____, next He selected the family of _____Matri_____, and finally He chose _____Saul_____, the son of Kish.

- The wording "was taken" in verses 20 and 21 suggests that Samuel probably used the lot to select Saul. Joshua 7:16–18 describes a similar occasion. Samuel already knew whom God had chosen, but the public selection confirmed to the people that Saul was God's choice.

Lesson 1

In This Lesson

Scope: 1 Samuel 10–16

Main Events
- The people ask for a king, and God chooses Saul.
- Saul organizes Israel and defeats the Ammonites.
- Saul offers a sacrifice himself instead of waiting for Samuel.
- Saul defeats the Amalekites, but he does not obey God's command to completely destroy them.
- God rejects Saul and sends Samuel to anoint David king.

Objectives
- The students should know
  —why the Israelites wanted a king. (They wanted to be like the nations around them instead of letting God be their king.)
  —how Saul's humility made him a good king, but how his pride and stubbornness destroyed his usefulness. (See Part A, numbers 5–18.)
  —why Saul failed as a king. (See Part C.)
  —how Saul seriously disobeyed God twice. (He offered a sacrifice himself instead of waiting for Samuel, and did not completely destroy the Amalekites and all their cattle as God had commanded him to do.)

2. Which statement tells why Saul hid when the people wanted to make him king?

  a. Saul was too proud to let Samuel anoint him.

  b. Saul refused to be made king of Israel.

  (c.) Saul was a humble man at this time.

3. What did the people shout when they first looked upon their tall new king? _____

  _"God save the king."_____

4. a. Who despised Saul? _the children of Belial_____

  b. What did they refuse to do? _They refused to bring presents for Saul._____

  c. What did Saul do about this refusal? _Saul held his peace._____

Saul's First Battle

After Saul was chosen to be king, he went back home to help on the farm. But his peaceful life did not last long. During the first year of his reign, the Israelites in Jabesh-gilead faced a serious threat.

1 Samuel 11:1–13

5. The men of (a) _____Jabesh (gilead)_____ wanted to make a covenant with the Ammonites. But the

  Ammonites said that they would make no covenant with them unless they could pluck out their

  (b) _____right_____ _____eyes_____. This would bring shame to all Israel.

6. Saul heard about the Ammonites' threat one evening as he came from the _____field_____

  with the herd.

7. The _____Spirit_____ _of_ _____God_____ came upon Saul when he heard the message.

8. Saul quickly sent out a call to the Israelites, and a total of _____330,000_____ men from Israel

  and Judah arrived to help fight the Ammonites.

9. After the battle, some Israelites wanted to kill the men who had disrespected _____Saul_____.

Samuel gathered the people again and warned them not to turn away from God. The LORD sent thunder and rain that day, even though it usually did not rain during the time of wheat harvest (1 Samuel 12:16–19). The people understood that the LORD did not want them to follow their king instead of Him.

Saul Disobeys God

1 Samuel 13:5–14

Saul chose three thousand men to serve in his regular army. Jonathan took one thousand of these men and attacked a Philistine garrison. This angered the Philistines, and they prepared to attack Israel. Saul also prepared to fight. But Samuel told Saul to wait for him to offer a sacrifice before Israel went to battle.

10. How long did Saul wait for Samuel? _seven days_____

11. What excuse did Saul give for offering the sacrifice before Samuel arrived? _Saul said that the____

  _people had scattered from him, and that Samuel had not come._____

12. What punishment did Samuel pronounce upon Saul for his disobedience? _Samuel told Saul that__

  _the kingdom would be given to another man._____

- The meaning of 1 Samuel 13:1 is somewhat obscure, but apparently the events in 1 Samuel 13 took place early in Saul's reign. If this is true, Jonathan must have been much older than David, since Jonathan was already an army captain. David was only thirty years old at the end of Saul's reign.

- The students should memorize the names of the Old Testament books. They will need to know the spelling and order of the Books of Moses for the Chapter 1 Test.

Truths to Instill

- "Pride goeth before destruction, and an haughty spirit before a fall" (Proverbs 16:18).
  —Pride destroys a man's usefulness. When Saul was humble, God anointed him king and helped him defeat the Ammonites. As a humble man, Saul dealt wisely with critics and gained the people's confidence. But when Saul became proud, God rejected him.
  —Popularity leads to pride if one takes credit to himself. Contrast what Saul and David each did with their popularity.
  —Unthankfulness fosters pride. Saul forgot who had helped him win his victories.

✎ Write true *or* false. *Correct each false statement on the lines after the sentence.*

1 Samuel 15:1–3, 7–9

This account clearly shows Saul's disregard for God's commandments. It also shows that God rejects those who refuse to obey His instructions. Although Saul did not realize it, this was his last chance to correct his previous mistakes.

_____true_____ 13. The Amalekites had fought against the Israelites before Saul's time. _____

_____false_____ 14. Saul and the people obeyed God's orders in their battle with the Amalekites. _Saul and the people *spared Agag and all the good animals* in their battle with the Amalekites._

1 Samuel 15:13–23

_____true_____ 15. Saul tried to cover up his disobedience by saying that he had obeyed. _____

_____true_____ 16. Saul tried to shift the blame for his disobedience to others. _____

_____false_____ 17. Samuel said that sacrifice to God is more important than obedience. _____
Samuel said that *obedience* to God is more important than *sacrifice*.

_____true_____ 18. God rejected Saul because Saul had rejected God's word. _____

Samuel Anoints a New King

When Samuel pronounced God's judgment on Saul, he also told Saul that he would never see him again. This was a sign that God had completely departed from Saul. But Samuel still loved Saul, and he mourned for him until God told him that it was time to stop.

God had already planned that David would replace Saul. We do not know how old David was when Samuel anointed him. He was evidently quite young, yet he was old enough that God's Spirit came on him after leaving Saul. Perhaps David was in his teens.

1 Samuel 16:1–13

_____false_____ 19. Samuel did not want to go to Bethlehem, because he was afraid of the Bethlehemites. _Samuel did not want to go to Bethlehem, because he was afraid of *Saul*._

_____false_____ 20. The elders of Bethlehem rejoiced when they saw Samuel come. _The elders of Bethlehem *trembled* when they saw Samuel come._

_____true_____ 21. Samuel thought Eliab would surely be the new king. _____

_____true_____ 22. David was out caring for the sheep when Samuel came to Bethlehem. _____

To help avoid confusion while checking, you might want to have the students orally correct the false statements in numbers 13–22 in class.

In the rewritten sentences for numbers 13–22, the corrections are in italics. The pupil's sentences may vary somewhat.

✎ *Circle the letter of the correct answer.*

23. Eliab's outward features made him appear well qualified to be the next king. Which statement tells why God chose David instead?

   a. God thought that David's outward features were even more outstanding than Eliab's.

   (b.) God looked into David's heart and saw that he would make a better king than Eliab.

   c. God knew that by the time Saul died, Eliab would be too old to be king.

B. BIBLE WORD STUDY

✎ *Match these definitions with the Bible words or phrases on the right. All references are from 1 Samuel.*

_e_ 1. To control or rule harshly (10:18)	a. reproach
_h_ 2. To ask (10:22)	b. salute
_j_ 3. A Bible term meaning "persons of little worth; wicked men" (10:27)	c. covenant
_c_ 4. A binding agreement (11:1)	d. utterly
_a_ 5. Something that brings shame or disgrace (11:2)	e. oppress
_i_ 6. A delay or rest (11:3)	f. strait
_f_ 7. Great need or distress (13:6)	g. supplication
_b_ 8. To greet (13:10)	h. enquire (inquire)
_g_ 9. A humble request (13:12)	i. respite
_d_ 10. Completely (15:3)	j. children of Belial

When LORD is written with all capital letters in our English Old Testaments, it stands for *Jehovah,* one of God's names. When *Lord* is written with only the first letter capitalized, it is a title of respect, meaning *Master.* This workbook uses LORD for *Jehovah* to help you remember the difference between the use of LORD and *Lord* in the Old Testament.

11. Which of these two terms did Samuel use in 1 Samuel 13:13? _____ LORD (Jehovah) _____

12. Using the information above, give the meaning of the first phrase in Psalm 8:9. _____

   O Jehovah our Master

C. THINKING ABOUT BIBLE TRUTHS

Why Was King Saul a Failure?

King Saul was a tragic failure. He was rejected by God, his kingdom was taken from him, his sons were killed by the Philistines, and in the end he was wounded so seriously that he fell on his own sword to avoid being captured. When he died, his country was in shambles and under Philistine oppression.

However, it could have easily been different. God had lifted Saul up and appointed him king. While King Saul followed God, God supported him and blessed him. He could have reigned successfully and died in peace, leaving behind a glorious kingdom for his son. But he did not. This exercise will help you to see why Saul died a failure.

1. Read Proverbs 16:18. King Saul had a haughty spirit. He thought that his own ideas were as good as God's commands. He had _____pride_____ in his heart that led to his _____destruction_____. If Saul had stayed humble and had listened to God, these things would not have happened to him.

2. Read 1 Samuel 28:18. In this verse Samuel told Saul that God would punish him because he did not _____obey_____ God's voice. Saul could have avoided this punishment and failure.

3. Read 1 Samuel 15:23. King Saul was guilty of rebellion and _____stubbornness_____. Because of these sins, he rejected the word of God, and God rejected him. Saul should have listened to God's commands and Samuel's advice instead of doing his own will.

4. Read Proverbs 28:13. If King Saul had willingly _____confessed_____ his sins and _____forsaken_____ them, God would have had mercy on him. Instead, he tried to cover them and denied that he had done anything wrong. Even when he finally admitted his sin, he did not truly repent of it. Because of this, God could not bless Saul, and he died a failure.

D. LEARNING MORE ABOUT THE BIBLE

Old Testament Books

✎ *The thirty-nine books of the Old Testament are often divided into five groups. Memorize the Old Testament books and their divisions. You will need to know the order and the spelling of the Books of Moses for the Chapter 1 Test.*

The Books of Moses
Genesis
Exodus
Leviticus
Numbers
Deuteronomy

The Books of History
Joshua
Judges
Ruth
1 & 2 Samuel
1 & 2 Kings
1 & 2 Chronicles
Ezra
Nehemiah
Esther

The Books of Poetry
Job
Psalms
Proverbs
Ecclesiastes
Song of Solomon

The Major Prophets
Isaiah
Jeremiah
Lamentations
Ezekiel
Daniel

The Minor Prophets
Hosea
Joel
Amos
Obadiah
Jonah
Micah
Nahum
Habakkuk
Zephaniah
Haggai
Zechariah
Malachi

Review the Old Testament books and their divisions together in class as needed. The students will need to know the order and the spelling of the Books of Moses for the Chapter 1 Test.

Music in Old Testament Times

Saul met a company of prophets singing and prophesying.

They used a psaltery, a tabret, a pipe, and a harp (1 Samuel 10:5).

Men and women singers provided by far the most important and most beautiful music of Old Testament times. No instrument has ever been made that sounds better than the human voice. The messages of the Old Testament songs were what pleased God. The New Testament says that we should sing and make melody in our hearts.

1. What Old Testament book includes 150 songs? (Clue: It is the longest book of the Bible.)   Psalms

2. On what occasion did Moses and the Israelites sing? (Exodus 14:26–15:1) _____

   after the LORD had delivered them through the Red Sea

3. David employed 288 singers (1 Chronicles 25:7). How did the singers help to dedicate the temple?

   (2 Chronicles 5:12, 13)   They stood at the east end of the altar and praised and thanked the LORD.

   _____

4. What pleases God more: music from instruments or singing by people who love Him? (Read and

   think about 1 Corinthians 13:1 and Ephesians 5:19.)   singing by people who love Him

5. Read Psalm 100 and list two reasons the psalmist gave for praising God.

   a.   —The LORD is God.   —He has made us.   —The LORD is good.

   b.   —We are His people (and the sheep of His pasture).
        —His mercy is everlasting.   —His truth endureth to all generations.

The priests and other leaders used trumpets made of rams' horns (1 Samuel 13:3).

David played a harp for King Saul (1 Samuel 16:23).

15

Lesson 2. David the Fugitive

In Lesson 1 you saw how the Israelites demanded a king like the kings of the nations around them. God granted their request and chose King Saul, who was tall and handsome. He looked the way that the people thought a king should look. But Saul had weaknesses that kept him from being the kind of king God wanted him to be. In the end, he failed both God and his people.

When God appointed a king to replace Saul, He was not looking for a man of outstanding appearance. Instead, He was looking for someone that He knew had the kind of character a godly king needed.

David had many good characteristics. He was willing to stay at home and herd sheep while his brothers did more important things. When his older brother accused him falsely, David did not become angry.

David was also brave. When a lion and a bear threatened the sheep, he killed them. When Goliath threatened the Israelite army and everyone else was afraid, including big, strong King Saul, David had faith that God would be with him. He defeated the giant with a sling and a stone.

David became a mighty soldier, but he did not become proud. Even after living in the king's house for a while, he was willing to go back home and herd his father's sheep.

Because of his own failure, King Saul became jealous of David. God allowed him to persecute David so much that David became a fugitive. Perhaps God wanted to use these trials to help David become a better man. God also may have been testing David to see how he would react when everything seemed to go against him.

David was not perfect. He sinned on several occasions, but each time he admitted his errors and made them right. God could use a man like David.

Note for schools outside the United States. To keep this workbook simple, metric measures have not been included in the lessons. However, the table of measures in the back of the workbook gives metric equivalents, and the answer key gives answers in metric units. If you normally use the metric system, tell your students to give all answers involving measure in metric form.

A. ANSWERS FROM THE BIBLE

David and Goliath

According to 1 Samuel 16, David had spent some time at King Saul's home before he killed Goliath. An evil spirit had afflicted Saul after God rejected him, and David was able to give Saul relief by playing a harp. Samuel had already anointed David as the next king of Israel, but most people did not know it yet. Apparently David had returned home for quite a while before he offered to fight Goliath, because King Saul did not seem to recognize him.

1 Samuel 17:1–11, 32–37

The Bible calls David a youth and a stripling. Evidently he was too young to be in the army, but he had more faith and courage than the grown men.

1. What did Goliath challenge the Israelites to do? _____
   <u>He challenged them to send a man to fight against him.</u>

2. How did Saul and the Israelite soldiers feel about Goliath's challenge?_____
   <u>They were dismayed and greatly afraid.</u>

3. How did David respond to Goliath's challenge? _____
   <u>David offered to fight with Goliath.</u>

Lesson 2

Oral Review

These optional questions are for use during the class period. If you wish, you may duplicate the questions and hand them to the students for written work or for personal study.

The numbers in brackets tell which lessons are being reviewed.

1. Why did Saul hide when the people wanted to make him king? [1] **Saul was a humble man.**
2. Why did Saul gather the Israelites to fight against Ammon? [1] **The Ammonites were threatening to pluck out the right eyes of the men of Jabesh.**
3. What did Samuel say was more important than sacrifice? [1] **obedience**
4. What does the LORD look at rather than just the outward appearance of a person? [1] **the person's heart**
5. What are the five Books of Moses? (Be sure you know the correct order and spelling.) [1] **Genesis, Exodus, Leviticus, Numbers, Deuteronomy**
6. What pleases God more: music from instruments or singing by people who love Him? [1] **singing by people who love Him**

4. Why did David feel so confident that God would give him victory? _____

　God had helped him kill a lion and a bear, and he trusted God to help him kill Goliath too.

1 Samuel 17:38–51

5. David refused to wear Saul's armor because
    a. he knew that a sling was a better weapon than a sword.
    b. he had not practiced using the armor.
    c. he did not want to wear anything that belonged to Saul.

6. Goliath felt insulted when
    a. he saw a boy coming to meet him.
    b. David mentioned the God of Israel.
    c. no Israelites dared to come and meet him.

7. David's testimony to Goliath shows that
    a. he was not afraid of anything.
    b. he trusted completely in God.
    c. he was ready to die for his country.

David and Saul

David was very popular after he killed Goliath. Saul asked him to live in the king's house again. Jonathan, the king's son, became his close friend. Everyone in the country looked up to him, and Saul made him a captain in the army in spite of his young age. However, things soon changed for the worse.

1 Samuel 18:1–12

8. Jonathan gave his robe to David because
    a. David and Jonathan were very good friends.
    b. David did not have any good clothes to wear.
    c. Saul planned to send David back home.

9. King Saul was very angry when David
    a. refused to obey his instructions.
    b. wanted to marry his daughter.
    c. became more popular than he was.

10. While David was playing his harp for Saul,
    a. a good spirit from the LORD came upon Saul.
    b. Saul threw a javelin at David.
    c. Saul asked David to prophesy.

11. Saul suffered fits of strange behavior and discouragement. The Bible says that
    a. Saul had a mental illness.
    b. the LORD had left Saul.
    c. Saul should have been treated more kindly.

In This Lesson

Scope: 1 Samuel 17–31; 2 Samuel 1

Main Events

- David kills Goliath.
- Saul, consumed with jealousy, tries to destroy David.
- David becomes a fugitive. During this time he spares Saul's life.
- Saul consults a witch and loses his life in battle.

Objectives

- The students should know
    —the story of David and Goliath. (See Part A, numbers 1–7.)
    —why Saul hated David and tried to kill him. (David became more popular than Saul.)
    —how David showed respect for Saul. (He refused to kill Saul.)
    —why Saul went to a witch for direction. (He received no answer from the LORD.)
    —how Saul died. (in a battle with the Philistines)
    —what David did when he heard that Saul and Jonathan had been killed. (He mourned and fasted.)

David Becomes a Fugitive

Saul tried many times to kill David. Once he promised David that he could marry his daughter if he killed one hundred Philistines. Saul hoped David would lose his life in battle, but God helped David kill two hundred Philistines for good measure.

Finally, David had to flee from King Saul. He received a sword and some bread from the priests of the LORD. Then he escaped to the land of the Philistines, and later he fled to the wilderness.

✎ *Match the right ending to each of these sentences. All references except the last one are from 1 Samuel.*

___c___ 12. (22:1, 2) David the fugitive was joined by

___e___ 13. (22:17, 18) When Saul learned who had helped David, he told Doeg to kill

___a___ 14. (24:4–10) By sparing Saul's life, David showed his respect for

___g___ 15. (24:16–20) Saul realized by this time that David would someday become

___b___ 16. (28:5–8) When Saul was old and could receive no answer from the LORD, he went to see

___d___ 17. (31:1–6) Saul and his sons died during a battle with

___f___ 18. (2 Samuel 1:11, 12) David mourned and fasted when he heard about the death of

a. the LORD's anointed.

b. a witch.

c. many other fugitives.

d. the Philistines.

e. the priests of the LORD.

f. Saul and Jonathan.

g. the next king of Israel.

B. BIBLE WORD STUDY

✎ *Find the meanings of these words in a dictionary or Bible dictionary. Then answer each question based on how the word is used in the verse given.*

1. *Assay* (1 Samuel 17:39). Did David start to go, try to go, or refuse to go with Saul's armor? _____
   David started to go with Saul's armor.

2. *Ruddy* (1 Samuel 17:42). Was David reddish and healthy looking, rough and poorly dressed, or shy and soft-spoken? _____
   David was reddish and healthy looking.

3. *Staves* (1 Samuel 17:43). Did Goliath accuse David of fighting with slings, spears, or sticks? _____
   Goliath accused David of fighting with sticks.

4. *Javelin* (1 Samuel 18:11). Did Saul throw a sword, a spear, or a club at David? _____
   Saul threw a spear at David.

5. *Stay* (1 Samuel 24:7). Did David stop his men, kill his men, or encourage his men? _____
   David stopped his men.

Truths to Instill
- Selflessness prepares one for true service.
  —Because David was unselfish, he was able to do great things for the LORD.
  —As Saul became self-centered, he turned away from God and progressively lost wisdom and understanding. The more he served himself, the more he harmed himself.

- In contrast, the more David trusted and obeyed the LORD, the more the LORD blessed him and made him great. The following are examples of David's trust in the LORD rather than in himself.
  —He was obedient to his father.
  —He responded to Goliath's challenge.
  —He refused to wear Saul's armor.
  —He remained humble in spite of his growing fame.
  —He respected Saul's kingship even though Saul persecuted him.

18   Chapter One   Israel Becomes a Kingdom

✎ *Do these exercises together in class.*

6. Read 1 Samuel 17:4. (1 cubit = about 18 inches; 1 span = about 9 inches)

   About how many feet tall was Goliath? about 10 feet (9 feet 9 inches) (about 3 m)

7. Read 1 Samuel 17:5, 7. (1 shekel = about ⅖ ounce; 100 shekels = about 2½ pounds)

   a. About how many pounds did Goliath's metal coat weigh? about 125 pounds (about 56.5 kg)

   b. About how many pounds did the head of his spear weigh? about 15 pounds (about 6.8 kg)

C. THINKING ABOUT BIBLE TRUTHS

Differences Between Saul and David

King Saul and David were very different from each other. This exercise will help you see some of these differences.

✎ *Find phrases in these verses that contrast David with the phrases written about King Saul. The first one has been done for you. All references are from 1 Samuel.*

1. Saul: "The Spirit of the LORD departed from Saul" (16:14).

   David: *"The Spirit of the LORD came upon David"*
   _____ (16:13).

2. Saul: "When Saul and all Israel heard those words, . . . they were dismayed" (17:11).

   David: "Let no man's heart fail because of him; thy servant will go and fight with this Philistine."
   _____ (17:32).

3. Saul: "Saul . . . was afraid of him [David]" (18:15).

   David: "David behaved himself wisely in all his ways."
   _____ (18:14).

4. Saul: "Saul spake . . . that they should kill David" (19:1).

   David: "The LORD forbid that I should stretch forth mine hand against the LORD's anointed."
   _____ (26:11).

5. Saul: "Seek me a woman that hath a familiar spirit, that I may . . . enquire of her" (28:7).

   David: "And David enquired at the LORD."
   _____ (30:8).

If time permits, do numbers 6 and 7 together in class. Note that the tables of equivalent measures and weights are approximate. Weights and measures probably varied slightly over the centuries.

Answers may vary slightly.

D. LEARNING MORE ABOUT THE BIBLE

David's Fugitive Years

While fleeing from Saul, David became well acquainted with the land of Israel. From Moab in the east to Philistia in the west, David and his men hid in cities, in mountain forests, in deserts, and in dry canyons along the Dead Sea.

✎ *Fill in each blank on the map of David's fugitive years. You can find the names by reading the following sentences.*

1. David was born at Bethlehem (1 Samuel 16:1, 11).
2. He served King Saul at Gibeah (1 Samuel 10:26; 18:2).
3. He fled to Samuel at Ramah (1 Samuel 19:18).
4. He received help from the priests at Nob (1 Samuel 21:1).
5. He pretended to be insane at Gath (1 Samuel 21:10–15).
6. Then he fled to Adullam (1 Samuel 22:1).
7. David took his parents to Mizpeh in the land of Moab (1 Samuel 22:3).
8. After hiding in a stronghold, David found refuge in the forest of Hareth (1 Samuel 22:5).
9. David fought the Philistines at Keilah (1 Samuel 23:5).
10. Then he fled into the wilderness areas of Ziph and Maon (1 Samuel 23:14, 24).
11. From there David found his way to Engedi, a secluded canyon in the wilderness along the Dead Sea (1 Samuel 23:29).
12. David returned to both Maon and Gath, and eventually settled at Ziklag (1 Samuel 25:2; 27:2, 6).
13. Finally, David came to Hebron, where he was crowned king (2 Samuel 2:1–4).

If the students do not write in their workbooks, they will need to trace this map.

To help the students see how much David traveled, you could have them draw lines connecting the places in sequence on the map.

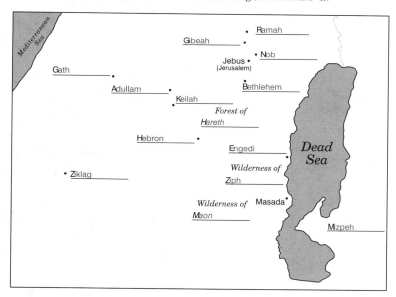

20

Lesson 3. David the King

You have studied some reasons God chose David to replace King Saul. God looked at David's heart rather than at his outward appearance. God said that David was a man after His own heart (1 Samuel 13:14).

Why could God say this about David? One important reason is that David loved God and served Him with all his heart. Because he loved God, he wanted to do what is right.

David also had great faith in God. When Goliath defied God's people, David knew that no one, not even a giant, could stand before the mighty God of Israel. His faith helped him lead God's people after he became king.

David's respect for the LORD's anointed kept him from sinning against King Saul. By behaving wisely toward Saul, David earned the respect of others. They could see that he was not trying to make himself king.

In this lesson you will study some other good things that David did while he was king. You will also see that David sinned, and that he later repented. God forgave David, but David reaped a bitter harvest.

Both Saul and David sinned, and both later admitted that they had done wrong. Why did God reject Saul and not David? Although we do not understand all of God's ways, we can see that David's repentance was different from Saul's. Saul made excuses and blamed others. He thought that his sin was not very serious. David humbly confessed that *he* had sinned and done evil in God's sight. He asked God to forgive him and to wash his heart whiter than snow.

God can use godly men with hearts like David's. People like David are humble. They love God and obey Him. If they fall into sin, they repent and seek complete cleansing.

God seeks godly men to lead His people.

A. ANSWERS FROM THE BIBLE

David Reigns at Hebron

Soon after Saul's death, the tribe of Judah anointed David as their king. But the other tribes of Israel did not accept David immediately. Abner, the general of Saul's army, made Saul's son Ishbosheth king over the northern tribes. For seven and a half years, David ruled in Hebron over the tribe of Judah alone.

✎ *Match the letter of each fact with the correct Bible reference.*

_b_	1. 2 Samuel 2:4	a. Abner makes peace with David.
_e_	2. 2 Samuel 2:8, 9	b. David is anointed king over the house of Judah.
_d_	3. 2 Samuel 3:8–11	c. Ishbosheth is murdered on his bed.
_a_	4. 2 Samuel 3:17–21	d. Ishbosheth angers Abner.
_c_	5. 2 Samuel 4:5–8	e. Ishbosheth is crowned king of Israel.

- According to 2 Samuel 2:10, Ishbosheth reigned for only two of the seven years that David reigned at Hebron. Abner appears to have had more power than Ishbosheth. Abner set him up as king, and when Abner turned to David, Ishbosheth's authority crumbled. Note Ishbosheth's response to David in 2 Samuel 3:14, 15.

Lesson 3

Oral Review

1. What excuse did Saul give for offering a sacrifice before Samuel arrived? [1] **He said that the people had scattered and Samuel had not come.**

2. Where was David when Samuel came to anoint him? [1] **He was out caring for his father's sheep.**

3. What do the words *covenant* and *supplication* mean? [1] *covenant:* **a binding agreement;** *supplication:* **a humble request**

4. Why did David feel confident that God would help him defeat Goliath? [2] **God had helped him kill a lion and a bear, and he trusted God to help him kill Goliath too.**

5. Why did Saul become angry with David? [2] **Saul was jealous that David was more popular than he was.**

6. When did Saul seek counsel from a witch? [2] **when he was old and could receive no answer from God (before his last battle with the Philistines)**

7. How did David show his respect for the LORD's anointed? [2] **He spared Saul's life.**

Lesson 3. David the King   **21**

David Is Anointed King Over All Israel

2 Samuel 5:1–5

6. Who came to Hebron to make David king over all Israel? _____
   all the elders of Israel (all the tribes of Israel)

7. David was _____thirty_____ years old when he began to reign. He reigned _____seven_____ years and _____six_____ months in Hebron over Judah alone, and _____thirty-three_____ years in Jerusalem over all Israel and Judah.

David Strengthens the Kingdom

2 Samuel 5:6–9

8. After David became king of all Israel, he moved his capital city closer to the northern tribes.

   a. Which city did David choose as his new capital? _____Jerusalem_____

   b. What tribe of Canaanites was living in the city, which David had to conquer before he could move there? _____the Jebusites_____

The Canaanites had controlled this city for many years. But after David conquered them, this city became the most important one in Israel. Solomon built the temple there, and a thousand years later, Jesus was crucified outside the city walls.

2 Samuel 5:17–21

When Saul died, Israel was weak and defeated. David fought many wars with the nations around him. He asked God for strength and victory, and the LORD helped him defeat all his enemies. Under David's leadership, Israel grew stronger than it had ever been before.

9. These verses tell about one battle David fought against the Philistines. Circle the letters of the three statements below that give reasons for David's success in war.

   (a.) David asked counsel of the LORD before going to battle.
   b. David made sure he had more soldiers than his enemies had.
   (c.) David gave God the credit for his victories.
   (d.) David destroyed the idols that he captured.

2 Samuel 7:1

The Bible tells about many other battles that David fought against the Philistines, the Moabites, the Syrians, the Edomites, and other nations.

10. Because David was faithful, God gave him _____rest_____ round about from all his _____enemies_____.

David Restores True Worship

At the end of Eli's life, his sons had removed the ark of the covenant from the tabernacle at Shiloh. The Philistines had captured the ark during a battle, and after they returned it to Israel, it had been kept in a private house. The ark represented God's presence among His people. David decided to move it to Jerusalem, where all Israel could meet to worship God.

- Both Bethlehem and Jerusalem are called the City of David. Bethlehem was David's native town, and Jerusalem was his capital.

- Although the heathen Jebusites controlled Jerusalem during the time of the judges and King Saul, the city had been an early center of true worship. Melchizedek, king of Salem in Abraham's time, was a priest of the most high God (Genesis 14:18). And Abraham offered Isaac on a mountain in the land of Moriah (Genesis 22:2), possibly at the place where Solomon later built the temple (2 Chronicles 3:1).

In This Lesson

Scope: 2 Samuel 2–7, 12–18; 1 Kings 1

Main Events

- David reigns 7½ years over Judah alone. During this time Saul's son Ishbosheth reigns over the rest of Israel.
- David becomes king over all Israel. With God's blessing, David extends the kingdom by conquering Jerusalem and many of Israel's enemies.
- After an initial failure, David brings the ark of God to Jerusalem. This helps to establish Jerusalem as the center of Hebrew worship.

- David wants to build a temple for God, but God says no. Instead, God tells David that He will establish David's kingdom forever.
- David sins but repents. As a result of his sin, he suffers the loss of two sons and has other family troubles.
- David writes many psalms of praise and worship to God.

2 Samuel 6:2–7; 1 Chronicles 15:1–3

11. David made a serious mistake the first time he tried to take the ark to Jerusalem. He placed the ark on a new cart instead of following God's plan for moving it. A man named _____Uzzah_____ touched the ark to steady it, and God slew him.

12. David carefully read the Law before trying to move the ark again. He saw that God wanted the _____Levites_____ to carry the ark on their shoulders. By following God's plan, David was able to bring the ark safely to Jerusalem.

David wanted to build a temple for God, but God said that David's son would build it instead. However, David gathered much building material for the temple and planned how the priests and the Levites would serve in it.

God Establishes David's Kingdom

God was pleased with David's desire to honor and worship Him. He honored David by promising to establish his kingdom forever. This was one of the most important Old Testament covenants.

2 Samuel 7:12–16

13. Which of these statements tells what God meant when He promised to establish David's kingdom forever?
   (a.) One of David's descendants would reign forever.
   b. God would keep David from growing old and dying.
   c. David would have a very long and prosperous reign.

Later in this course you will learn more about how God kept His covenant with David.

David Sins and Receives Judgment

For most of his reign, David was a very good king. But he made some mistakes, and one time he sinned grievously. First he took Uriah's wife, and then he took Uriah's life. God could not tolerate adultery and murder. He sent Nathan the prophet to David with a message of judgment.

2 Samuel 12:5–10, 13

14. Nathan told David a parable about a rich man who stole a poor man's lamb. When David angrily declared that the rich man must die, Nathan replied, "Thou _____art_____ _____the_____ _____man_____."

15. David had sent Uriah into battle to be killed with a sword. Because of this, Nathan said that the _____sword_____ would never depart from David's house. This meant that David would reap trouble, rebellion, and death within his own family.

16. In verse 13, David confessed, "_I have sinned against the LORD._____." Because David sincerely repented, God forgave his sin. David again served God with all his heart, but his sin remained a dark stain upon his life.

- Numbers 4:1–6, 15 gives instructions for moving the ark. The priests were to cover it and insert the staves; and the Kohathites, a division of the Levites, were to carry it. God warned, "They shall not touch any holy thing, lest they die." Moses gave wagons to the other Levites for transporting the tabernacle, but God commanded the Kohathites to bear the articles of the tabernacle "upon their shoulders" (Numbers 7:6–9).

- God's covenant with David established the lineage through which Christ would come. Revelation 5:5 speaks of Christ as "the Lion of the tribe of Juda, the Root of David." Although He is the eternal, almighty Son of God, He is not ashamed to be identified with His saints.

  Between David's time and the fall of Jerusalem, some Israelites probably thought this promise meant that David's earthly dynasty would never end. It is true that God allowed David's descendants to rule much longer than any dynasty in the northern kingdom. However, Jeremiah 33:15–17 shows that God's promise to David extended far beyond his earthly kingdom. The ultimate fulfilment of 2 Samuel 7:16 is Christ's eternal kingdom. This eternal fulfilment is mentioned in exercise C5 of Lesson 21.

Objectives
- The students should know
  —why David did not become king over all Israel immediately after Saul's death. (Only the tribe of Judah accepted him as king at first. Abner made Saul's son Ishbosheth king over the northern tribes.)
  —what happened seven years after David began to reign, which gave him rule over all Israel. (See Part A, numbers 3–6.)
  —who was king over Israel while David reigned over Judah alone. (Ishbosheth)
  —why David was successful on his second attempt to bring the ark of the covenant to Jerusalem. (He followed God's plan by having the Levites carry the ark.)
  —what covenant God made with David after He told him his son would build the temple. (that David's kingdom would be established forever)
  —what was the result of King David's sin. (He reaped many troubles in his older years, even though he had repented.)

David Reaps a Sad Harvest

The New Testament says, "Be not deceived; God is not mocked: for whatsoever a man soweth, that shall he also reap" (Galatians 6:7). But long before the New Testament was written, this law of God was already in effect. King David learned this by experience.

David repented of his sin when he realized what he had done. He did not keep on sinning. But the wrong he had done still bore fruit. David reaped a sad harvest from that seed.

✎ *Study your Bible to discover who did what in this long, sad series of events. All references are from 2 Samuel unless shown otherwise.*

Amnon, King David's oldest son, fell into sin. David was furious when he heard about it, but he did not punish his son according to the Law. The Law of God said that he should have been put to death.

Two years later another one of David's sons, (17) _____Absalom_____, murdered Amnon to get even with him (13:28). After this murder he fled to Geshur for three years. Again King David failed to punish the wrongdoer according to the Law. Instead, he became very lonesome for his son. So (18) _____Joab_____, the general of David's army (14:2), used a wise woman to trick King David into bringing this son back home to Jerusalem. But he was not allowed to visit the king until two years later.

During the next several years, (19) _____Absalom_____ used his handsome looks and his crafty ways to win the favor of the people (15:6). When he had enough support, he announced that he was king. King David had to flee from Jerusalem.

King David and his men fled across the Jordan River to the city of Mahanaim. From there David's men set out to fight against Absalom's army. Absalom was caught by his head in a tree, and (20) _____Joab_____ killed him (18:14).

When David was very old, (21) _____Adonijah_____, another son, tried to take the kingdom (1 Kings 1:5). Joab and Abiathar the priest sided with this son in spite of their long friendship with David. Bathsheba, Solomon's mother, and Nathan the prophet came to tell King David about it. David told (22) _____Zadok_____, the other priest, to take oil and quickly anoint (23) _____Solomon_____ to be the next king (1 Kings 1:39). After this, David died and was buried in Jerusalem.

B. BIBLE WORD STUDY

✎ *Match these definitions with the Bible words on the right. All references are from 2 Samuel.*

__h__	1. Very angry (3:8)	a. apparel
__d__	2. To go for and bring back (4:6)	b. establish; stablish
__f__	3. An agreement between two or more parties (5:3)	c. feign
__b__	4. To make firm or secure (7:12, 13)	d. fetch
__g__	5. To help in time of need (8:5)	e. kindled
__e__	6. Aroused; stirred up (12:5)	f. league
__a__	7. Clothes (14:2)	g. succour
__c__	8. To pretend (14:2)	h. wroth

Truths to Instill
- "Thou shalt love the LORD thy God with all thine heart" (Deuteronomy 6:5).
  —David's love for God stirred up his desire to worship God. He brought the ark to Jerusalem, and he made preparations for building the temple.
  —David's love for God is manifest in the psalms he wrote.
- David's courage helped him overcome opposition and difficulties. He had the courage to face problems correctly—in the fear of God.

- "Be not deceived; God is not mocked: for whatsoever a man soweth, that shall he also reap" (Galatians 6:7).
  —David reaped blessings because of his faithfulness. God subdued his enemies and established his kingdom forever.
  —David reaped a bitter harvest for his sin, even though he genuinely repented.
  —David received forgiveness because he repented. God did not reject David as He had rejected Saul.
- David's failure to observe a detail in the Law caused Uzzah's death. God expects us to do and teach even the least commandment (Matthew 5:19).

24   Chapter One   Israel Becomes a Kingdom

C. THINKING ABOUT BIBLE TRUTHS

The Psalms of David

David was more than just a brave king. The Bible calls him a "man after [God's] own heart" (1 Samuel 13:14) and "the sweet psalmist of Israel" (2 Samuel 23:1). David loved God and wrote many beautiful psalms of praise, trust, and worship. Even after David sinned, he expressed his longing for God by writing psalms of repentance.

The Book of Psalms is one of the best-loved books of the Bible. The Jews used it as a hymnbook. Jesus sang psalms and showed His disciples how the Psalms prophesied of Him. And Christians still find comfort and encouragement by reading the psalms that David wrote.

Psalm 23

1. In what kind of paths did David want God to lead him?   the paths of righteousness

2. How long did David want to live close to God?   forever

Psalm 34:1–7

3. What kind of people were glad that David made his boast in God?   the humble

4. What kind of people does the angel of the LORD protect?   those that fear the LORD

Psalm 51

David wrote this psalm after he had committed adultery and murder.

5. How clean did David want his heart to be? (51:7)   whiter than snow

6. What did David say God wants rather than sacrifice? (51:16, 17)

   a broken spirit (a broken and a contrite heart)

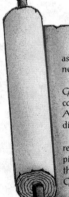

God used David's experiences as a shepherd boy to prepare him to lead His people as a king. Being a shepherd taught David to care for others. When he became king, he needed to care for all the people in Israel.

As a shepherd, David also learned to trust God to deliver him from danger. With God's help, he killed a lion and a bear who threatened his sheep. This gave him Him courage to fight against Goliath when Goliath mocked the Israelites and their God. As king, David sought God's direction and blessing before leading the Israelite soldiers to battle. He conquered many enemies who had long threatened Israel.

Perhaps the most important thing David learned while tending his flock was to recognize God as His shepherd. David wrote his thoughts about this in Psalm 23. He pictured God leading him safely through life, just as he had led his sheep, cared for their needs, and delivered them from evil. David's love for God and dependence on God caused other Israelites to love, worship, and serve God too.

D.   LEARNING MORE ABOUT THE BIBLE

David's Family

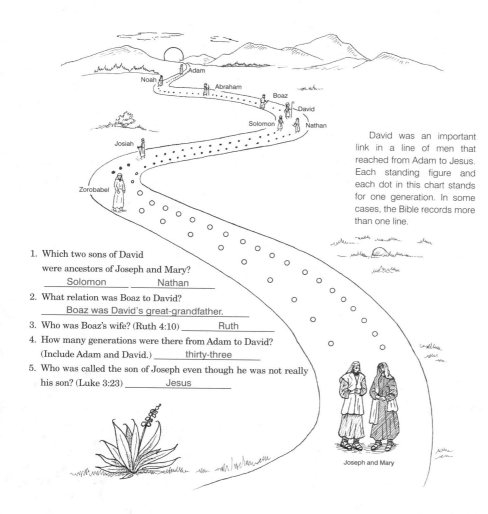

David was an important link in a line of men that reached from Adam to Jesus. Each standing figure and each dot in this chart stands for one generation. In some cases, the Bible records more than one line.

Joseph and Mary

1. Which two sons of David were ancestors of Joseph and Mary?
   _____Solomon_____   _____Nathan_____

2. What relation was Boaz to David?
   _____Boaz was David's great-grandfather._____

3. Who was Boaz's wife? (Ruth 4:10)   _____Ruth_____

4. How many generations were there from Adam to David? (Include Adam and David.)   _____thirty-three_____

5. Who was called the son of Joseph even though he was not really his son? (Luke 3:23)   _____Jesus_____

- This drawing is based on genealogical records given in the Old Testament, Matthew 1, and Luke 3. From David to Christ, Luke gives a genealogy through David's son Nathan, while Matthew gives the genealogy through Solomon and the kings of Judah.

  Matthew does not list every generation; he omits four kings of Judah (Ahaziah, Joash, Amaziah, and Jehoiakim). This may explain why Luke gives more generations between Zerubbabel and Joseph than Matthew does.

  Luke's genealogy might be Mary's lineage. If this is correct, Joseph was the son-in-law of Heli (Luke 3:23) and the son of Jacob (Matthew 1:15).

  Luke includes a Cainan who is not listed in Genesis 11 (Luke 3:36). This name is not included on the drawing, because it does not appear in the Hebrew Old Testament.

26

Lesson 4. Solomon's Wisdom, Wealth, and Wicked Wives

As a young boy, Solomon did not have many books to read. Few people in those days had books. The books they had were handwritten scrolls of parts of the Old Testament.

Solomon did not have textbooks like the ones you use. He studied the Law of God and the history of his people. His parents taught him how to live and to serve God. But Solomon did not get his wisdom from men. He asked God for wisdom, and God made him wise.

Knowledge is very necessary. Students need to memorize arithmetic facts, practice spelling, and learn to find places on a map. But such knowledge alone is not true wisdom. Wisdom is knowing how to use knowledge for God's glory and the good of others.

The Bible says that not many wise, mighty, or noble men after the flesh are called (1 Corinthians 1:26). Many well-known scientists, doctors, college professors, and authors openly disobey God. Their "wisdom" is often "earthly, sensual, devilish" (James 3:15).

Only those who ask God for wisdom find true wisdom (James 1:5). Wisdom from God is "first pure, then peaceable, gentle, and easy to be intreated, full of mercy and good fruits, without partiality, and without hypocrisy" (James 3:17).

God calls wise men to lead His people.

A. ANSWERS FROM THE BIBLE

Solomon's Good Beginning

Solomon was king during the Golden Age of Israel. God gave King Solomon the privilege to ask Him for anything he wanted. Solomon realized that he would need God's help to rule His people properly, so he asked God for wisdom. God was very pleased with Solomon's request, and He granted him his desire.

1 Kings 4:29–32

1. How many proverbs did Solomon speak? _____3,000_____

2. How many songs did he write? _____1,005_____

3. King Solomon is known as the wisest man who ever lived. He was wise because
   a. he had a better education than the other people of his time had.
   (b) he depended on God to give him true wisdom.
   c. his father, King David, was a man after God's own heart.

Solomon's Projects

King Solomon was an ambitious and industrious man. He did much trading with many lands and brought great wealth to Israel. He built cities, extended the walls of Jerusalem, and constructed many buildings. His most important project was building the temple.

1 Kings 5:8–18

4. a. What did Solomon buy from Hiram, king of Tyre, for the temple? _____
   cedar and fir trees _____

   b. What did Solomon give Hiram as pay? ___wheat and pure oil (food for Solomon's household)___

- King Solomon ruled during the Golden Age of Israel, when God blessed the Israelites with a period of relative peace. King David had defeated the Philistines, the Egyptians were in a period of weakness, the Hittite Empire had collapsed, and the Assyrians and Babylonians were not yet strong enough to be a serious threat.

Lesson 4

Oral Review

1. How did Saul disobey God in his battle with the Amalekites? [1] **Saul spared the king and all the good animals.**

2. Why did Saul command Doeg to kill the priests of the LORD? [2] **The priests had helped David.**

3. How did David feel when he heard about the death of Saul and Jonathan? [2] **He felt very sad. He mourned and fasted.**

4. Who reigned over Israel while David reigned over Judah alone? [3] **Ishbosheth**

5. Why did the prophet Nathan pronounce judgment on David? [3] **David had committed adultery and murder.**

6. Who was killed by Joab while trying to take the kingdom from his father? [3] **Absalom**

7. Why is David's family line important to us today? [3] **Jesus came through David's line.**

5. How many workmen did Solomon send to Lebanon each month? _____ 10,000 _____

6. How many carriers of burdens did Solomon employ? _____ 70,000 (threescore and ten thousand) _____

7. How many men hewed (cut) rocks out of the mountains? _____ 80,000 (fourscore thousand) _____

✎ *Read the verses and answer these questions.*

8. How much gold did Solomon use to decorate the inside of the temple? (2 Chronicles 3:8) _____
   600 talents, or about 22½ tons (20.4 metric tons)

9. How much brass (bronze) did Solomon use to make objects for the temple? (2 Chronicles 4:18) _____
   an amount so great they did not measure it

10. How many animals did Solomon offer to God at the dedication of the temple? (2 Chronicles 7:5) _____
    22,000 oxen and 120,000 sheep (142,000 animals)

After Solomon finished building the temple, he built houses for himself and his wives. By the time Solomon died, many Israelites were tired of working for the king and paying high taxes to support his projects (1 Kings 12:4).

11. Solomon spent seven years building the temple. How many years did he spend building his palace?
    (1 Kings 7:1) _thirteen years_

12. What did Solomon build for his heathen wives? (1 Kings 11:7, 8) _____
    high places (for heathen worship)

Solomon's Wisdom and Foolishness

Solomon was the wisest man on earth, yet he did some foolish things that led him away from God. According to the teachings in the Bible, which of the following acts of Solomon were wise and which were foolish?

✎ *Write* W *for wise or* F *for foolish.*

_F_ 13. Solomon marries Pharaoh's daughter (1 Kings 3:1; also see 1 Kings 11:1–3).

_W_ 14. Solomon asks God for wisdom (1 Kings 3:9).

_W_ 15. Solomon tells his servants to divide a living child with a sword (1 Kings 3:16–28).

_W_ 16. Solomon dedicates the temple (2 Chronicles 6:2).

_W_ 17. Solomon answers hard questions for the Queen of Sheba (1 Kings 10:1–3).

_F_ 18. Solomon acquires very many horses (1 Kings 10:26; also see Deuteronomy 17:14–16).

_F_ 19. Solomon marries many wives (1 Kings 11:1–3).

Solomon's Downfall

Solomon made some serious mistakes. For example, God had specifically commanded the kings of His people that they were not to have many wives, but Solomon deliberately ignored this command. He married seven hundred wives and had three hundred concubines (secondary wives)! Solomon's heathen wives led him into serious sin that caused his downfall. When people disobey God, they cannot expect that He will help them to be victorious.

In This Lesson

Scope: 1 Kings 3–5, 7, 10, 11; 2 Chronicles 3, 4, 6, 7

Main Events

• God gives Solomon wisdom.
• Solomon builds a temple at Jerusalem.
• Solomon marries many wives and gathers great riches.
• Solomon turns away from God in his old age.
• God tells Solomon that He will take ten tribes from his son.
• Solomon writes the Book of Ecclesiastes and many proverbs and songs.

Objectives

• The students should know
  —why the LORD gave Solomon his great wisdom. (Solomon asked God for wisdom to rule God's people properly.)
  —that Solomon built the temple.
  —why Solomon turned away from God when he was old. (He married heathen wives, who led him into sin.)
  —that Solomon learned (perhaps too late) that riches do not satisfy.

20. What serious mistake did Solomon make when he was old? (1 Kings 11:4–6) _____

   He worshiped the gods of his heathen wives. _____

   _____

21. What punishment did God pronounce upon Solomon? (1 Kings 11:11) _____

   God said that He would take the kingdom away from Solomon. _____

   _____

22. What promise did God make for David's sake? (1 Kings 11:13) _____

   God promised to give one tribe to Solomon's son. _____

   _____

B. BIBLE WORD STUDY

✎ *Match these definitions with the Bible words on the right. Use the tables of measure in the back of this workbook to find the meaning of* talent.

c	1. Twenty (1 Kings 4:22)	a. train
e	2. Control or rule (1 Kings 4:24)	b. ruby
g	3. A person who cuts out or shapes stones (1 Kings 5:15)	c. score
a	4. A caravan or group of people (1 Kings 10:2)	d. talent
d	5. A Bible weight equal to about 75 pounds (2 Chronicles 3:8)	e. dominion
f	6. A place to live (2 Chronicles 6:2)	f. habitation
b	7. A valuable, deep-red stone (Proverbs 3:15)	g. hewer

✎ *Read 1 Kings 4:22, and then use the tables of measure to give the answers.*

8. The *measures* of 1 Kings 4:22 were cors. A cor was a large measure equal to a homer.

   a. One cor equals about _____8 (282 l)_____ bushels.

   b. Solomon's household used about _____240 (8,460 l)_____ bushels of fine flour each day.

   c. They also used about _____480 (16,920 l)_____ bushels of meal (coarse flour).

Truths to Instill

• "If any of you lack wisdom, let him ask of God" (James 1:5).
  —God will bless us with wisdom as He did Solomon, if we seek after it. "For the LORD giveth wisdom: out of his mouth cometh knowledge and understanding" (Proverbs 2:6).
  —Biblical wisdom is practical. The Book of Proverbs gives many specific details on how to be a wise person. Biblical wisdom consists of doing the right thing, not just knowing the right thing.
  —If one has wisdom but does not act accordingly, he will suffer as Solomon did. In Proverbs, Wisdom says, "But ye have set at nought all my counsel, and would none of my reproof: I also will laugh at your calamity; I will mock when your fear cometh" (Proverbs 1:25, 26).
• Wealth and possessions do not bring satisfaction. Happiness is found in serving God and helping others. The Book of Ecclesiastes illustrates the unhappiness that comes from serving self.

C. THINKING ABOUT BIBLE TRUTHS

Solomon's Writings

God inspired King Solomon to write part of the Bible. He probably wrote most of the Book of Proverbs, and the Books of Ecclesiastes and Song of Solomon.

The Book of Proverbs contains hundreds of proverbs. These proverbs are short, wise sayings that give practical advice for everyday living.

Ecclesiastes shows that the things of this world do not satisfy. Solomon was a wealthy king who could afford anything he wanted. If wealth brings happiness, he should have been happy. But he discovered that the more a person has, the more he wants. Near the end of his life, he wrote the Book of Ecclesiastes to tell how unhappy his possessions had made him.

Solomon also wrote more than one thousand songs (1 Kings 4:32). One of them, the Song of Solomon, is a book of the Old Testament.

✎ *Read Proverbs 3:13–18. Notice that all these verses refer to the same subject.*

1. Name three things that wisdom is better than. silver, gold, and rubies

2. What do the pronouns *she* and *her* in verses 15–18 refer to?   wisdom

✎ *Read Proverbs 10:1–5. Notice that the beginning and the end of each verse tell about opposite things.*

3. What word in the middle of each verse shows a contrast between two things?   but

4. Name two things that a wise son does. He makes his father glad. He gathers in summer.

✎ *Read Ecclesiastes 12:1, 13, 14.*

5. When should we start living for God?
   now (in the days of youth)

6. What is our duty to God?
   Fear God, and keep His commandments.

✎ *Think about what you have studied in this lesson to answer these questions.*

7. a. Did Solomon always follow the good advice he gave in his writings?   no

   b. What do you think was one of the main reasons for Solomon's downfall? (Sample answer)
   Solomon married many heathen wives, and they turned his heart away from the LORD.

D. LEARNING MORE ABOUT THE BIBLE

King Solomon's World

✎ *Along which routes did the following items come to King Solomon at Jerusalem?*

1. A wealthy queen (1 Kings 10:1) <u>Route B; Sheba to Jerusalem</u>
2. Gold, silver, ivory, tin, apes, peacocks (1 Kings 10:22) <u>Route A; Tarshish (Tharshish) to Jerusalem</u>
3. Horses (1 Kings 10:28) <u>Route D; Egypt to Jerusalem</u>
4. Chariots (1 Kings 10:29) <u>Route D; Egypt to Jerusalem</u>
5. Gold (1 Kings 9:28) <u>Route C; Ophir to Jerusalem</u>

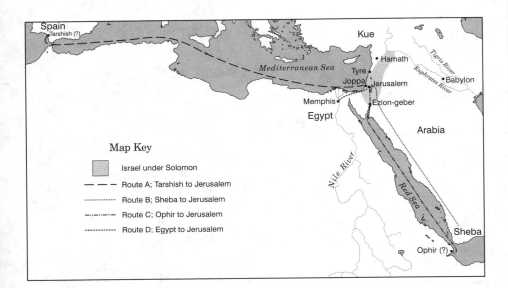

King Solomon's Collection

By the time Solomon was old, he realized that riches do not satisfy. The more he had, the less he enjoyed what he had. Many people today are like Solomon. They try to find satisfaction in wealth, sports, and other worldly pleasures; but they become more and more unhappy. Only God can give true, lasting satisfaction.

6. Read these verses. For each line, write one thing Solomon owned besides the possessions mentioned in the section "King Solomon's World."

(Answers may vary slightly.)

Ecclesiastes 2:4–8		**1 Kings 10:25–27**	
2:4	houses	10:25	vessels of silver
2:4	vineyards	10:25	vessels of gold
2:5	gardens	10:25	garments
2:5	orchards	10:25	armour (armor)
2:6	pools of water	10:25	spices
2:7	servants	10:25	mules
2:7	maidens	10:26	horsemen
2:7	cattle	10:27	cedar trees
2:8	singers		
2:8	musical instruments		

7. By the end of his life, Solomon realized that "he that loveth _____silver_____ shall not be satisfied with _____silver_____; nor he that loveth _____abundance_____ with increase" (Ecclesiastes 5:10).

32

Chapter One Review

A. ORAL REVIEW

✎ *Be sure you know the answers to these questions. Answer as many as you can from memory. If you need help, you may check the reference or lesson given in brackets.*

Why >>

1. Why did David feel confident that God would help him defeat Goliath? [1 Samuel 17:32–37]
2. Why did Jonathan give his robe to David? [1 Samuel 18:1–4]
3. Why did Saul become angry with David? [1 Samuel 18:8]
4. Why did Saul go to see a witch? [1 Samuel 28:6, 7]
5. Why was David successful in overcoming his enemies? [2 Samuel 5:19; 7:1]
6. Why did David suffer much trouble, rebellion, and death in his own family? [2 Samuel 12:9]
7. Why is David's family line important to us today? [Luke 2:4]

How >>

8. How long did Saul wait for Samuel before offering a sacrifice himself? [1 Samuel 13:7, 8]
9. How did Saul disobey God in his battle with the Amalekites? [1 Samuel 15:9]
10. How did David show his respect for the LORD's anointed? [1 Samuel 24:10]
11. How did David feel when he heard about the death of Saul and Jonathan? [2 Samuel 1:12]
12. How long did King David reign (including his reign over Judah alone)? [2 Samuel 5:4]
13. How clean did David want God to wash his heart from sin? [Psalm 51:7]
14. How did Solomon become the wisest man? [1 Kings 3:11, 12]

Who

15. Who was the enemy when Saul first gathered the Israelites to fight? [1 Samuel 11:1–8] the Ammonites
16. Who reigned over Israel while David reigned over Judah alone? [2 Samuel 2:10] Ishbosheth
17. Who decided to take the ark of God to Jerusalem? [2 Samuel 6:15] David
18. Who sold cedar and fir trees to Solomon? [1 Kings 5:8] Hiram, king of Tyre
19. Who tested Solomon with hard questions? [1 Kings 10:1] the Queen of Sheba
20. Who spoke 3,000 proverbs and wrote 1,005 songs? [1 Kings 4:30–32] Solomon

1. God had helped him kill a lion and a bear, and he trusted God to help him kill Goliath too.
2. David and Jonathan were very good friends.
3. David was more popular than he was.
4. The LORD no longer answered him.
5. David trusted in God, and God gave him victory over his enemies.
6. David had sinned (by committing adultery and murder).
7. Jesus came through David's line.
8. seven days
9. Saul spared the king and all the good animals.
10. David spared Saul's life.
11. very sad
12. forty years
13. whiter than snow
14. He asked God for wisdom.

Chapter One Review

This review is divided into two parts, an oral review and a written review. The oral review is intended for class discussion, but students could also use it for self-study.

B. WRITTEN REVIEW

✎ *Write the answers to these questions. Do as many as you can from memory. If you need help, you may check the reference or lesson given in brackets.*

What

1. What excuse did Saul give for offering a sacrifice before Samuel arrived? [1 Samuel 13:8, 11] _____
   He said that the people had scattered and Samuel had not come within the seven days that he had appointed.

2. What excuse did Saul make for not destroying all the Amalekites' sheep and oxen? [1 Samuel 15:15]
   He said that the people had spared the best sheep and oxen to sacrifice to the LORD.

3. What did Samuel say is more important than sacrifice? [1 Samuel 15:22] _____
   to obey

4. What does the LORD look at rather than just the outward appearance of a person? [1 Samuel 16:7]
   the person's heart

5. What pleases God more: music from instruments or singing by people who love Him? [Lesson 1] ___
   singing by people who love Him

6. What are the five Books of Moses? (Be sure to use the correct order and spelling.) [Lesson 1] _____
   Genesis, Exodus, Leviticus, Numbers, Deuteronomy

7. What city did David capture from the Jebusites for his capital? [2 Samuel 5:6, 7] _____ Jerusalem _____

8. What covenant did God make with David? [2 Samuel 7:16] _____
   God promised to establish David's kingdom forever.

9. What did Solomon realize about riches by the end of his life? [Ecclesiastes 5:10] _____
   Riches do not satisfy.

10. What do these words mean? [Lessons 1–4]

    a. covenant a binding agreement

    b. supplication a humble request

    c. succour to help in time of need

    d. league an agreement between two or more parties

    e. score twenty

    f. shekel about ⅖ ounce

    g. talent a Bible weight equal to about 75 pounds

When

11. When did Saul throw a javelin at David? [1 Samuel 18:10, 11] _____

    while David was playing his harp

12. When did Solomon turn away from serving God? [1 Kings 11:4] _____

    when he was old

Where Is It Found?

So far this year you have studied passages from 1 Samuel, 2 Samuel, and 1 Kings. This outline reviews some main events from the Israelites' request for a king to King Solomon's death.

✎ *Match these chapters with the events they record. The headings in your Bible may help you.*

<u>c</u> 13. 1 Samuel 8–10

<u>f</u> 14. 1 Samuel 11–15

<u>b</u> 15. 1 Samuel 16–31

<u>e</u> 16. 2 Samuel 1–10

<u>a</u> 17. 2 Samuel 11–20

<u>d</u> 18. 2 Samuel 21–24

<u>g</u> 19. 1 Kings 1–11

a. David commits adultery and murder. David's sons Amnon and Absalom bring him much trouble.

b. Samuel anoints David, and David behaves wisely. Saul becomes jealous and tries to kill David, but he finally kills himself.

c. Samuel is old, and the people ask for a king. Samuel anoints Saul.

d. God sends famine because of the Gibeonites. David's words and mighty men are recorded. David sins by numbering Israel.

e. Saul dies. David becomes king and conquers Israel's enemies.

f. Saul defeats the Ammonites. Later he disobeys God twice.

g. Solomon reigns wisely and prospers until he falls into sin.

35

Lesson 5. What Did People Wear?

People in Bible times did not have closets hanging full of clothes. Clothes were scarce in those days. It took a very long time to make one garment. Every thread had to be spun by hand, and then it was woven into cloth on simple looms. Some people wore the same garments day and night, taking them off only to wash them.

Even footwear was scarce. Most people wore sandals made of pieces of leather tied to the feet with leather thongs. People took off their sandals when they were mourning or when they entered a house or a holy place.

A. ANSWERS FROM THE BIBLE

Introduction

1. Why would John the Baptist's teaching in Luke 3:11 have seemed difficult to most Jews? (Read the verse and the lesson introduction.) _____

   Clothes were scarce and valuable. Giving away a second coat would have been a sacrifice.

2. For what price did the Israelites sell poor people as slaves in Amos's time? (Amos 2:6) _____

   a pair of shoes

3. What did John the Baptist say about Jesus' sandals? (Luke 3:16) _____

   He was unworthy to unloose them.

Men's Clothing

Tunic

The most important article of clothing for men and boys of Bible times was the *tunic.* A tunic was a loose, sacklike shirt that came down to the knees or ankles. It had slits in the sides for the arms and a hole in the top for the head. A leather or rough cloth belt, called a *girdle,* kept the tunic in place around the waist.

Sometimes, for greater freedom to work, men lifted the hems of their tunics and stuffed them into their girdles. This was called girding up one's loins.

4. The soldiers who crucified Jesus divided most of His clothes among themselves, but they cast lots for His tunic (coat). How had Jesus' tunic been made? (John 19:23, 24) _____

   It had been woven without a seam.

5. The girdle also served as a pouch or a handy place to carry tools or weapons. What did the men mentioned in 2 Samuel 20:8 and Mark 6:8 keep in their girdles (also called purses if they had pouches in them)? _____ a sword _____   _____ money _____

Girding up one's loins

Life in Bible Times

Lesson 5

Oral Review

1. Why did Saul hide when the people wanted to make him king? [1] **Saul was a humble man.**
2. When did Saul throw a javelin at David? [2] **while David was playing his harp**
3. Why was David successful in overcoming his enemies? [3] **David trusted in God, and God gave him victory over his enemies.**
4. How did Solomon become the wisest man? [4] **He asked God for wisdom.**
5. Who tested Solomon with hard questions? [4] **the Queen of Sheba**
6. When did Solomon turn away from serving God? [4] **when he was old**
7. Who spoke 3,000 proverbs and wrote 1,005 songs? [4] **Solomon**

In This Lesson

Main Points

• This lesson gives a description of clothes worn in Bible times.
• The Bible gives commandments about dress.
• Bible study books give helpful information, but they must be used with discretion.

Cloak

Men often wore a heavy outer *cloak* (also called a *mantle,* a *coat,* or *raiment*) when they were not working. When evening came, men and boys loosened their girdles and slept in their tunics, using their cloaks for extra warmth.

6. What fell from Elijah as he was taken up to heaven? (2 Kings 2:13) _____
   his mantle

7. What Old Testament law referred to the practice of men sleeping in their cloaks? (Exodus 22:26, 27) _If they took a neighbor's raiment (Hebrew:_ _mantle or cloak), they were to return it to the owner before evening._

8. The LORD wanted the Israelites to keep His commandments and to be his holy, special people. What did He tell them to make on their cloaks to remind them of this? (Numbers 15:38, 39) _____
   fringes with ribbands of blue (tassels made with blue thread)

Priests wore a coat over their tunics while they served in the tabernacle or temple. This coat, called an *ephod,* was made according to the Law. Sometimes other men or boys wore ephods when they were near God's holy ark or tabernacle.

Ephod

9. Who wore an ephod as a young child? (1 Samuel 2:18)
   _____ _Samuel_

Women's Clothing

Cloak

Tunic

Women of Bible times also wore tunics, but their tunics reached down to their ankles. Over this they wore cloaks. Women's tunics and cloaks were often made of finer material than men's.

Women covered their heads and hid their hair. Only wicked women displayed their hair for men to see. The New Testament explains that women should cover their heads as a sign of submission.

Many women of Bible times veiled their faces in the presence of strangers. They stayed hidden in the back rooms of their tents or houses. Women still do this in some parts of the Middle East today.

10. What did God say about women who wore men's clothing or about men who wore women's clothing? (Deuteronomy 22:5) _____
    They are an abomination to Him.

11. When did Rebekah veil her face? (Genesis 24:64, 65) _____
    when she met Isaac, her husband

12. What does a woman do if she prays or prophesies with her head uncovered? (1 Corinthians 11:5) ___
    She dishonors her head.

Life in Bible Times

Objectives

- The students should know
  —the names and descriptions of the basic garments that people wore in Bible times. (See Part A.)
  —how the Bible commands God's people to dress. (modestly and distinctively)

Truths to Instill

- God wants His people to dress modestly, in keeping with character qualities of decency and quietness. We are to avoid displaying our bodies or drawing attention to ourselves.
- There should be a difference between the appearance of men and women.
- Women's hair is not to be displayed.

God rebuked women of Bible times who wore fancy and expensive attire. Some women wore bracelets and earrings, and chains around their necks. Some painted their eyes and arranged their hair elaborately. Both men and women sometimes wore rings on their fingers.

13. What did God say that He would do to all this unnecessary display? (Isaiah 3:18–24) _____

   God said that He would take away their fancy clothes and bring them shame.

14. In 1 Peter 3:3, 4, God tells women to avoid wearing fancy hairstyles, gold, or expensive clothes. Instead, godly women should adorn themselves with the inner ornament of a _____ meek _____ and _____ quiet _____ _____ spirit _____, which is of great price in God's sight.

In Bible times, the Israelites' clothes were washed by men called *fullers,* who trampled on them in water. They used a soda-like soap (Malachi 3:2) to clean clothes.

15. a. Whose field was near the end of the conduit of the upper pool in Jerusalem? (Isaiah 7:3) _____

   the fuller's

   b. Why would a fuller want to work near a good supply of water? _____

   A fuller needed a good supply of water for washing clothes.

B. BIBLE STUDY BOOKS

The Bible is the most important book ever written. It is God's message to us, telling how men turned away from God and how God made a way for men to come back to Him. Everyone needs the message of the Bible.

Because the Bible is so important, men have prepared books to help others better understand it. A Bible concordance lists Bible words and tells where they are found. A Bible dictionary defines Bible words and terms. A Bible atlas contains maps of Bible lands which show the locations of countries, cities, mountains, rivers, and bodies of water that are mentioned in the Bible.

Bible study books must be used carefully. They are not perfect like the Bible. The people who write Bible dictionaries define words according to their understanding. The maps and text of Bible atlases are based on what people have learned about Bible lands, but sometimes they do not know for sure where a city or boundary was. Concordances are usually dependable, since they mainly list references for Bible words. But some concordances include dictionaries that may not be perfect. This workbook is not perfect either, even though it has been carefully checked with the Bible and with other sources. Only God's Word is perfectly true, perfectly dependable, and forever settled in heaven.

✎ *Use Bible study books to learn more about the Hirams who helped Solomon.*

1. Find *Hiram* in a Bible dictionary. *Hiram* was the name of several men in the Bible.

   a. One Hiram was the king of _____ Tyre _____, who sent cedar and fir trees to Solomon.

   b. Another Hiram helped Solomon build the _____ temple _____ at Jerusalem.

   c. *Hiram* is sometimes spelled _____ Huram _____.

Life in Bible Times

If the students have not studied the Grade 5 book of this series, you may need to introduce the use of Bible dictionaries, concordances, and Bible atlases.

2. Use a large concordance to list all the Bible chapters that mention the name *Hiram*. (Be sure to check both spellings.) The first three have been done for you.

a. _2 Samuel 5_   g. _1 Chronicles 8_

b. _1 Kings 5_   h. _2 Chronicles 2_

c. _1 Kings 7_   i. _2 Chronicles 4_

d. _1 Kings 9_   j. _2 Chronicles 8_

e. _1 Kings 10_   k. _2 Chronicles 9_

f. _1 Chronicles 14_

3. Find a map of Solomon's kingdom in a Bible atlas or in the back of a Bible.

a. Was the city of Tyre north, south, east, or west of Jerusalem? _____ north _____

b. Tyre was an important city of what country? _____ Phoenicia _____

CHAPTER TWO

The Northern Tribes
Set Up a Separate Kingdom

I am the LORD,
and there is none else,
there is no God beside me:
I girded thee,
though thou hast not known me:
that they may know
from the rising of the sun,
and from the west,
that there is none beside me.
I am the LORD,
and there is none else.
Isaiah 45:5, 6

TIME LINE—Chapter Two

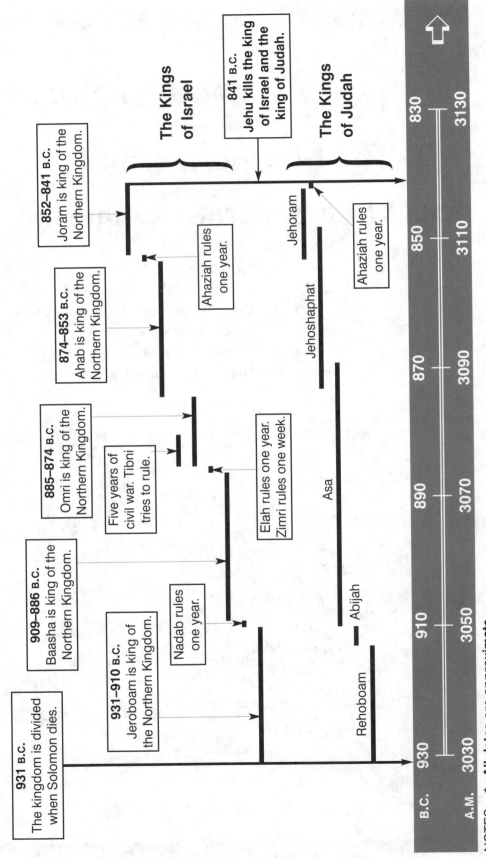

931 B.C.
The kingdom is divided when Solomon dies.

931–910 B.C.
Jeroboam is king of the Northern Kingdom.

Nadab rules one year.

909–886 B.C.
Baasha is king of the Northern Kingdom.

885–874 B.C.
Omri is king of the Northern Kingdom.

Five years of civil war. Tibni tries to rule.

Elah rules one year. Zimri rules one week.

874–853 B.C.
Ahab is king of the Northern Kingdom.

Ahaziah rules one year.

852–841 B.C.
Joram is king of the Northern Kingdom.

841 B.C.
Jehu kills the king of Israel and the king of Judah.

The Kings of Israel

The Kings of Judah

Jehoram

Ahaziah rules one year.

Jehoshaphat

Asa

Abijah

Rehoboam

| B.C. | 930 | 910 | 890 | 870 | 850 | 830 |
| A.M. | 3030 | 3050 | 3070 | 3090 | 3110 | 3130 |

NOTES:
* All dates are approximate.
* According to 1 Kings 15:25 and 1 Kings 16:8, Nadab and Elah each reigned two years. However, these figures must include part years, because 1 Kings 15:25, 28 and 1 Kings 16:8, 10 indicate that both of these kings were killed in the years after they began to reign.

41

Lesson 6. The Northern Tribes Rebel

Rehoboam received great responsibilities after the death of his father, Solomon. Solomon had been king of the twelve tribes of Israel and had controlled all the land from the Euphrates River to the Gulf of Aqaba (Red Sea). Certainly Rehoboam needed much good advice to rule so great a nation.

At first Rehoboam went to a good source. He consulted the men who had helped his father. These old, experienced men had learned much from Solomon's wisdom, but they had also seen the results of Solomon's mistakes. They gave Rehoboam good advice.

But Rehoboam did not listen to the old men. Instead, he consulted younger men who had grown up with him. These men did not have much experience. They did not care what was good for God's people. They gave Rehoboam poor advice. Because he listened to them, he lost almost all of his large kingdom.

Although most young people today are not called to rule, as Rehoboam was, we all receive some responsibilities while we are young. The younger we are, the more we need the counsel of older people. We also need God's Word, the source of all true wisdom. Our parents, church leaders, and teachers can help us follow the Bible's instructions.

God's people need sound counsel.

- Chapters 2 and 3 are mainly a study of the Northern Kingdom of Israel. The history of Judah is taken up in Chapter 4.

A. ANSWERS FROM THE BIBLE

God's Judgment on Solomon

The Golden Age of Israel did not last long. Because of Solomon's sin, God said that Solomon's descendants would not rule over the whole nation. However, God remembered David's faithfulness and the promise He had made to him. For David's sake, God said that the judgment would not fall in Solomon's time, and that David's descendants would continue to rule over the tribe of Judah.

Before Solomon's death, the prophet Ahijah promised Jeroboam, one of Solomon's young officers, that God would give him ten tribes of Israel to rule. After Solomon died, the Israelites asked Jeroboam to help them try to persuade Rehoboam to make life easier for them.

1 Kings 11:40

1. Solomon tried to _____kill_____ Jeroboam, but he escaped and fled to _____Egypt_____.

Rehoboam's Big Mistake

Rehoboam had seen his father grow wealthy and powerful, and he thought that he could follow in his father's footsteps. However, God had other plans for him.

1 Kings 12:1–5

2. All Israel gathered together to make Rehoboam king at
   (a) Shechem.   b. Jerusalem.   c. Gibeah.
3. Jeroboam and the Israelites asked Rehoboam
   a. for money to pay their taxes.
   b. to be their servant.
   (c) to make their burdens lighter.

Lesson 6

Oral Review

The numbers in brackets tell which lessons are being reviewed.

1. What excuse did Saul give for offering a sacrifice before Samuel arrived? [1] **He said that the people had scattered and Samuel had not come.**
2. What covenant did God make with David? [3] **God promised to establish David's throne forever.**
3. How did Solomon become the wisest man? [4] **He asked God for wisdom.**
4. What was one of the main reasons for Solomon's downfall? [4] **He married many heathen women who turned his heart away from God.**
5. What did Solomon realize about riches by the end of his life? [4] **Riches do not satisfy.**
6. What was a tunic? a cloak? an ephod? [5] *tunic:* **an inner, sacklike garment;** *cloak:* **a heavy outer coat;** *ephod:* **a special coat worn by priests**
7. According to 1 Peter 3:4, what ornament does the New Testament tell godly women to adorn themselves with? [5] **a meek and quiet spirit**

1 Kings 12:6–14

These verses show what kind of man Rehoboam was. God had already said that He would take the kingdom from him because of Solomon's sin, but it is clear that Rehoboam did not deserve to be king over all Israel.

4. Rehoboam asked for advice

   (a.) from both old and young men.

   b. from only the old men.

   c. from only his young friends.

5. Rehoboam decided to

   a. do what was best for the people.

   b. seek the LORD's counsel on the matter.

   (c.) make the people's burdens even heavier.

6. Rehoboam's decision shows that he

   a. knew the people were rebellious and needed to be dealt with firmly.

   (b.) was more concerned about his own plans than about the people's needs.

   c. was even wiser than his father Solomon had been.

1 Kings 12:16–20

7. When Rehoboam sent Adoram, the tax collector, to Israel,

   (a.) the Israelites stoned him to death.

   b. the Israelites sent him back empty-handed.

   c. Adoram overcharged the people.

8. Rehoboam got into his chariot and

   a. killed the leaders of the rebellion.

   (b.) fled to Jerusalem.

   c. collected the taxes himself.

1 Kings 12:21–24

9. How did Rehoboam plan to regain control of all Israel? _____

   <u>He planned to fight against the house of Israel.</u>_____

10. When the LORD sent a prophet to tell Rehoboam to return home, Rehoboam

   (a.) accepted the prophet's message and obeyed God.

   b. listened to the prophet but became very angry.

   c. rejected the prophet's message and disobeyed God.

Jeroboam's Big Mistake

Jeroboam knew that God had given him part of Rehoboam's kingdom because of Solomon's sin. He should have learned from this warning. Instead, he led the Israelites into even worse sins than Solomon had. Maybe he thought God would not punish him, but God never overlooks sin.

- Although God took the ten tribes from Rehoboam because of Solomon's sin, it also seems evident that Rehoboam lacked the character he would have needed to hold the kingdom together. We cannot put all the blame on Solomon.

8. What kind of book gives references for words in the Bible? [5] **a Bible concordance**

In This Lesson

Scope: 1 Kings 11:26–14:20

Main Events

- God promises Jeroboam that he will rule ten tribes of Israel.
- When Rehoboam becomes king, he decides to treat the Israelites with a heavy hand.
- The ten northern tribes, led by Jeroboam, rebel when Rehoboam refuses to lighten their tax burden.

God tells Rehoboam to return home without trying to subdue the Israelites.

- Jeroboam establishes a substitute religion, mixing idolatry with the worship of God. In spite of warnings, he persists in leading Israel astray.

Objectives

- The students should know
  —why God took ten of the tribes away from Rehoboam. (Solomon had sinned.)
  —what made the ten tribes decide to rebel and follow Jeroboam. (Rehoboam decided to make the people's burdens heavier instead of lightening them.)

1 Kings 12:25–33

11. Jeroboam feared that if the Israelites went up to Jerusalem to worship, they would return to Rehoboam. To keep this from happening, he

   a. told the Israelites to worship the LORD at Bethel and Dan.

   b. built a high wall from Bethel to Dan.

   (c.) made two golden calves and set them in Bethel and Dan.

12. God had said that only Aaron's descendants should be priests, but Jeroboam made priests of the _____lowest_____ of the people.

13. Instead of sending the Israelites to observe the feasts of the LORD at Jerusalem, Jeroboam

   (a.) made another feast at Bethel and Dan.

   b. encouraged his people to worship the LORD at home.

   c. told the people that feasts were not necessary.

1 Kings 13:1–5

14. Who came to warn Jeroboam about his sins? __a man of God__

15. What did this man say would happen to the altar at Bethel? __It would be rent, and the ashes would be poured out.__

16. What happened to Jeroboam and the altar when Jeroboam tried to stop the man from giving his warnings? __Jeroboam's hand dried up, and the altar was rent (split).__

Jeroboam's Son

The Bible says that "whatsoever a man soweth, that shall he also reap" (Galatians 6:7). Jeroboam discovered that he too would have to suffer for his sins.

✎ *Underline the correct words in the parentheses.*

1 Kings 14:1–17

17. Jeroboam's son (<u>Abijah</u>, Ahijah) became sick. Jeroboam sent his (mother, <u>wife</u>) to (Abijah, <u>Ahijah</u>) the prophet. Jeroboam told her to put on (<u>a disguise</u>, her queenly garments) and to take the prophet some bread and (wine, <u>honey</u>). When Jeroboam's (<u>wife</u>, mother) came to the prophet, he (<u>heard</u>, saw) her and recognized her. He told her that God was (pleased, <u>displeased</u>) with the (righteous, <u>wicked</u>) acts of Jeroboam. He also said that God would bring (blessings, <u>evil</u>) upon their house and that (<u>Abijah</u>, Ahijah) would (<u>die</u>, recover) when she returned home.

—why Jeroboam set up the golden calves in Israel. (He was afraid that if the Israelites went to Jerusalem to worship, they would return to Rehoboam.)

Truths to Instill

• Neglecting to heed good counsel brings tragedy. Three characters in this lesson failed to profit from counsel and warnings.

  —Solomon did not listen to God (1 Kings 11:9–11, 40).

  —Rehoboam did not listen to wise counselors (1 Kings 12:8).

  —Jeroboam did not listen to God's prophet (1 Kings 13:1–4).

• Listening to wrong advice is also dangerous. Both Rehoboam (1 Kings 12:8) and Jeroboam (1 Kings 12:28) took advice, but it was the wrong kind.

• It is important to do what is right, whatever the cost, rather than seeking an easier way. Rehoboam took the counsel of the young men rather than suffer a loss in income. Jeroboam set up a false religion rather than suffer the loss of his people. Both eventually lost what they were trying to save.

44   Chapter Two   The Northern Tribes Set Up a Separate Kingdom

B. BIBLE WORD STUDY

✎ *The King James Bible uses some expressions that are not used in modern speech. Judging from how these expressions are used in the following verses, underline the best definition.*

1. Jeroboam *lifted up his hand* (1 Kings 11:26).

   a. motioned to stop

   b. waved good-bye

   c. rose up in rebellion

2. Solomon *repaired the breaches* (1 Kings 11:27).

   a. fixed the gaps

   b. mended the trousers

   c. rebuilt the bridges

3. Jeroboam was *a mighty man of valour* (1 Kings 11:28).

   a. an aged, wealthy man

   b. a strong, courageous man

   c. a tall, heavy man

4. Ahijah had *clad himself* (1 Kings 11:29).

   a. bathed himself

   b. struck himself

   c. clothed himself

5. The Israelites said that Solomon had *made their yoke grievous* (1 Kings 12:4).

   a. oppressed them

   b. made fun of them

   c. offended them

6. The Israelites said that they *had no portion in David* (1 Kings 12:16).

   a. had received no goods from David

   b. had no share in David's kingdom

   c. had no grudge to hold against the family of David

7. Jeroboam built up the *high places* (1 Kings 12:31).

   a. centers of idol worship on hilltops

   b. palaces on mountain peaks

   c. stone-capped pyramids

C. THINKING ABOUT BIBLE TRUTHS

God Requires Obedience

God requires obedience from His people. He will always punish disobedience sooner or later. The kings of Israel and Judah are illustrations of this principle. So far you have studied the lives of five kings: Saul, David, Solomon, Rehoboam, and Jeroboam. Each of these men sinned and was punished for it, but they did not all react in the same way.

1. Read Deuteronomy 13:4. When people obey God, they _____walk_____ after Him and _____fear_____ Him. They _____keep_____ His commandments and serve Him. Of the five kings whom you have studied this year, the one that best followed this verse was _____David_____.

2. Read Jeremiah 7:23. When people are obedient to God's voice, He will be their _____God_____ and they will be His _____people_____ . If God's people walk according to His commands, it will go _____well_____ for them. According to this verse, God would have blessed the Israelites if they had always obeyed His _____voice_____.

3. Read Deuteronomy 11:26–28. In these verses God gave the Israelites a choice between a blessing and a curse.

   a. They would receive a curse if they _____
      _(Sample answer) did not obey God's commandments_____.

   b. They would receive a blessing if they _____
      _(Sample answer) obeyed God's commandments_____.

4. Which of these statements gives a reason why the sins of a leader are especially serious?

   a. When a leader sins, the people under his rule always fall into sin too.

   (b.) Many people are influenced by the sins of a leader, and this often causes much trouble.

   c. God expects men to always obey their leaders, even if the leaders ask them to do evil.

D. LEARNING MORE ABOUT THE BIBLE

Old Testament Books

✎ *Review the Old Testament books and their divisions. (See Lesson 1 if you need help.) You will need to know the order and spelling of the Books of History for the Chapter 2 Test.*

✎ *Study and complete the chart on the following page to learn more about Death and Burial in the Old Testament.*

Review the Old Testament books and their divisions together in class as needed. The students will need to know the order and spelling of the Books of History for the Chapter 2 Test.

46   Chapter Two   The Northern Tribes Set Up a Separate Kingdom

Death and Burial in the Old Testament

Solomon was buried in Jerusalem (1 Kings 11:43). Rehoboam was buried with his fathers (1 Kings 14:31). A false prophet buried a man of God in his own grave (1 Kings 13:29–31). To understand how the Israelites buried their dead in Old Testament times, do the exercise below.

The Egyptians believed that the souls of the dead lived on in their bodies. Because of this, they made their tombs as beautiful as they could afford.

People who believe the Bible know that when a Christian dies, his soul departs to be with Christ. On the Last Day, his body will be raised back to life and be reunited with his soul.

The bodies of the wicked will also be raised, and they will suffer forever in hell.

1. Israelite families buried their own dead.

   a. Who buried Abraham? (Genesis 25:9) ____Isaac and Ishmael____

   b. Who buried Isaac? (Genesis 35:29) _____Esau and Jacob_____

   c. Who buried Samson? (Judges 16:31) _____
   __his brothers and all of his father's house__

2. Some Israelite funerals became noted for their loud crying. Whom did wealthy families hire to cry for them? (Jeremiah 9:17, 18) _____
   __mourning women__

3. When Israelites died, their relatives wore coarse clothing made from goats' hair (sackcloth). What did they do to their clothes? (2 Samuel 3:31)
   __They tore their clothes.__

4. Because Jesus rose from the dead, Christians no longer need to be as sad about death. Paul wrote: "But I would not have you to be ignorant, brethren, concerning them which are _____asleep_____ [dead], that ye sorrow not, even as others which have no ____hope____. For if we ____believe____ that Jesus died and _____rose_____ again, even so them also which sleep in _____Jesus_____ will God bring with him" (1 Thessalonians 4:13, 14).

Funerals and proper burials were very important to the Israelites. They knew that God had made man in His own image.

Therefore they treated their bodies with respect. They did not normally burn dead bodies as some of their ungodly neighbors did.

They wrapped the dead in long pieces of cloth, sometimes with spices and oils, before laying the bodies in tombs.

The Israelites often used caves dug out of rocky hillsides for tombs. Caves held the bodies of entire families and were closed with a large stone.

Lesson 7. The Course of the Kingdom of Israel

Small decisions can have long-lasting effects.

Many years ago, a French Canadian man rode on horseback through wooded southern Ontario. Seated in front of him on the saddle rode his little boy, Louis. Perhaps Louis's mother had died. Perhaps he was tired of riding and wanted to get down. Perhaps he was cold, sick, or hungry. No one remembers. But when the two on horseback came to a clearing in the woods, Louis's father made a hasty decision.

In the clearing stood the house of David and Leah Snyder, Mennonite pioneers in the Grand River valley. Louis's father decided to leave his little boy with them. He rode on—and never came back.

Louis Bichet grew up in the Snyder home, married a Christian woman, and had nine children. Many of his descendants have become ministers, bishops, Sunday school teachers, and faithful church members. Far and wide, God has blessed the church through the grandchildren and great-grandchildren of the French-Canadian boy dropped off by his father.

King Jeroboam also made a far-reaching decision, but his did not turn out so well. When Jeroboam saw his people traveling to Judah to worship at Jerusalem, he decided to stop them. He made golden calves to worship and set them up at Bethel and Dan. He chose new priests and changed the worship feasts. He told his people that it was too much for them to go to Jerusalem to worship.

Jeroboam's plan helped him keep his people from going to Judah, but it brought evil results. Soon the ten northern tribes were worshiping the calves instead of the LORD.

In Lesson 6, you saw how Jeroboam's decision had bad effects while he lived. In this lesson you will see how it had much worse effects long after he died. Many Bible verses speak of Jeroboam as the king "who made Israel to sin." Because of his bad decision, Israel started down the wrong course and was eventually destroyed. Thousands of men, women, and children were carried from their homes or killed. Most of those taken into captivity never returned to Canaan.

Some decisions we make today also have results that are long-lasting—even eternal.

God's people need to make good decisions.

It is good for sixth grade students to realize what the results of sin are. However, the teacher must be careful not to arouse premature feelings of guilt in students. Some of your students may have reached a point of personal accountability to God, but others may not have yet. As you teach, concentrate on general principles of sowing and reaping. The Holy Spirit can use these truths to bring personal conviction when the student is mature enough.

A. ANSWERS FROM THE BIBLE

FIVE BAD KINGS

Jeroboam made a bad decision, and the kings who followed him continued making bad decisions. The nation of Israel (the Northern Kingdom) moved further and further away from God. In this lesson you will learn about five wicked kings who followed Jeroboam.

Nadab—the Idol Worshiper

1 Kings 15:25–27

1. Who was Nadab's father? _____ Jeroboam _____

2. What was the sin Nadab committed by following his father's example? (If you need help, turn back to 1 Kings 12:28–30.) _Nadab continued the worship of the golden calves at Bethel and Dan._

Lesson 7

Oral Review
1. What did Samuel say was more important than sacrifice? [1] **obedience**
2. Who decided to take the ark of God to Jerusalem? [3] **David**
3. What trouble did David reap, even though he repented of his sin? [3] **much fighting and death in his own family**
4. When did Solomon turn away from serving God? [4] **when he was old**
5. How did the Israelites make their cloaks look different from those of other people? [5] **They made fringes with ribbands of blue on the hems of their cloaks.**
6. What did the ten northern tribes ask of Rehoboam? [6] **to make their burdens lighter**
7. What kind of man is a mighty man of valor? [6] **a strong, courageous man**
8. What are the twelve Books of History? (Be sure you know the correct order and spelling.) [1, 6] **Joshua, Judges, Ruth, 1 Samuel, 2 Samuel, 1 Kings, 2 Kings, 1 Chronicles, 2 Chronicles, Ezra, Nehemiah, Esther**

3. What city were Nadab and all Israel attacking at the time of Nadab's death? _Gibbethon_

Baasha—the Murderer

1 Kings 15:28–34

4. Whom did Baasha kill besides King Nadab? _all the house of Jeroboam_

5. In what city did Baasha live while he reigned over all Israel? _Tirzah_

6. How was Baasha like Jeroboam? _Baasha walked in the way of Jeroboam and in his sin._
   (He continued to promote the idol worship at Bethel and Dan.)

7. a. What did the prophet Jehu say would happen to Baasha's family? (1 Kings 16:3, 4) ____
   (Sample answer) The LORD would make Baasha's house like Jeroboam's house—all his
   descendants would die. (Those that died in the city the dogs would eat, and those that died in
   the field the birds would eat.)
   b. Why did God plan to bring this judgment upon them? (1 Kings 16:7) ____
   Baasha provoked the LORD to anger by being like the house of Jeroboam.

Elah—the Drunkard

1 Kings 16:8–10

8. Who was Elah's father? _Baasha_

9. Who conspired against Elah? _Zimri_

10. What was Elah doing when he was killed? _drinking himself drunk_

11. How did the LORD feel about the sins of Baasha and Elah—especially their sin of continuing the idol
    worship that Jeroboam had started? (There is a phrase in 1 Kings 16:13 that will help you.) ____
    The LORD was provoked to anger by their sin.

Zimri—the Conspirator

1 Kings 16:12–18

12. What did Zimri do to the house of Baasha? ____
    He destroyed all the house of Baasha.

13. How long did Zimri reign? _seven days_

14. Against what city was the army of Israel encamped at the time? _Gibbethon_

15. What did the people in the army camp do when they heard of Zimri's conspiracy? ____
    They made Omri king over Israel.

In This Lesson

Scope: 1 Kings 15:25–16:28

Main Events

- The kings of Israel continue to walk in the sins of Jeroboam, "who made Israel to sin."
- Baasha destroys Jeroboam's family and reigns, but he follows in the sins of Jeroboam.
- Zimri kills Baasha's family and reigns for seven days.
- Omri takes the kingdom from Zimri, but he does "worse than all that were before him."

Objectives

- The students should know
  —why the nation of Israel experienced so much turmoil during this period. (They had sinned. They could have avoided these troubles by submitting to God.)
  —what were the far-reaching effects of Jeroboam's decision to promote idolatry. (It started Israel down the wrong course, which ended in their destruction.)
  —what is always the result of sin. (punishment)

16. a. Why did Zimri kill himself? _____

    He saw that Tirzah was taken (and that he would soon be killed).

    b. How did he kill himself? _____

    He went into the king's house and burnt the house and himself with fire.

Omri—the King Worse Than All Before Him

After Zimri killed himself, half of the Israelites followed Omri and the other half followed another man. They fought each other for several years, but finally Omri overcame his opponent and established himself as king.

1 Kings 16:21–24

17. Who were the leaders of the two sides after Zimri's death? _____Tibni_____ and

    _____Omri_____

18. Omri built a new capital city for Israel. What did he name it? _____Samaria_____

Omri was a powerful king. His name appears in ancient records that have been found in the Middle East. Omri conquered Moab, made an alliance with the king of Tyre, and built elaborate forts and palaces in his new capital city.

19. Omri probably seemed great to many men of his time, but God viewed him differently. What does the

    Bible say about Omri in 1 Kings 16:25? _____

    "[He] wrought evil in the eyes of the LORD, and did worse than all that were before him."

A Little Brother Follows Me

A careful boy I want to be;
A little brother follows me.
I do not dare to go astray
For fear he'll go the selfsame way.

I cannot once escape his eyes;
Whate'er he sees me do, he tries;
Like me he says he's going to be—
That little brother following me.

He thinks that I am good and fine;
Believes in every word of mine.
The bad in me he must not see—
That little brother following me.

I must remember as I go,
Through summer's sun and winter's snow,
I'm building for the years to be
That little brother following me.

Truths to Instill
- It is important to make right decisions.
  —Some decisions are hard to reverse. Jeroboam's successors never changed the course he set.
  —People who make wrong decisions often do not intend to begin a wrong course. They simply fail to make the right decision because of a lack of courage, faith, or fear of God. This weakness leads them on a downward course away from God.

50 Chapter Two The Northern Tribes Set Up a Separate Kingdom

B. BIBLE WORD STUDY

✎ *Fill in each blank with a word from the list that means about the same as the other words in that row. All references are from 1 Kings.*

conspire (15:27)   provoke (16:13)   host (16:16)   wrought (16:20)
posterity (16:3)   chronicles (16:14)   besiege (16:17)   prevail (16:22)

1. besiege   surround   blockade
2. triumph   prevail   overcome   conquer
3. offspring   children   descendants   posterity
4. troops   army   host   soldiers   throng
5. did   accomplished   worked   wrought
6. accounts   chronicles   histories   records
7. incite   provoke   kindle   stir up   excite   arouse
8. plan   plot   conspire   devise   scheme

C. THINKING ABOUT BIBLE TRUTHS

The Result of Wicked Leaders

Sin is a dreadful thing. It creates problems for everyone who allows it to stay in his life, yet many people continue practicing it. The five kings in this lesson were like that. In spite of the warnings that they received from God, they persisted in living in sin and in causing God's people to sin.

The sins of these kings brought much violence in Israel. Five of the first seven kings of Israel rebelled against the king who reigned before them. Several destroyed the entire family of the king they overthrew.

1. Why did the LORD allow Baasha to kill all of Jeroboam's descendants? (1 Kings 15:29, 30) _____
   Jeroboam had sinned and provoked the LORD to anger.

2. What words are used again and again to describe the kings of Israel? (For examples, see 1 Kings 15:26, 34; 16:19, 26. As you read about more kings of Israel in the next lessons, notice how often these words are repeated.) _"[He] walked in the way of Jeroboam, and in his sin wherewith he made_
   Israel to sin."

3. Nadab, Baasha, Elah, Zimri, Tibni, and Omri ruled the northern kingdom after Jeroboam. Use the lesson comments and the Scripture references in Part A of this lesson to answer these questions.

   a. Which two of these kings received the kingdom from their fathers?
      _____ Nadab _____ and _____ Elah _____

   b. Which four took (or tried to take) the kingdom from someone else? _____
      Baasha, Zimri, Tibni, and Omri

4. When a country has a series of rulers who rise up and overthrow the previous rulers, it usually indicates that the country has serious problems. Circle the letters of the *five* statements that give reasons for the trouble and changing dynasties in Israel.

   (a.) Most Israelites did not respect their leaders as David had respected King Saul.

   (b.) The kings of Israel cared more about themselves than they did about others.

   c. The Israelites wanted to follow only the leaders anointed by a prophet of God.

   (d.) God could not bless His people with good leaders because most of the Israelites served idols.

   (e.) The kings who came after Jeroboam did not have enough courage to destroy the idols he had set up.

   (f.) Because the Israelite kings sinned the same way Jeroboam had sinned, they reaped the same judgment God had brought upon him.

D. LEARNING MORE ABOUT THE BIBLE

The Divided Kingdom

After Solomon died, the Israelites divided into two kingdoms: Israel and Judah. All the kings of Judah were descendants of David. But many of the kings of Israel were usurpers who seized the throne, killed the previous king and his family, and began a new dynasty (family line of kings). On the chart, the first king of each dynasty is marked with an asterisk (*).

The dates given are the approximate years B.C. (before Christ). Determining the exact dates is difficult, even though the Bible tells how many years each king reigned. Sometimes a son began reigning while his father was still living, and both kings counted the years they ruled together. Also, a king's first and last years were usually counted as whole years, even if they were only short parts of years.

1. Who was king of Israel while Rehoboam and Abijah reigned in Judah? _____Jeroboam_____

2. Who was king of Judah during the reigns of Nadab, Baasha, Elah, Zimri, and Omri? _____Asa_____

3. Only two dynasties in Israel lasted for more than two generations. Who was the first king in each of these dynasties? _____Omri_____   _____Jehu_____

4. Which prophet shown on the chart prophesied during the first part of Ahab's reign? _____Elijah_____

5. About how many years before Christ did Baasha and Asa reign? _900 (More exact figures are also acceptable.)

- Because Ahaziah had no sons, his brother Joram (Jehoram) reigned after him (2 Kings 1:17). This means Omri's dynasty spanned only three generations, even though it had four kings.

More About the Kings of Israel and Judah

—On the average, the kings of Judah reigned much longer than the kings of Israel. This is partly because many kings of Israel were killed by usurpers. Both kingdoms had about the same number of kings, even though Judah lasted more than one hundred years longer than Israel.

—A comparison of this chart with the chart in Lesson 19 shows that God blessed many of the righteous kings of Judah with longer reigns. Asa, Jehoshaphat, Uzziah, Jotham, Hezekiah, and Josiah were among the best kings of Judah. Joash and Amaziah were also good kings during the first parts of their reigns. These eight kings reigned during a large part of the time between Solomon's death and the Fall of Jerusalem.

—Mannaseh is an exception to the rule that righteous kings ruled longer than wicked kings. Mannaseh was known as one of the most wicked kings, yet he ruled longer than any other king in Israel and Judah. Nevertheless, we see God's mercy in this, for Mannaseh repented later in life. Mannaseh lived to see the birth of his grandson Josiah, who would become one of the best kings of Judah.

—Jehu was probably the best king in Israel, yet even he continued to worship Jeroboam's golden calves. Nevertheless, God rewarded him for overthrowing Baal worship in Israel (See 2 Kings 10:30). Jehu's dynasty (Jehu, Jehoahaz, Jehoash, Jeroboam, and Zechariah) reigned more than one-third of the time between Solomon's death and the fall of Samaria. You will read more about Jehu and his family in Lessons 13 and 14.

—Queen Athaliah was the only queen to rule in Israel or Judah. She was also the only ruler of Judah who was not of David's dynasty.

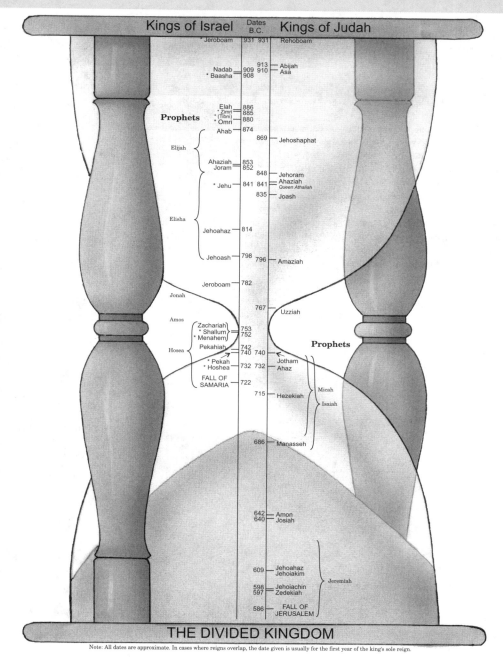

Kings of Israel	Dates B.C.	Kings of Judah
Jeroboam	931 931	Rehoboam
Nadab	909 913	Abijah
* Baasha	908 910	Asa
Elah	886	
* Zimri (Tibni)	885	
* Omri	880	
Ahab	874	
	869	Jehoshaphat
Ahaziah	853	
Joram	852	
	848	Jehoram
* Jehu	841 841	Ahaziah / Queen Athaliah
	835	Joash
Jehoahaz	814	
Jehoash	798 796	Amaziah
Jeroboam	782	
	767	Uzziah
Zachariah	753	
* Shallum	752	
* Menahem		
Pekahiah	742	
	740 740	Jotham
* Pekah	732 732	Ahaz
* Hoshea		
FALL OF SAMARIA	722	
	715	Hezekiah
	686	Manasseh
	642	Amon
	640	Josiah
	609	Jehoahaz / Jehoiakim
	598	Jehoiachin
	597	Zedekiah
	586	FALL OF JERUSALEM

Prophets (Israel): Elijah, Elisha, Jonah, Amos, Hosea

Prophets (Judah): Micah, Isaiah, Jeremiah

THE DIVIDED KINGDOM

Note: All dates are approximate. In cases where reigns overlap, the date given is usually for the first year of the king's sole reign.

- *Joram* is a shortened form of *Jehoram*. The Bible uses both forms to name two different kings who reigned about the same time. Ahab's son Joram (Jehoram) was a king of Israel; Jehoshaphat's son Joram (Jehoram) was a king of Judah. (See the chart of the kings of Israel and Judah in Lesson 7.) This is explained to the students in Lesson 13, where they study these kings.

- *Joash* is a shortened form of *Jehoash*. The Bible uses both forms to name two different kings. Jehoahaz's son Jehoash (Joash) was a king of Israel; Jehoram's son Joash (Jehoash) was a king of Judah. This is explained to the students in Lesson 17, where they study these kings.

54

Lesson 8. God's Judgment Foretold on the House of Ahab

The Old Testament speaks of many who did not obey God. The kings of Israel were especially known as disobedient, unfaithful, selfish, and ungodly men.

King Omri of Israel, who "did worse than all that were before him," had a son and two grandsons who became kings of Israel. Altogether, they reigned more than forty years.

Ahab, the son of Omri, was even worse than his father. He not only worshiped Jeroboam's calves but also married the daughter of a heathen king and helped her promote the shameful worship of Baal. He built a temple and set up an altar to Baal. The Bible says, "Ahab the son of Omri did evil in the sight of the LORD above all that were before him" (1 Kings 16:30).

In those days of wicked kings in Israel, Jehoshaphat, the king of Judah, was an outstanding contrast. Jehoshaphat was such a good king that the Bible says he walked in the ways of his father David.

But even though Jehoshaphat was good, he was not always wise. He made friends with wicked Ahab and went out to battle with him. God was not pleased with that kind of friendship. Jehoshaphat suffered harm because of his friendship with Ahab, but even more serious results came in the next generations. His son married Ahab's daughter Athaliah, who was a Baal worshiper like her mother. Later Athaliah killed all but one of Jehoshaphat's remaining descendants.

Many good people have come to ruin because of bad friends. Many husbands, like Ahab, have fallen further into sin because they married wicked wives.

God's people need to choose good friends.

A. ANSWERS FROM THE BIBLE

Ahab—the Worshiper of Baal

Sin has no convenient stopping place. It tends to get worse and worse. This was true in the lives of the kings of Israel. While Omri, Ahab's father, was the most sinful king that Israel had had up to that time, Ahab purposely went even further into sin.

1 Kings 16:29–33

1. Ahab married _____Jezebel_____, the daughter of Ethbaal, king of the _____Zidonians_____.
   (Sidonians)
2. Ahab served and worshiped _____Baal_____.
3. Ahab set up an _____altar_____ for Baal in a temple that he had built in _____Samaria_____.
4. Ahab did more to provoke the LORD to _____anger_____ than all the _____kings_____ before him.

Elijah Challenges Ahab

Even though Ahab was the most wicked king that Israel had ever had, God still gave him a chance to repent. He sent the prophet Elijah to show him that the God of Israel was more powerful than the heathen gods that Ahab and Jezebel worshiped.

Lesson 8

Oral Review

1. What are the five Books of Moses? (Be sure you know the correct order and spelling.) [1] **Genesis, Exodus, Leviticus, Numbers, Deuteronomy**
2. How clean did David want God to wash his heart from sin? [3] **whiter than snow**
3. What do the words *score*, *shekel*, and *talent* mean? [2, 4] *score:* **twenty**; *shekel:* **a Bible weight equal to about 2/5 ounce**; *talent:* **a Bible weight equal to about 75 pounds**
4. Why did Jeroboam make golden calves at Bethel and Dan? [6] **He wanted to keep the northern tribes from returning to Jerusalem.**
5. What happened to Jeroboam and the altar at Bethel when the prophet spoke to him? [6] **Jeroboam's hand dried up and the altar was rent.**
6. What happened to the house of Jeroboam? [7] **Baasha killed all of Jeroboam's descendants.**
7. What words does the Bible use again and again to describe Jeroboam? [7] **"He made Israel to sin."**
8. What two dynasties in Israel lasted for more than two generations? [7] **Omri's and Jehu's**

✎ *Write* true *or* false. *Correct each false statement on the lines after the sentence.*

1 Kings 18:17–20, 36–40

_____ true _____ 5. Ahab thought Elijah was troubling Israel. _____

_____

_____ false _____ 6. Jezebel fed 400 prophets of Baal and 450 prophets of the grove at her table. _____

Jezebel fed *450* prophets of Baal and *400* prophets of the grove at her table.

_____ true _____ 7. Ahab gathered the Israelites and the false prophets together on Mount Carmel. ___

_____

_____ false _____ 8. Elijah asked the LORD to hear him and send fire from heaven to prove to the people

that Ahab was a bad king. Elijah asked the LORD to hear him and send fire from

heaven to prove to the people that *the* LORD *is the true God of Israel.*

_____ false _____ 9. Ahab kept Elijah from killing the false prophets. _____

Ahab *did not keep* Elijah from killing the false prophets.

Ahab—the King Who Sulked

For some time after the false prophets' defeat on Mount Carmel, Ahab did better. He followed the advice of a prophet of the LORD. God helped him win two great victories over the Syrians. But Ahab soon forgot. Besides his palace in the capital city of Samaria, Ahab had another palace in a city called Jezreel. Nearby was a vineyard that he coveted, and when he could not get it lawfully, he listened again to Jezebel's evil advice. She led him into a sin even more dreadful than the ones he had committed before.

1 Kings 21:1–14

10. Why did Naboth not want to sell his vineyard to Ahab? _____

Naboth had inherited the vineyard from his father.

11. What did Ahab do after he entered his house? _____

He lay down on his bed, turned his face toward the wall, and refused to eat. (He sulked.)

12. How did Jezebel have Naboth killed? _____

Jezebel wrote letters to the leaders of the city, telling them to have two false witnesses accuse

Naboth of blaspheming God and the king. Then they were to stone Naboth.

The Bible says, "Be sure your sin will find you out" (Numbers 32:23). Although killing Naboth had been Jezebel's idea, Ahab was guilty too. The judgment that God pronounced upon Ahab and his family was so terrible that even wicked King Ahab was shaken. He humbled himself, but he did not fully forsake his evil ways.

1 Kings 21:17–19

13. Where was Ahab when the LORD sent Elijah to meet him? in Naboth's vineyard

14. What did the LORD say would happen to Ahab? _____

The dogs would lick Ahab's blood where they had licked Naboth's.

In the rewritten sentences for numbers 5–9, the corrections are in italics. The pupil's sentences may vary somewhat.

- The Bible does not say so, but evidently Ahab just stood by and let Elijah kill the prophets. When he went home that night, he told Jezebel all that Elijah had done.

- Samaria was the official capital of Israel during Ahab's reign (1 Kings 16:24; 20:1), but Ahab and Jezebel also had a palace in Jezreel (1 Kings 21:1). Ahab rode to Jezreel after the contest on Mount Carmel (1 Kings 18:45). Later, Elijah met him again in Naboth's vineyard (1 Kings 21:16–18). About twelve years after Ahab's death, Jehu killed Jezebel and her son Joram at Jezreel (2 Kings 9:14–37).

In This Lesson

Scope: 1 Kings 16:29–33; 18:17–20, 36–40; 20:1–22:40 (Note that these passages overlap with those in Lesson 9. This lesson focuses on Ahab, and Lesson 9 focuses on Elijah.)

Main Events
- Ahab is worse than all the kings before him. He marries the wicked Jezebel and promotes Baal worship.
- God sends prophets to warn Ahab, who does "more to provoke the LORD God of Israel to anger than all the kings of Israel that were before him" (1 Kings 16:33).
- Ahab sulks when Naboth refuses to sell his vineyard. His wife gets the vineyard for him by having Naboth murdered. But God sends Elijah to Ahab with a terrible sentence of judgment.
- Ahab is killed in battle, and the dogs lick his blood just as Elijah had prophesied.

Objectives
- The students should know
  —the evil effect that Jezebel had on King Ahab and on Israel. (She led them into deeper sin, including Baal worship.)
  —why Jehoshaphat should not have been such close friends with Ahab. (See the lesson introduction.)

15. What did the LORD say would happen to Ahab's house? (21:22) _____

    It would become like the houses of Jeroboam and Baasha.

16. What did the LORD say would happen to Jezebel? (21:23) _____

    The dogs would eat her by the wall of Jezreel.

1 Kings 21:25–29

17. What did Ahab sell himself to do? _____

    to do wickedness in the sight of the LORD

18. What did Ahab do after he heard how God would punish him and his wife? _____

    He rent his clothes, put on sackcloth, fasted, lay in sackcloth, and went softly (humbly, meekly).

19. How did the LORD soften Ahab's punishment? _____

    The LORD said that He would wait to punish Ahab's house until after Ahab's death.

Ahab and Jehoshaphat

Jehoshaphat, the good king of Judah, came to see King Ahab. Ahab invited Jehoshaphat to join him in fighting against Syria.

20. What did Jehoshaphat say? (1 Kings 22:4) _____

    "I am as thou art, my people as thy people, my horses as thy horses."

Jehoshaphat wanted to know what the LORD thought about their plans. Ahab called in about four hundred false prophets. They all said that the Lord would help Ahab and Jehoshaphat conquer the Syrians. But Jehoshaphat did not trust these prophets. He wondered if there was a prophet of the LORD whom they could ask. So Ahab called in one true prophet.

21. Why did Ahab hate Micaiah? (1 Kings 22:8) _____

    Micaiah prophesied evil things about Ahab.

At first Micaiah pretended to agree with the other prophets. He knew Ahab would disregard the LORD's message. But then Micaiah prophesied that the LORD wanted Ahab to be killed in battle and that Israel would be like sheep without a shepherd. However, Ahab and Jehoshaphat went to battle anyway.

22. What happened to Ahab? (1 Kings 22:34) _____

    He was (mortally) wounded by an arrow that a certain man shot into the air at random.

23. How was Elijah's prophecy concerning Ahab fulfilled? (1 Kings 22:38) _____

    Someone washed Ahab's blood from his chariot, and the dogs licked it up.

- Note that the four hundred false prophets first said that Adonai (the Lord) rather than Jehovah (the LORD) would help Ahab and Jehoshaphat conquer the Syrians. However, after Jehoshaphat asked for a prophet of Jehovah, Zedekiah changed his emphasis and claimed his message was from Jehovah. Also note that the officer who called Micaiah misquoted the false prophets on this point.

—how Elijah's prophecy against Ahab was fulfilled. (When Ahab's blood was washed from his chariot, the dogs licked it up.)

Truths to Instill
- Association with evil leads one to sin.
  —Ahab's marriage to Jezebel brought him into close association with paganism. It resulted in his leading Israel deeper into sin, in the murder of Naboth, and in the destruction of his whole family.
  —Jehoshaphat's friendship with Ahab put him into uncomfortable situations. He did not really wish to go to battle without God's approval, nor did he wish to displease Ahab. He ended up doing what

he did not wish to do.

"Can two walk together, except they be agreed?" (Amos 3:3).

"Be not deceived: evil communications corrupt good manners" (1 Corinthians 15:33).

B. BIBLE WORD STUDY

✎ *Match these definitions with the Bible words or phrases on the right. All references are from 1 Kings.*

d 1. Not serious; having little importance (16:31)	a. at a venture
f 2. To set up (16:32)	b. blaspheme
c 3. Very close to (21:1)	c. hard by
e 4. An important man (21:8)	d. light (thing)
b 5. To curse or speak evil of (21:10)	e. noble
g 6. To tear (21:27)	f. rear
h 7. Coarse cloth worn by mourners (21:27)	g. rend
a 8. By chance; at random (22:34)	h. sackcloth

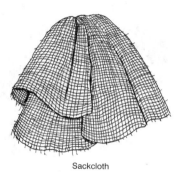

Sackcloth

Man dressed in sackcloth

C. THINKING ABOUT BIBLE TRUTHS

Ahab's Wicked Reign

1. Ahab was wicked, but his wife Jezebel urged him to do even worse than he would have done alone. Read these verses, and list additional sins of Jezebel that help show why God pronounced a terrible judgment upon her.

   a. (1 Kings 18:4) Jezebel killed __the prophets of the LORD__.

   b. (1 Kings 19:2) She tried to kill ____Elijah____.

   c. (1 Kings 21:25) She ____stirred____ ____up____ the wickedness of her husband.

   d. (2 Kings 9:22) She practiced whoredoms and ____witchcrafts____.

   e. (2 Kings 9:30) She ____painted____ her face and tired (adorned) her ____hair (head)____.

2. How was Naboth's death also Ahab's fault, and not just Jezebel's? <u>(Sample answer) Ahab sulked</u> <u>because Naboth would not sell his vineyard. When Jezebel devised her evil plan, Ahab did not</u> <u>stop her. And after Naboth's death, Ahab went to take possession of the vineyard.</u>

3. Why do you think Ahab considered Elijah his enemy in 1 Kings 21:20? _____ <u>(Sample answer) Elijah spoke against Ahab's wicked deeds.</u>

_____

4. In 1 Kings 22:8, what should Jehoshaphat have done besides just reproving Ahab? (For a clue, read 2 Chronicles 19:1, 2.) _____ <u>(Sample answer) Jehoshaphat should have refused to help Ahab.</u>

_____

D. LEARNING MORE ABOUT THE BIBLE

Israel During Ahab's Reign

Ahab reigned over the Northern Kingdom about sixty years after Solomon's death. His country was much different from what it had been in Solomon's time. Most of the foreigners subdued by David had rebelled, and the Hebrews had split into the two nations of Israel and Judah.

✎ *Use the clues to label the map with these names: Bethel, Damascus, Dan, Jerusalem, Jezreel, Mount Carmel, Ramoth-gilead, Samaria, Shechem, Tirzah, and Zidon (Sidon). If you need help, you may use the references given or a map from a Bible atlas. All references are from 1 Kings.*

1. City ruled by Jezebel's father (16:31)
2. Capital of Ben-hadad the Syrian (20:34)
3. Northern city where Jeroboam had set up golden calf worship (12:29)
4. Place where Elijah gathered the Israelites for a contest (18:19)
5. City of Naboth, where Ahab had a palace (21:1)
6. City where Ahab was fighting when he was wounded by an arrow (22:29)
7. Early capital of Israel, where Zimri had burned the king's house and himself (16:17)
8. Ahab's capital city, which his father Omri had built (16:24)
9. City where the northern tribes had rejected Rehoboam as their king (12:1)
10. Southern city where Jeroboam had set up golden calf worship (12:29)
11. Capital of Judah, where Jehoshaphat ruled (22:42)

• The inscriptions of Shalmaneser III expand our knowledge of Ahab's time. If your students have time, you might want to assign a research project on this subject. See "Shalmaneser III" in a Bible dictionary or "The Battle of Qarqar" in *The Moody Atlas of Bible Lands* (pages 132, 133). Remind students that while inscriptions such as these give us more information about Old Testament times, they are not as reliable as God's Word.

According to Shalmaneser's records, he fought against a coalition of kings that included King Ahab of Israel and kings from Syria, Arabia, Egypt, and other countries. Shalmaneser's records state that Ahab supplied two thousand chariots and ten thousand soldiers. Shalmaneser claimed a great victory, but apparently he also suffered losses, because he needed to return home.

The following are several other items of interest from his inscriptions, which could be discussed in class.

—Shalmaneser's monuments include the famous Black Obelisk, the Monolith Inscription, and several other inscriptions.

—Shalmaneser's inscriptions provide a link between secular history and Biblical history.

—Ahab was apparently killed soon after the Battle of Qarqar.

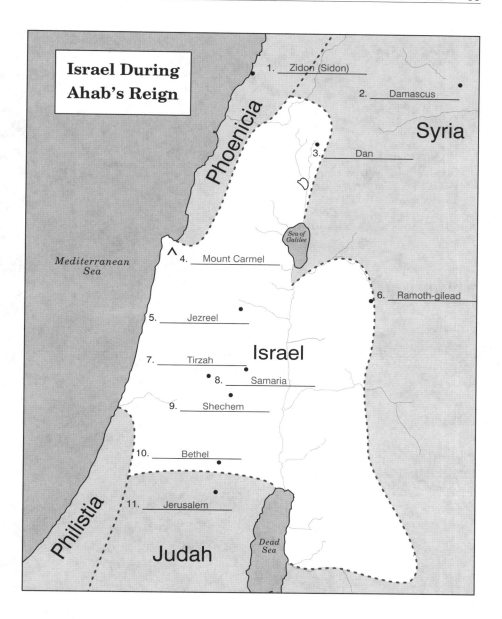

Israel During Ahab's Reign

Phoenicia

Syria

1. _____ Zidon (Sidon) _____

2. _____ Damascus _____

3. _____ Dan _____

Mediterranean Sea

Sea of Galilee

4. _____ Mount Carmel _____

6. _____ Ramoth-gilead _____

5. _____ Jezreel _____

Israel

7. _____ Tirzah _____

8. _____ Samaria _____

9. _____ Shechem _____

10. _____ Bethel _____

11. _____ Jerusalem _____

Philistia

Judah

Dead Sea

60

Lesson 9. Elijah's Ministry and Miracles

The Bible tells about different kinds of preachers. Some, like the apostles at Jerusalem, preached the good news of salvation. Some, like Jonah and Jeremiah, preached a message of warning and doom.

Preachers in Bible times lived in many places and spoke in different ways. Daniel witnessed in a king's palace. John the Baptist preached in the wilderness. Peter preached to thousands in Jerusalem. Philip spoke to one man in a chariot. Paul preached in jail.

God does not mind that preachers are different from each other. What matters to God is that preachers live and preach the truth. True men of God always speak the truth, whether people like it or not. Elijah was such a man of God.

Few people liked to hear Elijah preach. King Ahab and his wife Jezebel especially hated his plain, forceful messages about what is right and what is wrong. They hated to hear about the LORD's coming judgments on their sin. But Elijah kept on speaking the truth.

Because Elijah's message was true, the wicked Israelites could not escape it. His prophecies came to pass. The LORD carried out the judgments he foretold through Elijah. The people learned to respect and fear Elijah more than King Ahab because God was with Elijah.

God's people need to hear the truth.

A. ANSWERS FROM THE BIBLE

Stories of Elijah

The Bible tells many stories of men and women who lived for or did not live for God. God preserved these stories in the Bible to help us learn how to live. Several stories were written about Elijah.

✎ *Using the Scriptures as a guide, number the events of each story in the correct order.*

1 Kings 17:1–24

1. Elijah in the Dry Years

   __4__ Elijah asks the widow for some water and bread.

   __1__ Elijah predicts a drought.

   __3__ The LORD sends Elijah to a widow of Zarephath.

   __5__ The widow's meal and oil are not used up.

   __6__ Elijah raises the widow's son back to life.

   __2__ The ravens feed Elijah by the Brook Cherith.

Lesson 9

Oral Review

1. What did the ten northern tribes ask of Rehoboam? [6] **They asked him to make their burdens lighter.**
2. Whom did Jeroboam choose to be his priests? [6] **the lowest of the people**
3. Who conspired against Elah and the house of Baasha? [7] **Zimri**
4. How does the Bible describe Omri? [7] **"[He] did worse than all that were before him."**
5. How many false prophets ate at Jezebel's table? [8] **850**

6. How did Ahab show his disappointment about not getting Naboth's vineyard? [8] **He lay down with his face toward the wall and refused to eat. (He sulked.)**
7. What did Elijah prophesy about Ahab's and Jezebel's deaths? [8] **The dogs would lick Ahab's blood, and the dogs would eat Jezebel.**
8. What did Ahab do after Elijah told him how God would punish him and his wife? [8] **He tore his clothes, put on sackcloth, and fasted.**

1 Kings 18:17–46

2. Elijah and the Baal Worshipers

___2___ Elijah tells Ahab to gather the prophets to Mount Carmel.

___5___ Elijah commands the people to kill the false prophets.

___/___ Ahab blames Elijah for troubling Israel.

___6___ Elijah prays and the LORD sends rain.

___4___ The LORD sends fire to consume Elijah's sacrifice.

___3___ The false prophets receive no answer from Baal.

1 Kings 19:1–18

3. Elijah in the Desert

___4___ The LORD sends wind, an earthquake, and fire.

___5___ The LORD speaks to Elijah in a still, small voice.

___/___ Elijah flees to Beersheba to escape Jezebel.

___6___ The LORD sends Elijah back to Israel.

___2___ An angel of the LORD provides food for Elijah in the wilderness.

___3___ Elijah travels to Mount Horeb.

1 Kings 22:51–53; 2 Kings 1

4. Elijah and Ahaziah

___/___ Ahaziah becomes king of Israel after Ahab's death.

___4___ Elijah sends God's message to Ahaziah.

___6___ Ahaziah dies and his brother reigns.

___3___ Ahaziah falls through a lattice.

___2___ Moab revolts against Ahaziah.

___5___ Ahaziah's men are burned with fire when they try to capture Elijah.

1 Kings 19:19–21; 2 Kings 2:1–18

5. Elijah and Elisha

___3___ Elijah and Elisha cross the Jordan.

___5___ Elijah's mantle falls from him, and Elisha takes it up.

___2___ Elijah and Elisha go to Gilgal, Bethel, and Jericho.

___4___ Elijah is taken up into heaven by a whirlwind.

___6___ The men of Jericho look for Elijah but cannot find him.

___/___ Elijah calls Elisha to be his servant.

In This Lesson

Scope: 1 Kings 17–19; 22:51–53; 2 Kings 1:1–2:11 (Note that part of this scope overlaps with Lessons 8 and 11. This lesson focuses on Elijah's ministry.)

Main Events
• God shows His power by performing miracles through Elijah.
• God uses Elijah to counteract Baal worship.
• Elijah flees from Jezebel to Mount Horeb, where he hears God's still, small voice. At God's command, he returns to his work in Israel.
• Elijah tells King Ahaziah he will die because he did not depend on the LORD.
• Elijah calls Elisha, after which God takes Elijah up into heaven by a whirlwind.

Objectives
• The students should know the stories outlined in the lesson, including these details.
  —The two places Elijah stayed during a famine, and how God supplied Elijah's needs. (He stayed by the Brook Cherith, where ravens fed him; and at a widow's house in Zarephath, where the meal and oil did not run out.)

Extra Activity

✎ *Choose one of the stories above for a report. (Your teacher will tell you whether your report should be written or oral.) Different students in your class may want to choose different stories. Be sure to include details about the main points that are given above. Also include a lesson the story teaches. If you want, you may draw a sketch to illustrate your report.*

B. BIBLE WORD STUDY

✎ *Match these definitions with the Bible words on the right. All references are from 1 Kings unless marked otherwise.*

__e__	1. Meat (17:6)	a. bullock
__j__	2. A piece of food (17:11)	b. chamber
__i__	3. Flour (17:12)	c. cruse
__c__	4. A jug (17:12)	d. dress
__d__	5. To prepare food (17:12)	e. flesh
__k__	6. To be used up (17:14)	f. lancet
__b__	7. A room (17:23)	g. lattice
__a__	8. A bull (18:23)	h. mantle
__f__	9. A small spear (18:28)	i. meal
__h__	10. A cloak or robe (19:13)	j. morsel
__g__	11. A framework of strips that cross each other in a regular pattern (2 Kings 1:2)	k. waste

✎ *Use the table of measure in the back of this book to complete this exercise.*

12. The word *measures* is used in our King James Bibles for several different Hebrew words. The measures in 1 Kings 18:32 are *seahs*. Two *seahs* equal about __2 (about 18 l)__ pecks. (Note: 1 peck = ¼ bushel.)

The optional story assignment can provide a profitable diversion for your Bible class. Be sure the students understand the assignment. The lesson will be best covered by having different students write or talk about different stories.

If you assign the stories, exercises 1–5 could be omitted, but be sure to discuss the major points of each story in class. The reviews and test include questions about the stories.

—Where Elijah met the prophets of Baal, and what he did with them after the contest. (He met them on Mount Carmel. He killed them.)
—How God spoke to Elijah on Mount Horeb. (in a still, small voice)
—What Elijah did when Ahaziah sent groups of soldiers to capture him. (He called for fire from heaven to burn the first two groups. At God's direction, he went with the third group.)
—How Elijah went to heaven, and who saw him go. (by a whirlwind; Elisha)

Truths to Instill
• It is always necessary to tell the truth, even though others might not appreciate it.
• The truth will solidly stand forever. The untruth will soon come to nothing.
• One man standing for the truth is more powerful than a king with a whole nation behind him.

C. THINKING ABOUT BIBLE TRUTHS

Elijah prophesied during a difficult time. Most of the Israelites were worshiping Baal and other idols. King Ahab hated the true prophets of the LORD, and his wife Jezebel killed many of them.

God gave special courage to Elijah and performed many miracles through him. Elijah served God faithfully, and at the end of his life, God took him up into heaven by a whirlwind.

Elijah's Miracles

1. List the miracles that God performed through and for Elijah.

   a. 1 Kings 17:1 _____
      No dew or rain fell.

   b. 1 Kings 17:6 _____
      The ravens fed Elijah.

   c. 1 Kings 17:16 _____
      The widow's meal and oil did not run out.

   d. 1 Kings 17:19–22 _____
      The widow's son was raised to life.

   e. 1 Kings 18:36–38 _____
      Fire from heaven burned Elijah's sacrifice.

   f. 1 Kings 18:41–45 _____
      God sent an abundance of rain after the drought.

   g. 2 Kings 1:10–12 _____
      Fire from heaven consumed captains and men.

   h. 2 Kings 2:8 _____
      The waters of Jordan parted.

   i. 2 Kings 2:11 _____
      Elijah went up into heaven by a whirlwind.

- There had been no rain for 3½ years (James 5:17).

Elijah's Departure

2. Elijah was taken to heaven without dying.

   a. What other man in Old Testament times did not die? (If you need help, see Genesis 5.) _____Enoch_____

   b. In the future, what group of believers will not die? (1 Thessalonians 4:15–17) _____
      those who are alive when the Lord comes again

64   Chapter Two   The Northern Tribes Set Up a Separate Kingdom

D. LEARNING MORE ABOUT THE BIBLE

Elijah's Ministry

✎ *Fill in each blank on the map to show where these events took place. They are numbered in the order they occurred.*

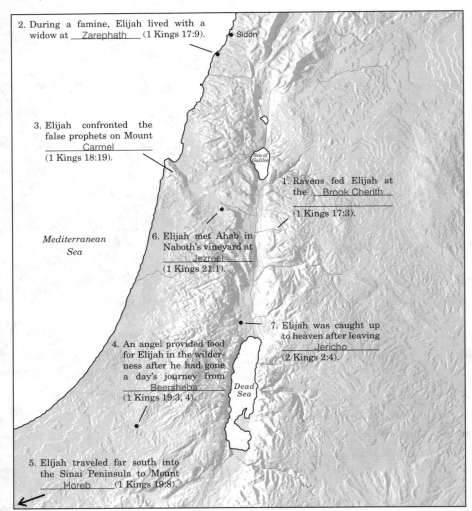

2. During a famine, Elijah lived with a widow at __Zarephath__ (1 Kings 17:9).

● Sidon

3. Elijah confronted the false prophets on Mount __Carmel__ (1 Kings 18:19).

Sea of Galilee

1. Ravens fed Elijah at the __Brook Cherith__ (1 Kings 17:3).

Mediterranean Sea

6. Elijah met Ahab in Naboth's vineyard at __Jezreel__ (1 Kings 21:1).

7. Elijah was caught up to heaven after leaving __Jericho__ (2 Kings 2:4).

4. An angel provided food for Elijah in the wilderness after he had gone a day's journey from __Beersheba__ (1 Kings 19:3, 4).

Dead Sea

5. Elijah traveled far south into the Sinai Peninsula to Mount __Horeb__ (1 Kings 19:8).

65

Chapter Two Review

A. ORAL REVIEW

✎ *Be sure you know the answers to these questions. Answer as many as you can from memory. If you need help, you may check the reference or lesson given in brackets.*

Why >>

1. Why did Jeroboam make golden calves at Bethel and Dan? [1 Kings 12:27, 28]
2. Why were both Ahab and Jezebel guilty of killing Naboth and taking his vineyard? [Lesson 8]
3. Why did Ahab hate Micaiah the prophet? [1 Kings 22:8]
4. Why did Elijah flee for his life? [1 Kings 19:1–3]

How >>

5. How did Jeroboam's wife find out that her son would die? [1 Kings 14:2]
6. How did people in Bible times express their grief when someone died? [Lesson 6]
7. How long did Zimri reign over Israel? [1 Kings 16:15]
8. How does the Bible describe Omri? [1 Kings 16:25]
9. How did Ahab respond when Elijah told him the terrible judgments God would bring upon him and his family? [1 Kings 21:27]

Who

10. Who met Jeroboam and told him he would be king? [1 Kings 11:29, 30] Ahijah
11. Whom did Jeroboam choose to be his priests? [1 Kings 12:31] the lowest of the people
12. Who conspired against Elah and the house of Baasha? [1 Kings 16:8, 9] Zimri
13. Who built the capital city of Samaria? [1 Kings 16:23, 24] Omri
14. Who married Jezebel and worshiped Baal? [1 Kings 16:30, 31] Ahab

When >>

15. When did Rehoboam flee to Jerusalem? [1 Kings 12:18]
16. When did Rehoboam accept good advice and obey God? [1 Kings 12:24]
17. When did Elijah kill the false prophets? [1 Kings 18:40]
18. When did King Ahab die? [1 Kings 22:34–37]

B. WRITTEN REVIEW

✎ *Write the answers to these questions. Do as many as you can from memory. If you need help, you may check the reference or lesson given in brackets.*

What

1. What did King Solomon do after he learned that Jeroboam had been anointed? [1 Kings 11:40] ____

   He tried to kill Jeroboam.

---

1. He wanted to keep the northern tribes from returning to Jerusalem.
2. Jezebel planned and commanded the killing of Naboth. Ahab did not stop her wicked plans, and he went to take possession of the vineyard after Naboth was killed.
3. Micaiah prophesied evil things about Ahab.
4. Jezebel sought to kill him after he had killed her false prophets.
5. She went to Ahijah the prophet.
6. (Sample answer) They cried, tore their clothes, and put on sackcloth.
7. seven days
8. "[He] did worse than all that were before him."
9. He tore his clothes, put on sackcloth, and fasted.

15. after the Israelites killed Adoram, his tax collector
16. when God told him not to fight against Jeroboam
17. after the LORD sent fire upon the altar on Mount Carmel
18. after he was wounded in a battle with the Syrians

Chapter Two Review

This review is divided into two parts, an oral review and a written review. The oral review is intended for class discussion, but students could also use it for self-study.

66   Chapter Two   The Northern Tribes Set Up a Separate Kingdom

2. What did the ten northern tribes ask of Rehoboam? [1 Kings 12:2–4] _____
   They asked him to make their burdens lighter.

3. What happened to the house of Jeroboam? [1 Kings 15:27–29] _____
   Baasha killed all of Jeroboam's descendants.

4. What words does the Bible use again and again to describe Jeroboam? [1 Kings 16:19, 26] _____
   "He made Israel to sin."

5. What two dynasties in Israel lasted for more than two generations? [Lesson 7] _____
   Omri's and Jehu's

6. What did Ahab do when Naboth refused to sell his vineyard? [1 Kings 21:4] _____
   He lay down with his face toward the wall and refused to eat.

7. What did Elijah prophesy about Ahab's and Jezebel's deaths? [1 Kings 21:19, 23] _____
   The dogs would lick Ahab's blood, and the dogs would eat Jezebel.

8. What did Ahab sell himself to do? [1 Kings 21:25] _____
   wickedness in the sight of the LORD

9. What did Elijah do when Ahaziah sent groups of soldiers to capture him? [2 Kings 1:10] _____
   He called down fire from heaven to burn them up.

10. What are the twelve Books of History? (Be sure to use the correct order and spelling.) [Lessons 1, 6]
    Joshua   Ruth   2 Samuel   2 Kings   2 Chronicles   Nehemiah
    Judges   1 Samuel   1 Kings   1 Chronicles   Ezra   Esther

11. What do these words mean? [Lessons 8, 9]
    a. blaspheme: to curse or speak evil of _____
    b. sackcloth: coarse cloth worn by mourners _____
    c. mantle: a cloak or robe _____
    d. morsel: a piece of food _____

Where

12. Where did Elijah stay during the years of drought? (Give two places.) [1 Kings 17:5, 9] _____
    near the Brook Cherith and with a widow at Zarephath

13. Where did Elijah meet the priests of Baal? [1 Kings 18:19] on Mount Carmel _____

14. Where did Elijah hear the still, small voice? [1 Kings 19:8, 12] on Mount Horeb _____

Where Is It Found?

This is a brief outline of the events that you have studied in this chapter.

✎ *Match these chapters with the events they record. Fill in the blanks from memory if you can. The headings in your Bible may help you.*

<u>c</u> 15. 1 Kings 12

<u>g</u> 16. 1 Kings 13, 14

<u>a</u> 17. 1 Kings 15

<u>d</u> 18. 1 Kings 16

<u>f</u> 19. 1 Kings 17, 18

<u>b</u> 20. 1 Kings 19–21

<u>e</u> 21. 1 Kings 22

<u>h</u> 22. 2 Kings 1, 2

a. Israel and Judah war against each other. Baasha kills all the house of Jeroboam.

b. Elijah flees for his life and hears God's voice at Mount Horeb. Later he returns and rebukes Ahab for taking Naboth's life and vineyard.

c. The kingdom of Israel is divided. Jeroboam sets up golden calves at Dan and Bethel.

d. Zimri destroys Baasha's house, but after reigning seven days he is defeated by Omri. Later Omri's son Ahab marries Jezebel, a heathen princess.

e. Jehoshaphat and Ahab fight against Syria, and Ahab is killed in battle.

f. God cares for Elijah during a famine. Elijah confronts the prophets of Baal on Mount Carmel.

g. A prophet prophesies against Jeroboam's idolatry. Jeroboam's son becomes sick and dies.

h. Elijah rebukes Ahaziah. Elijah is taken into heaven by a whirlwind.

Map Review

✎ *Fill in each blank on the map with the correct name from the list.*

Bethel
Damascus
Dan
Jerusalem
Jezreel
Ramoth-gilead
Samaria
Zidon (Sidon)
Zarephath

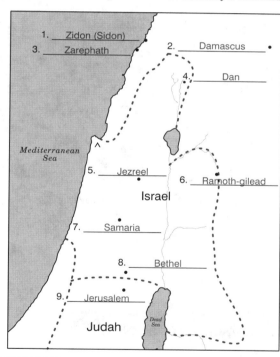

1. Zidon (Sidon)
3. Zarephath
2. Damascus
4. Dan
Mediterranean Sea
5. Jezreel
6. Ramoth-gilead
Israel
7. Samaria
8. Bethel
9. Jerusalem
Judah
Dead Sea

68

Lesson 10. The Israelite Family

A. ANSWERS FROM THE BIBLE

Hebrew Families

Early Hebrew families did not live in separate homes as most families do today. Instead, parents, children, grandparents, uncles and aunts, married brothers and sisters, and servants usually lived in one large compound of tents. The leader of the compound decided when to move from place to place for new pasture. He made plans for weddings, work, and warfare. The leader's eldest son, or first-born, usually took over the leadership after his father died.

1. Abraham was the leader of a large household. When he wanted to fight against his enemies, how many servants could he call together? (Genesis 14:14) _____318_____ (If most of these men had families, Abraham might have had several thousand people in his household.)

Even after the Israelites settled in towns and villages of Canaan, they still considered themselves part of large family groups.

2. As a child, Jesus traveled to Jerusalem with his family. What proves that the group of relatives and friends was large? (Luke 2:44) _____
   His parents did not notice that he was not with the group until they had gone a day's journey.

How Many Wives?

Sometimes a wealthy man had more than one wife. Divorce was also permitted. The Law allowed these practices in Old Testament times, but they often caused jealousy and hatred among the wives and children. When Jesus came, He restored God's original plan that one man and one woman should marry for life.

3. a. Solomon had _____seven hundred_____ wives and _____three hundred_____ concubines (1 Kings 11:3).

   b. What did Solomon's wives cause him to do? (1 Kings 11:4) _____
   They turned his heart away from God (and led him into idol worship).

4. Hannah's husband, Elkanah, had two wives. What did Elkanah's other wife do to Hannah? (1 Samuel 1:6) _She provoked Hannah sore and made her fret. (She angered Hannah and made_ _her irritated and miserable.)_

5. How many wives did God permit the early church leaders to have? (1 Timothy 3:2) _____one_____

6. Why did the Law allow divorce in Old Testament times? (Mark 10:4–6) _____
   because of the hardness of men's hearts

Life in Bible Times

Lesson 10

Oral Review

1. Who wrote many beautiful psalms of praise and worship? [3] **David**
2. What was a tunic? a cloak? an ephod? [5] *tunic:* **an inner, sacklike garment;** *cloak:* **a heavy outer coat;** *ephod:* **a special coat worn by priests**
3. According to 1 Peter 3:4, what ornament does the New Testament tell godly women to adorn themselves with? [5] **a meek and quiet spirit**
4. Who built Samaria, the capital city of Israel? [7] **Omri**
5. Who married Jezebel and worshiped Baal? [8] **Ahab**
6. Why did Ahab hate Micaiah the prophet? [8] **Micaiah prophesied evil things about Ahab.**
7. Where did Elijah hear the still, small voice? [9] **on Mount Horeb**
8. How did Elijah go to heaven? [9] **He went up by a whirlwind.**

Even though the Old Testament Law allowed more than one wife, most men in Bible times had only one. They could not afford to pay for more. The parents of Israelite brides received money (or valuable services or goods) from the young men who wanted to marry their daughters.

7. Who paid for his wives by working fourteen years? (Genesis 29:20, 30) _____ Jacob _____

Children—a Blessing From God

People in Bible times considered children a special blessing. If they could have no children, they thought they were under God's curse.

8. What was taken away from Elizabeth when she had a son? (Luke 1:24, 25) _____

   her reproach among men

9. Hannah had no children. While she was at the tabernacle, she _____ prayed _____ to the

   LORD, _____ wept _____ sore, and made a _____ vow _____ (1 Samuel 1:10, 11).

   When God answered her prayer, she gave her son (Samuel) back to Him.

Israelite babies were born at home. Their mothers wrapped them with long strips of white cloth (swaddling clothes).

10. Who found Jesus as a baby wrapped in swaddling clothes? (Luke

    2:8–12) _____

    the shepherds

Eight days after babies were born, they were named. When boys were forty days old and girls were eighty days old, their parents offered a lamb and a pigeon to God. Poor people offered two pigeons.

11. Judging by what they offered, were Joseph and Mary rich or poor? (Luke 2:24) _____ poor _____

Young children were taught at home by their mothers. Older boys were taught by their fathers, or by tutors if the parents were wealthy.

12. Who taught Timothy when he was a young child? (2 Timothy 1:5; 3:15) _____

    his mother (and grandmother)

13. God commands children to honor and obey their parents. What were parents commanded to do to a

    stubborn and rebellious son who refused to obey them? (Deuteronomy 21:18–21) _____

    They were to take him to the elders of his city to be stoned to death.

Life in Bible Times

- God's people were not to tolerate rebellion among themselves. Imagine how different Israel's history could have been if the rebellious had always been dealt with in their youth. On the other hand, how many of us were completely free from rebellion in our youth? By the Law is the knowledge of sin, and with that knowledge all the world becomes guilty before God (Romans 3:19, 20). As students mature toward the age of accountability, passages like this one from Deuteronomy will help them see the seriousness of sin in God's sight, and their personal need for salvation.

In This Lesson

Main Points

- Early Israelites lived together in large, extended family groups.
- The Law allowed divorce and polygamy, but Jesus restored God's original plan for marriage.
- People in Bible times considered children a special blessing.
- Bible names often had special meanings.

Objectives

- The students should know
  —that the Hebrews had close ties with their extended families.
  —why God allowed divorce in the Old Testament but no longer does in the New Testament. (See Part A, numbers 3–6.)
  —how families in the Old Testament felt about children. (They considered children a special blessing. If they could have no children, they thought they were under God's curse.)

70   Chapter Two   The Northern Tribes Set Up a Separate Kingdom

B. BIBLE STUDY BOOKS

Bible Names

People in Bible times did not choose names just because they sounded pretty. The names they used for both people and places were important. They had meanings that often served as testimonies to God's goodness. Many Israelite children were named after animals or objects.

✎ *Use a Bible dictionary to match these names with their meanings. (Note: The meanings given in Bible dictionaries sometimes vary. If your Bible dictionary gives other meanings, you may need to ask your teacher for help.)*

<u>c</u> 1. Barak   a. bee

<u>a</u> 2. Deborah   b. ewe

<u>b</u> 3. Rachel   c. lightning

Some children had the names of godly virtues. Use the clues given to find whose names meant the following.

4. Rest: _____Manoah_____   Samson's father (Judges 13:2)

5. Grace: _____Hannah_____   Samuel's mother (1 Samuel 1:2)

Some names were complete testimonies. Find a name in each verse to fit the blanks.

6. E l i m e l e c h : God is king. (Ruth 1:2)

7. J o n a t h a n : Jehovah has given. (1 Samuel 18:1)

Many Hebrew names began with the letters *El, Jo,* or *Je.* These were part of two names of God, *Elohim* and *Jehovah.* (Notice that the names in numbers 6 and 7 begin with *El* and *Jo.*)

✎ *Use a Bible dictionary to find additional names that begin with these letters. Be sure the meaning includes God's name. Write a name and its meaning for each set of letters.*

	Names	**Meanings**
8. El	Elijah—My God is Jehovah.	Elisha—God is his salvation.
9. Je	Jehoshaphat—Jehovah has judged.	Jehu—Jehovah is He.
10. Jo	Joab—Jehovah is father.	Jochebed—Jehovah her glory.

Answers for 8–10 may vary. Sample answers are given.

Life in Bible Times

Truths to Instill

• Children need to learn appreciation for their parents and for what they do in providing a home and giving them love, care, and guidance. Children should also recognize God's wisdom in planning marriage and the family.

• Children need to appreciate their brothers and sisters.

• Children should begin to realize that marriage is a sacred, lifelong commitment to be made by mature adults. (Avoid encouraging a premature interest in boy-girl friendships.)

CHAPTER THREE

Israel's Downfall

For the word of the LORD is right; and all his works are done in truth. He loveth righteousness and judgment: the earth is full of the goodness of the LORD. Psalm 33:4, 5

TIME LINE—Chapter Three

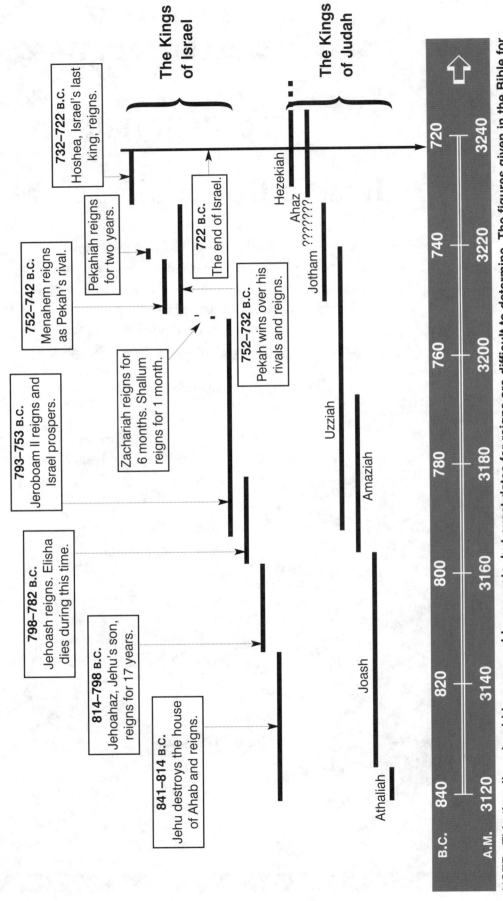

The Kings of Israel

The Kings of Judah

732–722 B.C. Hoshea, Israel's last king, reigns.

Pekahiah reigns for two years.

752–742 B.C. Menahem reigns as Pekah's rival.

722 B.C. The end of Israel.

793–753 B.C. Jeroboam II reigns and Israel prospers.

Zachariah reigns for 6 months. Shallum reigns for 1 month.

752–732 B.C. Pekah wins over his rivals and reigns.

798–782 B.C. Jehoash reigns. Elisha dies during this time.

814–798 B.C. Jehoahaz, Jehu's son, reigns for 17 years.

841–814 B.C. Jehu destroys the house of Ahab and reigns.

Hezekiah

Ahaz

Jotham ???????

Uzziah

Amaziah

Joash

Athaliah

B.C.	840	820	800	780	760	740	720
A.M.	3120	3140	3160	3180	3200	3220	3240

NOTE: This time line should be reasonably accurate, but exact dates for reigns are difficult to determine. The figures given in the Bible for these kings require either some overlapping reigns as shown above or some long gaps between kings.

73

Lesson 11. Elisha and the Sons of the Prophets

The sons of the prophets were men who were taught by prophets such as Samuel, Elijah, and Elisha. They prophesied or served under the prophet's leadership (1 Samuel 19:20; 2 Kings 9:1), and some of them probably became prophets themselves.

The sons of the prophets were not popular among many Israelites. They lived in a time when Israel was falling away from God. Thousands of Israelites were rejecting God's laws and living sinful lives. They worshiped idols, spent much time in feasting, and wore fancy clothing. But the sons of the prophets lived as God wanted them to live—in a quiet, decent, and orderly manner. They obeyed God's Law. No matter what most of the Israelites did, the sons of the prophets continued to serve God faithfully.

Elisha became the leader of the sons of the prophets. Because he was a faithful prophet, God was able to use him to speak to the Israelites.

Elisha performed many miracles, spoke fearlessly to kings, and provided an example for anyone who still wanted to know God's will. His wise leadership helped the sons of the prophets to be faithful.

God still looks for people who are not afraid to be part of a small, faithful group. He uses people who do what is right even when those around them are leaving the godly way.

- In Elisha's time, there were sons of the prophets at Bethel, Jericho, Gilgal, and other places (2 Kings 2:3, 5; 4:38; 5:22; 6:1). These men helped Elisha remind the Israelites that the LORD was the true God of Israel.

A. ANSWERS FROM THE BIBLE

A New Prophet in Israel

Elijah did not die. Instead, God took him to heaven by a whirlwind, and his servant Elisha saw him go. This was a sign from God that Elisha was to take Elijah's place as a prophet.

2 Kings 2:9–15

1. What request did Elisha make before Elijah was taken up into heaven? _____

   "Let a double portion of thy spirit be upon me."

2. What miracle did Elisha perform with Elijah's mantle? _____

   He parted the waters of Jordan.

When Elijah and Elisha had left Jericho earlier that day, fifty of the sons of the prophets followed them as far as the Jordan River. These sons of the prophets had looked to Elijah for leadership, but now they recognized Elisha as their leader. Perhaps they saw Elisha strike the Jordan as they waited for him to return.

3. What did the sons of the prophets say when they saw Elisha? _____

   "The spirit of Elijah doth rest on Elisha."

Lesson 11

Oral Review

The numbers in brackets tell which lessons are being reviewed.

1. What does the LORD look at rather than just the outward appearance of a person? [1] **the person's heart**
2. How did David show his respect for the LORD's anointed? [2] **He spared Saul's life.**
3. What covenant did God make with David? [3] **God promised to establish David's throne forever.**
4. What words does the Bible use again and again to describe Jeroboam? [7] **"He made Israel to sin."**
5. What two dynasties in Israel lasted for more than two generations? [7] **Omri's and Jehu's**
6. In what two places did Elijah stay during the years of drought? [9] **near the Brook Cherith, and with a widow at Zarephath**
7. What two practices did the Old Testament Law permit that were not according to God's original plan for marriage? [10] **having more than one wife, and divorce**
8. What shows that Joseph and Mary were probably poor? [10] **They offered two pigeons instead of a lamb and a pigeon.**

2 Kings 2:19–22

The men of Jericho also recognized Elisha as the new prophet of the LORD. They told him about the problem they had with their water supply.

4. The men of Jericho told Elisha that the "water is _____naught_____ (bad), and the ground _____barren_____." (Apparently the water was so bad that it harmed the soil if used for irrigation.)

5. What did Elisha throw into the water when he proclaimed that the LORD had healed it? _____salt_____

Elisha and the Shunammite Woman

Elisha apparently enjoyed spending time with others. These verses tell about one family that Elisha visited regularly during his travels around Israel.

2 Kings 4:8–37

✎ Write true or false. Correct each false statement on the lines after the sentence.

_____false_____ 6. Elisha asked the Shunammite woman and her husband to build a little room for him.
The Shunammite woman and her husband decided to build a little room for Elisha.

_____false_____ 7. The Shunammite reminded Elisha that she had no child. _____
Elisha's servant reminded Elisha that the Shunammite had no child.

_____false_____ 8. The boy died while he was with his father. _____
The boy died while he was with his _mother._

_____true_____ 9. The Shunammite did not tell her husband why she wanted to find Elisha. _____

_____false_____ 10. The boy came back to life when Gehazi laid Elisha's staff on him. _____
The boy came back to life when _Elisha prayed and laid himself on the child._

_____true_____ 11. Some years later, the king restored the Shunammite's land after Gehazi told him how her son had been restored to life (2 Kings 8:1–6). _____

In the rewritten sentences for numbers 6–11, the corrections are in italics. The pupil's sentences may vary somewhat.

Elisha's Miracles

God gave both Elijah and Elisha the ability to perform miracles. The miracles of both prophets reminded idol worshipers that the LORD is the true God, and they encouraged the sons of the prophets and other believers to remain faithful to God.

✎ Many of Elisha's miracles helped people in trouble. Complete this list of miracles that the LORD performed through Elisha. The ones you have studied in this lesson are given. You will study several more in Lesson 12. All references are from 2 Kings.

12. _The waters of Jordan were parted._ _____ (2:14)

13. _The water of Jericho was healed._ _____ (2:19–22)

In This Lesson

Scope: 2 Kings 2:1–6:18; 8:1–6; 13:20, 21

Main Events

• Elisha succeeds Elijah as a prophet of the LORD.
• The LORD performs many miracles through Elisha. Many of these helped the sons of the prophets and other faithful people. (All references are from 2 Kings.)
—The waters of Jordan were parted (2:14).
—The water of Jericho was healed (2:19–22).
—Water was supplied to kings (3:17, 20).
—A widow's oil increased (4:1–6).
—God gave the Shunammite woman a son (4:16, 17).
—The Shunammite woman's son was raised to life (4:33–35).
—The deadly pottage was healed (4:38–41).
—One hundred men were fed with a small amount of food (4:42–44).
—Naaman was healed of leprosy (5:10, 14).
—Gehazi was smitten with leprosy (5:27).
—An axe head floated (6:5, 6).
—Elisha told the Syrian king's secret plans (6:8–12).
—Elisha's servant saw chariots of fire (6:17).

14. __Water was supplied to kings._____ (3:17, 20)

15. __A widow's oil increased._____ (4:1–6)

16. __God gave the Shunammite woman a son._____ (4:16, 17)

17. __*The Shunammite woman's son was raised to life.*_____ (4:33–35)

18. __Deadly pottage was healed._____ (4:38–41)

19. __One hundred men were fed with a small amount of food._____ (4:42–44)

20. __Naaman was healed of leprosy._____ (5:10, 14)

21. __Gehazi was smitten with leprosy._____ (5:27)

22. __An axe head floated._____ (6:5, 6)

23. __Elisha told the Syrian king's secret plans._____ (6:8–12)

24. __Elisha's servant saw chariots of fire._____ (6:17)

25. __God smote the Syrians with blindness._____ (6:18)

The LORD worked a miracle through Elisha even after Elisha had died.

26. __A dead man was raised after touching Elisha's bones._____ (13:20, 21)

Challenge Exercise

✎ *Memorize the miracles of Elisha.*

If you require your students to memorize Elisha's miracles, you might want to require them to give them in the review and on the test.

B. BIBLE WORD STUDY

✎ *Match these definitions with the Bible words on the right. All references are from 2 Kings.*

__b__ 1. A person to whom money is owed (4:1)   a. constrain

__a__ 2. To urge or compel (4:8)   b. creditor

__h__ 3. To bring trouble or distress (4:27)   c. dearth

__c__ 4. A famine (4:38)   d. pottage

__e__ 5. To boil; cook (4:38)   e. seethe

__d__ 6. Soup or stew (4:38)   f. sojourn

__g__ 7. Small; confining (6:1)   g. strait

__f__ 8. To stay for a short time (8:1)   h. vex

✎ *Use a concordance to find verses in the New Testament that use the words* sojourn *and* strait *(without a suffix). Write one reference for each word.*

9. sojourn __Acts 7:6__

10. strait __(Any one) Matthew 7:13, 14; Luke 13:24; Philippians 1:23__

—God smote the Syrians with blindness (6:18).

—A dead man was raised after touching Elisha's bones (13:20, 21).

Objectives

• The students should know

—that the prophet Elijah was taken to heaven without dying.

—that Elisha performed many miracles.

—who recognized that the spirit of Elijah rested on Elisha. (the sons of the prophets)

—why God performs miracles. (to remind unbelievers that the LORD is the true God, and to encourage believers to remain faithful to God)

• Challenge Exercise: If you assign this optional exercise, students should memorize Elisha's miracles.

Truths to Instill

• God's people will always be a minority in this world (Matthew 7:13, 14; Luke 13:23, 24; Romans 11:5).

• Elisha and the sons of the prophets were a light in a dark place. They set an example of righteousness in the midst of an increasingly wicked people. Christians have a similar role in society today as they bear witness of God's call to holiness, both by their lives, and by their testimony (Philippians 2:15, 16).

C. THINKING ABOUT BIBLE TRUTHS

How Does God Use Miracles?

As you saw in this lesson, God used Elisha to perform a number of miracles. Many people today refuse to believe in miracles. They try to figure out natural explanations for the miraculous things that the Bible records. They do not have faith that God can do things such as making an iron axe head float on water, so they try to explain these things away. In this section you will look at some Bible principles regarding miracles.

1. Read Jeremiah 32:17. Since God created the heaven and the earth by His great _____ power _____, there is nothing too _____ hard _____ for him to do. It is not difficult for Him to temporarily change one of the laws of nature and make an iron axe head float on water. He made these laws, and they are under His control.

2. Read Mark 16:20. In the past, God has sometimes used signs (miracles) to _____ confirm _____ His word as it was preached by His messengers. For example, God made Jeroboam's altar break open as a sign, or proof, that what He had just told Jeroboam through a prophet would surely come to pass (1 Kings 13:3–5).

3. Read Exodus 7:5. At times God used miracles to prove to unbelievers who He is. God did a number of mighty miracles through Moses to show the Egyptians that He is the _____ LORD _____.

4. Sometimes God used a miracle to bring judgment on sinful people. In Noah's time God brought a _____ flood _____ on the earth to destroy it because of the sins of mankind.

5. Read Matthew 24:24. Not every miracle is from God. According to this verse, Satan will use miracles to try to _____ deceive _____ the very elect (God's people).

6. Circle the letter of the correct statement. If you need help, reread the comments and questions in this section.

   a. God performs miracles as often as He can.

   b. If a person can do miracles, it is evident that he is a true Christian, even if he does not obey the Bible.

   c. God can easily perform miracles whenever He wants, but usually He uses them only for special purposes.

- Elisha gave the LORD the glory for the miracles performed through him. We need to give God the glory for everything, whether great or small, that He accomplishes through our lives (1 Peter 4:10, 11).

D. LEARNING MORE ABOUT THE BIBLE

Old Testament Books

✎ *Review the Old Testament books and their divisions. (See Lesson 1 if you need help.) You will need to know the order and spelling of the Books of Poetry for the Chapter 3 Test.*

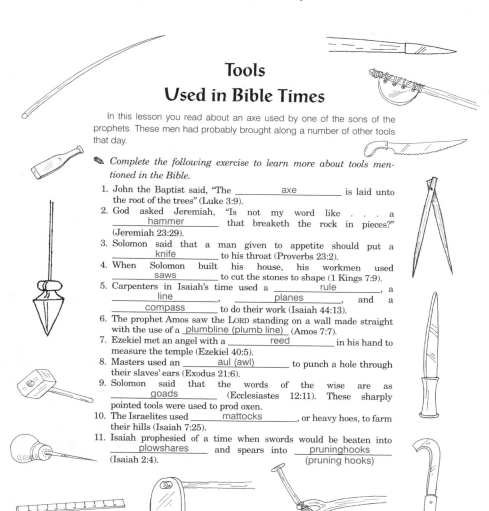

Tools
Used in Bible Times

In this lesson you read about an axe used by one of the sons of the prophets. These men had probably brought along a number of other tools that day.

✎ *Complete the following exercise to learn more about tools mentioned in the Bible.*

1. John the Baptist said, "The _____axe_____ is laid unto the root of the trees" (Luke 3:9).
2. God asked Jeremiah, "Is not my word like . . . a _____hammer_____ that breaketh the rock in pieces?" (Jeremiah 23:29).
3. Solomon said that a man given to appetite should put a _____knife_____ to his throat (Proverbs 23:2).
4. When Solomon built his house, his workmen used _____saws_____ to cut the stones to shape (1 Kings 7:9).
5. Carpenters in Isaiah's time used a _____rule_____, a _____line_____, _____planes_____, and a _____compass_____ to do their work (Isaiah 44:13).
6. The prophet Amos saw the LORD standing on a wall made straight with the use of a _plumbline (plumb line)_ (Amos 7:7).
7. Ezekiel met an angel with a _____reed_____ in his hand to measure the temple (Ezekiel 40:5).
8. Masters used an _____aul (awl)_____ to punch a hole through their slaves' ears (Exodus 21:6).
9. Solomon said that the words of the wise are as _____goads_____ (Ecclesiastes 12:11). These sharply pointed tools were used to prod oxen.
10. The Israelites used _____mattocks_____, or heavy hoes, to farm their hills (Isaiah 7:25).
11. Isaiah prophesied of a time when swords would be beaten into _____plowshares_____ and spears into _____pruninghooks_____ (pruning hooks) (Isaiah 2:4).

78

Lesson 12. Elisha Brings God's Message to Israel

In some ways, Elisha was not like Elijah. Elijah came from Gilead, a mountainous region east of the Jordan. He spent much time in the wilderness by himself. His work was to show men their sin and to help carry out God's judgment upon them.

Elisha spent more time in cities. He enjoyed being with people. His work was to help the poor, to heal the sick, and to show mercy to Israel's enemies.

Even though Elijah and Elisha were different, Elisha continued to serve the LORD faithfully, just as Elijah had done. Elisha kept bringing the LORD's message to the Israelites. He continued to prove God's power by performing miracles. And like Elijah, Elisha rebuked kings for their sin and told them what would happen in the future. God blessed Elisha's work, and thousands of people were helped through him.

God has called faithful leaders today to preach and to guide the church. As these faithful leaders grow older and die, God calls new leaders. These ministers do not speak exactly like the old ministers. They may have different gifts and abilities. But if they are true to God, they will preach sound doctrine and guide the church faithfully just as the older ministers have done. God will bless the faithful leaders of today, just as He blessed the faithful leaders in the past.

God can use people who value the good, proven ways of the past.

A. ANSWERS FROM THE BIBLE

Elisha spent most of his time with men and women who served the LORD. But sometimes he also prophesied to kings. Through miracles, Elisha proved to them that the LORD is the true God.

Elisha and Four Kings

2 Kings 3:1–9, 14–18, 26, 27

1. After King Ahab died, his son _____Jehoram_____ reigned in Samaria _____twelve_____ years.

2. Ahab's son was also evil, but he did put away the image of _____Baal_____ that Ahab had made.

3. Mesha, king of _____Moab_____, rebelled against Israel.

4. The king of Israel went out to fight against King Mesha. Jehoshaphat, the king of _____Judah_____, went along, and so did the king of _____Edom_____.

The kings found themselves in a dry place with no water for their men and animals. King Jehoram became fearful, but Jehoshaphat suggested that they ask Elisha for a message from the LORD.

5. Elisha told them to make the valley full of _____ditches_____, and God would send them water.

With the LORD's help, the three kings smote the Moabites. When King Mesha saw that the battle was going against him, he also looked to a god. But he looked to Chemosh, the god of Moab.

6. Mesha offered his _____oldest_____ _____son_____ as a burnt offering to Chemosh.

- Chemosh, the god of the Moabites, is not directly mentioned in 2 Kings 3. But in 1868 the Moabite Stone was discovered, which bears an inscription giving King Mesha's account of his revolt. King Mesha honors Chemosh in this inscription. Chemosh is also mentioned in a number of Bible verses, such as Judges 11:24 and 1 Kings 11:33.

Lesson 12

Oral Review

1. Why is David's family line important to us today? [3] **Jesus came through David's line.**
2. Why did Jeroboam make golden calves at Bethel and Dan? [6] **He wanted to keep the northern tribes from returning to Jerusalem.**
3. What did Elijah prophesy about Ahab's and Jezebel's deaths? [8] **The dogs would lick Ahab's blood, and the dogs would eat Jezebel.**
4. Where did Elijah hear the still, small voice? [9] **on Mount Horeb**
5. What does the name Jonathan mean? [10] **"Jehovah has given."**
6. What request did Elisha make before Elijah was taken up to heaven? [11] **"Let a double portion of thy spirit be upon me."**
7. What miracle performed by Elisha helped a poor widow to pay her debts? [11] **the increasing of the widow's oil**
8. What happened to the Shunammite woman's son one day? [11] **He died and was raised back to life.**

Elisha and Naaman

Elisha sometimes helped Israel's enemies. This showed that the LORD was not just the God of the Israelites, but that He is God of the whole earth. In this chapter Naaman learns about the true God.

✎ *Write* true *or* false. *Correct each false statement on the lines after the sentence.*

2 Kings 5:1–16

__true__ 7. Naaman was captain of the Syrian army. _____

_____

> *In the rewritten sentences for numbers 7–12, the corrections are in italics. The pupil's sentences may vary somewhat.*

__true__ 8. Naaman's wife had a maid from Israel who said that the prophet in Samaria could heal Naaman. _____

_____

The king of Syria did not know where to find the prophet, so he sent Naaman to the king of Israel. When Naaman arrived with his strange request for healing, the king of Israel thought that the king of Syria was trying to find an excuse to fight against him. Elisha told the king to send Naaman to him.

__true__ 9. At first Naaman was too proud to obey Elisha's instructions. _____

_____

__false__ 10. Naaman's servants suggested that he wash in the rivers of Damascus. _Naaman's servants suggested that he wash_ in the Jordan as Elisha had told him to do.

__false__ 11. Naaman paid Elisha for healing him. _Naaman did not pay_ Elisha for healing him. (_Elisha refused payment_ for healing Naaman.)

__true__ 12. Because Gehazi coveted and took Naaman's goods, he and his descendants were smitten with leprosy (2 Kings 5:20–27). _____

_____

Elisha and the Syrians

Elisha did not always help the Syrians. On several occasions he revealed their secret plans to the king of Israel.

✎ *Number these events in the order they happened.*

2 Kings 6:8–17

13. __4__ Elisha's servant is afraid.

__2__ The king of Syria sends his army to capture Elisha.

__1__ Elisha reveals the Syrians' plans.

__3__ The Syrians surround the city of Dothan.

__5__ The LORD lets Elisha's servant see the heavenly host.

In This Lesson

Scope: 2 Kings 3; 5; 6:8–7:20; 13:14–19

Main Events
- The kings of Israel, Judah, and Edom fight against Moab. Elisha gives the kings of Israel and Judah direction, and God provides water for them.
- Naaman comes to Elisha to be cured of his leprosy. Gehazi becomes covetous of Naaman's goods and is smitten with Naaman's disease.
- The Syrians try to capture Elisha, but they are blinded.
- The Syrians lay siege to Samaria. God miraculously delivers the city.
- Elisha prophesies the future of Jehoash.

Objectives
- The students should know
  —the stories about Elisha mentioned in "Main Events" above.
  —some lessons that we can learn from the lives of Elijah and Elisha. (See Part C.)

80   Chapter Three   Israel's Downfall

2 Kings 6:18–23

14. __5__ The Syrians return home in peace.

    __3__ Elisha tells the king of Israel not to smite the Syrians.

    __1__ Elisha asks the LORD to smite the Syrians with blindness.

    __4__ The king of Israel prepares food for the Syrians.

    __2__ Elisha leads the Syrians from Dothan to Samaria.

• The distance that Elisha led the blind Syrians was about ten miles.

Elisha in the Siege of Samaria

Sometime later the Syrians fought against Israel again. This time they surrounded Samaria, the capital city. The Israelites in Samaria became so desperate for food that they ate whatever they could find. When the king of Israel heard that two mothers had agreed to eat their own sons, he was distressed and angry. He blamed Elisha and the LORD, and he decided that Elisha must be put to death immediately. But Elisha told the king that the famine would end the next day.

2 Kings 7:1–17

15. Elisha prophesied that the next day a measure of fine _____ flour _____ would be sold for a

    _____ shekel _____.

16. Who doubted what Elisha said? __a lord on whose hand the king leaned__

    That night some lepers decided to go to the Syrian camp and ask for food. But when they came to the camp, they discovered that the Syrians had fled, leaving most of their belongings behind.

17. Why did the Syrians flee? __God had made the Syrians hear a noise of chariots, horses, and a__

    __great host. (They thought the Israelites had hired the Hittites and the Egyptians to help them.)__

18. How was Elisha's prophecy fulfilled? _____

    __The Israelites sold the Syrian goods for the prices Elisha had said.__

    _____

19. What happened to the man who had doubted Elisha's prophecy? _____

    __The people trampled him and he died.__

Elisha and King Jehoash

2 Kings 13:14–19

Elisha lived to be an old man. He saw the reigns of Ahab, Ahaziah, Joram (sometimes called Jehoram), Jehu, Jehoahaz, and Jehoash (sometimes called Joash). In these verses King Jehoash came to visit Elisha when he heard that Elisha was sick. He knew that Elisha would die soon.

20. Elisha asked King Jehoash to take a bow and shoot an arrow out the window. This was a sign that

    King Jehoash would smite the _____ Syrians _____.

21. Then Elisha asked Jehoash to hit the ground with the arrows. Jehoash smote the ground only

    _____ three _____ times. This meant he would defeat the Syrians _____ three _____ times.

22. Why was Elisha angry with Jehoash? __King Jehoash should have struck the ground five or six times.__

    __Then he would have destroyed the Syrians completely instead of just defeating them three times.__

Truths to Instill

• Elisha, in carrying on Elijah's work, also carried on his faith. (See 2 Kings 2:9, 14.) Will your students have the same desire to carry on the true faith?

• Elisha's ministry was a testimony of God's power in a time when many Israelites were apostatizing. Naaman learned that "there is no God in all the earth, but in Israel" (2 Kings 5:15). The lord on whose hand the king of Israel leaned learned (too late) that God's word must not be questioned. And the kings of several countries learned to respect the Word of the LORD that Elisha spoke.

Lesson 12. Elisha Brings God's Message to Israel   **81**

B. BIBLE WORD STUDY

✎ *Use the tables of measure in the back of this book to complete these exercises.*

During the siege of Samaria, the head of an ass (donkey) was sold for fourscore pieces of silver, and one-fourth of a cab of dove's dung (droppings) for five pieces of silver (2 Kings 6:25). Elisha prophesied that the next day a measure of fine flour would be sold for a shekel, and two measures of barley for a shekel (2 Kings 7:1).

1. A score equals ___20___. (See Lesson 4 if you need help.) Fourscore equals ___80___.

2. The pieces of silver mentioned in 2 Kings 6:25 were probably shekels of silver. A shekel weighs about

    __²/₅__ ounce(s).
    (11.3 g)

3. One cab equals about __2 ¾__ pint(s). One-fourth cab equals less than ___1___ pint(s).
    (1.5 l)   (0.4 l)

4. The *measures* of 2 Kings 7:1 were seahs. One seah equals about __¼__ bushel(s). Two seahs equals
                                                                      (9 l)
    about __½__ bushel(s).
         (18 l)

5. a. How many shekels (pieces of silver) did an ass's head sell for during the siege? (2 Kings 6:25) ___80___

   b. How many seahs (measures) of fine flour could be bought for the same price the day after the

      Syrians fled? ___80___

6. a. How many cabs equal one seah? ___6___

   b. After the Syrians fled, how many cabs of barley could be bought for a shekel? ___12___ How many

      cabs of barley could be bought for five shekels? ___60___ (Compare this with the amount of dove

      dung that cost five shekels the day before.)

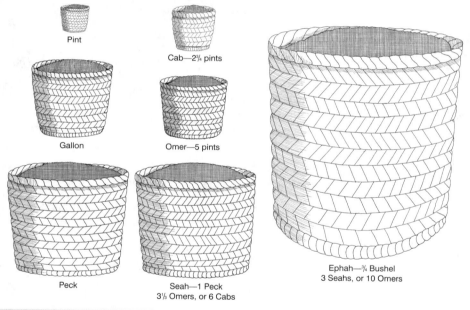

Pint

Cab—2¾ pints

Gallon

Omer—5 pints

Peck

Seah—1 Peck
3⅓ Omers, or 6 Cabs

Ephah—¾ Bushel
3 Seahs, or 10 Omers

Do Part B together in class if time permits. It is difficult to compare the value of money used in Bible times with modern currency, but the drastic drop in prices shows how expensive food had become during the siege.

C. THINKING ABOUT BIBLE TRUTHS

Lessons From Elijah and Elisha

In the last several lessons you have studied the lives of Elijah and Elisha. This section points out some lessons that you can learn from the example of their lives.

✎ *Circle the letter of the* best *answer. Be prepared to explain in class why you chose the answer you did.*

1. Elijah fled into the wilderness when he learned that Jezebel wanted to kill him. Here God spoke to him, not in the mighty storm, not in the earthquake, not in the fire, but in a still, small voice. From this we can learn that
   a. God often speaks to His people through small things in life rather than through great disasters or miracles.
   b. God speaks to His people only through disasters such as storms, earthquakes, or fires.
   c. God never allows His people to suffer from disasters such as storms, earthquakes, and fires.

2. Elijah and Elisha were both powerful prophets whom God used in many ways. But God took Elijah to heaven without dying, while Elisha became sick and died. This shows that
   a. Elijah was a better prophet than Elisha was, so God rewarded him by taking him to heaven without dying.
   b. God loved Elijah more than He loved Elisha. He showed this by taking Elijah to heaven and letting Elisha die a natural death.
   c. God's plan for one person might be very different from his plan for another person, even if both are faithful to Him.

3. Soon after Elijah was taken to heaven, some children followed Elisha and made fun of him. The Bible says that he cursed them in the Name of the LORD, and some bears came out of the woods and attacked them. From this we should learn that
   a. the bears in Israel were more dangerous than the bears in most countries of the world.
   b. mocking or showing disrespect toward someone is very wrong.
   c. Elisha did not like children.

4. Elisha seems to have been a prosperous farmer when Elijah called him to become his servant. The Bible says that he was plowing with twelve yoke of oxen. He probably needed servants to drive some of the oxen. However, when Elijah called him, Elisha left everything behind and followed Elijah. This shows that
   a. it is wrong for God's people to own farms or other possessions.
   b. God wants His people to be farmers before they are called into a special service.
   c. God's plan for a person's life is more important than anything else that he might be doing.

Part C points out a few lessons that students can learn from the lives of Elijah and Elisha. You may want to do these exercises together in class to be sure that the students understand them. You may also want to spend some time discussing these principles and making practical applications. The discussion could be broadened to include other lessons that the students might think of.

The "little children" of 2 Kings 2:23 were apparently old enough to realize what they were doing. The Hebrew word translated children (Strong's #5288) is used for an age range from infants to young men.

Lesson 12.   Elisha Brings God's Message to Israel   **83**

D. LEARNING MORE ABOUT THE BIBLE

Leprosy

In Bible times, leprosy was one of the most dreaded diseases that a person could get. It included various ailments of the skin and was not always the same disease that is called leprosy today. Leprosy in the Bible is a picture of sin.

Some types of leprosy healed by themselves. At other times, God healed lepers by working a miracle.

1. When a leper was healed, what did he need to offer to God? (Leviticus 14:2–4) two live, clean birds; cedar wood; scarlet; and hyssop >>

Read Leviticus 13:45, 46.

2. What was a leper required to do with his clothes? ___ tear them

3. What was a leper required to do to his head? ___ keep it bare

4. What was a leper required to do to his face? ___ cover his upper lip

5. Why did lepers cry "Unclean, unclean" when they met other people? ___ This warned other people to stay away from them. >>

6. Where did lepers live? ___ outside the camp

A house that got a patchy look from fungus growing on its walls was said to have leprosy. Sometimes the owner removed the infected stones and scraped, washed, and replastered the house.

7. What was done if the plague kept returning? (Leviticus 14:43–45) ___ The house was torn down, and the rubble was carried outside the city.

Clothes that got moldy spots had leprosy.

8. What was done to the garments if the mold could not be stopped by washing or mending? (Leviticus 13:52) They were burned.

Number 1. Additional offerings were required on the eighth day (Leviticus 14:10).

Number 5. Answer may vary. An exact answer is not given in this passage.

84

Lesson 13. God's Judgment on the House of Ahab

Everyone that knew Jehu also knew how he drove his chariot. One day the watchman at Jezreel saw a chariot in the distance. He knew it was Jehu because of the furious way that he was driving.

Jehu's whole character was like his driving. He had a great amount of energy. When God's prophet anointed him king of Israel and told him to smite the house of Ahab, Jehu announced it to his followers right away. That same day he set off for Jezreel to destroy Ahab's family. Before he entered the gate of Jezreel, he had already killed the king of Israel. Shortly after his arrival, the dogs were eating Queen Jezebel's body. Soon the heads of Ahab's seventy sons were piled by the city gate. When forty-two relatives of the king of Judah came to visit the former king, Jehu had them killed at a sheep-shearing house. And only a short while later, Jehu killed a great assembly of the worshipers of Baal and broke down Baal's temple and images.

Yes, Jehu had a great deal of energy. But like some other energetic people, he was not always careful. Because of Jehu's zeal in destroying Ahab's family, God promised that his descendants would reign over Israel for four generations. But Jehu did not carefully remove all idol worship. He never destroyed Jeroboam's golden calves. He did not walk in the Law of the LORD with all his heart. God was displeased with Jehu and "began to cut Israel short" (2 Kings 10:32). And after the four generations of Jehu's descendants had reigned, God cut off Jehu's dynasty.

God needs careful and obedient people to do His work.

A. ANSWERS FROM THE BIBLE

Elijah had foretold the terrible end of Ahab, Jezebel, and their family. Part of Elijah's prophecy was fulfilled when Ahab was killed in battle. The Scripture passages in this lesson show how God brought judgment on Jezebel and the rest of Ahab's family.

Jehu's Mission of Judgment

Elisha sent one of the sons of the prophets to Ramoth-gilead to anoint Jehu, an army captain, to be the next king of Israel. The messenger told Jehu that he was to totally destroy the house of Ahab. When Jehu's fellow captains heard what the young prophet had told Jehu, they made him king immediately.

2 Kings 9:16–30

King Joram, Ahab's son, was king of Israel. But he was at Jezreel because he had been wounded in a battle with Syria. His nephew Ahaziah, the king of Judah, was there to visit him. Jehu went to Jezreel right away to begin the job that God had given him.

Note: *Joram* is a shortened form of *Jehoram*. The Bible uses both forms to name two different kings who reigned about the same time. Be sure to notice the difference: Ahab's son Joram (Jehoram) was a king of Israel; Jehoshaphat's son Joram (Jehoram) was a king of Judah. (See the chart of the kings of Israel and Judah in Lesson 7.)

1. Joram and Ahaziah saw Jehu and his men coming to Jezreel. They sent out
   a. an army to attack him.
   b. two messengers to find out why he was coming.
   c. a warning for Jehu to do nothing rashly.

Lesson 13

Oral Review

1. What did Samuel say was more important than sacrifice? [1] **obedience**
2. What did Solomon realize about riches by the end of his life? [4] **Riches do not satisfy.**
3. What did the ten northern tribes ask of Rehoboam? [6] **They asked him to make their burdens lighter.**
4. What miracle did the LORD perform through Elisha after Elisha's death? [11] **He raised a dead man who touched Elisha's bones.**
5. To what tool did Jeremiah compare God's Word? [11] **a hammer**
6. Which two kings helped the king of Israel fight against the Moabites? [12] **the kings of Judah and Edom**
7. How did God break the siege on Samaria? [12] **He made the Syrians hear a noise of chariots, horses, and a great host.**
8. Where were lepers required to live? [12] **outside the camp**

2. The watchman of Jezreel thought the approaching chariots were led by Jehu because
    a. the king was expecting Jehu that day.
    b. Jehu had sent a messenger ahead of him.
    (c.) he knew that Jehu drove furiously.

3. King Joram and King Ahaziah went out to meet Jehu. When they discovered that he was trying to seize the kingdom, they tried to escape, but Jehu drew his bow and _____killed King Joram_____.

4. The king of Judah was wounded by Jehu's men, but he escaped and died at _____Megiddo_____.

5. When Jezebel heard that Jehu was coming, she
    a. prayed to Baal for protection and strength.
    b. called her servants and set her house in order.
    (c.) painted her face and adorned her hair.

2 Kings 9:34–37

As Jehu entered Jezreel, Jezebel looked out of a window. Jehu told several eunuchs to throw her down, and he rode over her with his horses. Thus died Jezebel, a wicked, foreign princess who had brought much trouble to Israel. Jehu went in to eat, and then he told his servants to bury Jezebel.

6. Jezebel could not be buried properly because
    a. no one was willing to help bury such a wicked person.
    (b.) the dogs had eaten most of her body.
    c. the servants could find no trace of her body.

7. Who had prophesied that God would punish Jezebel in this way? _____Elijah_____

Jehu and the Sons of Ahab

God had commanded Jehu to destroy the house of Ahab, and he did not stop until he had completed the job.

2 Kings 10:1–8

8. Ahab had _____seventy_____ sons who lived in _____Samaria_____.

9. Jehu told the men who cared for Ahab's sons to set one of them on his father's _____throne_____.

10. The men who cared for Ahab's sons were afraid of Jehu. They knew that if they made a new king, Jehu would fight against them. So they sent a message to Jehu instead, saying, "We are thy _____servants_____."

11. Jehu wrote back telling them to bring the heads of the king's sons to _____Jezreel_____ by the next morning.

Jehu and the Kings' Relatives

2 Kings 10:11–14

12. What did Jehu do to the house of Ahab? (Also see 10:17.) _____
    ___He killed all the rest of Ahab's family.___

- After Jehu killed Ahaziah, Athaliah seized the throne in Judah. This wicked queen was the daughter of Ahab and Jezebel. While Jehu was purging Israel of Baal worship, Athaliah was introducing it in Judah.

In This Lesson

Scope: 2 Kings 9, 10

Main Events
- Jehu is anointed king of Israel.
- Jehu zealously destroys Ahab's house and the Baal worshipers.
- Jehu fails to destroy the idols that Jeroboam had set up.

Objectives
- The students should know
    —that Jehu's actions fulfilled the prophecy made by Elijah years before.
    —that Jehu was not as zealous in obeying God in other things as he was in destroying the family of Ahab and the house of Baal. This would suggest that he had some self-interest in carrying out these commands.
    —that zeal can be good or bad, depending on one's motives and methods.
    —that although God can fulfill His purposes by using men who have wrong motives, such men will not receive the blessing they could have if they had wholly followed Him.

13. How many of King Ahaziah's relatives were killed by Jehu? __forty-two__

Ahab's daughter, Athaliah, was the mother of King Ahaziah. When she saw that Jehu had killed her son, she tried to kill all her remaining children and grandchildren, as well as all their other relatives, so that she could rule Judah herself. In this way Ahab's own daughter helped to fulfill the prophecy that all of Ahab's house would be destroyed.

Jehu and the Baal Worshipers

After destroying Ahab's family and relatives, Jehu turned his attention to the worshipers of Baal. These people had followed Jezebel and Ahab into the terrible sins that went with the worship of this heathen god. Jehu did right in God's sight by destroying Baal worship in Israel.

2 Kings 10:18–28

14. How did Jehu deceive the Baal worshipers? _____

 __He told them he wanted to serve Baal even more than Ahab had done.__

15. Where did the Baal worshipers gather? __in the house of Baal__

16. How did Jehu make sure he would not kill any righteous people? _____

 __He told the worshipers of Baal to search through the crowd to be sure there were no servants of__

 __the LORD among them.__

17. Who killed the Baal worshipers? __Jehu's guard and captains__

18. What did Jehu and his men do to the images and the temple of Baal? _____

 __They broke down the images of Baal and burned them, and they broke down the house of Baal.__

Jehu's Carelessness

2 Kings 10:29–32

Jehu was probably the best king the Northern Kingdom had after they became a separate nation. Jehu was anointed by a prophet of the LORD. He zealously obeyed God's command to destroy Ahab's family. He broke down Baal's temple and images, and he killed the worshipers of Baal.

Jehu seemed eager to obey the LORD in destroying Ahab's family and removing Baal worship from Israel, yet he refused to completely turn from sin and lead the nation to righteousness. God rewarded Jehu for the good that he had done. But because of his sin, God allowed Hazael, king of Syria, to take away part of Israel's land.

19. What idols did Jehu leave in Israel? _____

 __the golden calves at Bethel and Dan__

20. What promise did the LORD give Jehu as a reward for destroying the house of Ahab and the worship of Baal? _____

 __The LORD promised that four generations of Jehu's descendants would reign over Israel.__

21. Whose sins did Jehu continue to follow? __Jeroboam's__

Truths to Instill

- God wants us to do wholehearted, careful work.
  - —God commended Jehu's zeal in destroying the evil house of Ahab.
  - —Jehu's zeal did not reach all areas of his life. Jehu "took no heed to walk in the law of the LORD God of Israel with all his heart" (2 Kings 10:31). His zealousness did not compensate for his carelessness.
  - —Some people are naturally more zealous and some more careful. But whether naturally careful or not, we must all be careful in obeying God. There will be consequences if we are not.

B. BIBLE WORD STUDY

✎ *Write a word or phrase from the verse given to match each definition. All references are from 2 Kings.*

avenge	1. Punish in return for a wrong (9:7)
treachery	2. Unfaithfulness to someone's trust or confidence (9:23)
requite	3. Repay (9:26)
tired	4. Adorned; decorated (9:30)
subtilty	5. Craftiness; deceitfulness (10:19)
vestry	6. A place where garments are kept (10:22)
vestments	7. Clothes, especially robes worn during special ceremonies (10:22)
to cut Israel short	8. To make Israel smaller (10:32)

C. THINKING ABOUT BIBLE TRUTHS

Zeal and Carefulness

In this lesson you have seen that God used Jehu's zeal to destroy the house of Ahab and the Baal worshipers. However, Jehu's carelessness and sin make him a poor example for us to follow. This section will help you learn what the Bible says about zeal and carefulness.

1. Read Galatians 4:17, 18. These verses indicate that (choose two)

   a. it is possible to be zealous about the wrong things.
   b. it is always good to be zealous in good things.
   c. we should not be zealous when our leaders are somewhere else.
   d. it is always good to be excited about what others say.

Jehu's zeal was not the cause of his mistakes. He could have zealously destroyed all the idolatry in Israel, just as he destroyed Ahab's family and Baal worship. What a great revival he might have started had he wholly followed the Lord and restored true worship in Israel!

2. Jehu zealously destroyed Ahab's family and the worshipers of Baal, but he failed to walk in the Law of the Lord with all his heart and to destroy the idol worship of Jeroboam. This shows that

   a. Jehu thought that Jeroboam's idols were images of the Lord God of Israel.
   b. after destroying Ahab's family and the Baal worshipers, Jehu was too tired to do anything else.
   c. Jehu was more concerned about destroying Ahab and his family than about completely following God.
   d. Jehu was too zealous. If he had worked more slowly, he could have completely destroyed idolatry in Israel.

Being zealous for our own benefit can be a display of selfishness and pride. God wants us to be zealous in loving Him with all our hearts and in obeying all His commandments.

3. Read Romans 10:2, 3.

   a. The unbelieving Jews of Paul's day had zeal, but it was not according to _____ knowledge _____.

   b. These Jews made a mistake similar to Jehu's mistake. Rather than doing all that God wanted them to do, they tried to be righteous in their own way. Paul says that they "have not _____ submitted _____ themselves unto the righteousness of God."

4. Read 2 Corinthians 7:11. In this passage, Paul is commending the Corinthians for the way they had dealt with sin in the church. According to this verse, is it possible to be both zealous and careful? _____ yes _____

D. LEARNING MORE ABOUT THE BIBLE

Chariots

1. The first chariots the Bible tells about were in Egypt. Which young Israelite man rode in an Egyptian chariot? (Genesis 41:41–43) _____ Joseph _____

2. Egyptian chariots were made mostly of wood. They had no springs, but their floors were made of woven rope so that the men who stood in them would have a smoother ride. What did the LORD do to the Egyptians' chariots when they pursued the Israelites into the Red Sea? (Exodus 14:25, 28) _____ He took off the wheels and brought the water back upon them. _____

3. What kind of chariots did the Canaanites have? (Joshua 17:18) _____ iron chariots _____

4. The early Israelites usually fought on foot, but Solomon and some later kings had many chariots. How many chariots did Solomon own? (2 Chronicles 1:14) _____ 1,400 _____

5. What did the LORD want His people to trust in rather than in chariots? (Isaiah 31:1; Psalm 20:7) _____ He wanted them to trust in Him. _____

6. Read 2 Kings 9:16, 21, 24, 27, and 28.

   a. To what city did Jehu ride in a chariot? _____ Jezreel _____

   b. Who went out against Jehu in chariots? _____ Joram _____ and _____ Ahaziah _____

   c. Whose body was taken to Jerusalem in a chariot? _____ Ahaziah's _____

7. Read Acts 8:27–29. The Egyptian warriors stood in their chariots. How did the Ethiopian eunuch ride? _____ He sat in his chariot. _____

89

Lesson 14. The Collapse of Israel

The LORD loved His chosen people, the Israelites. He had made a special covenant with their father Abraham. He had delivered them from slavery in Egypt and had given them a good land. He had promised to bless them if they obeyed His commandments.

Sometimes, when the Israelites had a righteous leader, they worshiped God and obeyed Him. But often they forgot the LORD when that leader died. After the kingdom was divided, the northern tribes had no godly kings. Not one of their kings served the LORD with all his heart. Even Jehu, who stamped out Baal worship, failed to destroy Jeroboam's golden calves. Israel grew worse and worse.

God was grieved. He sent prophets to warn His chosen people. He sent droughts, swarms of insects, and enemy nations to remind them of their sin. Still His people refused to obey Him. God warned them that they were destroying themselves by their evil ways, but they continued living in sin until it was too late.

Finally God could withhold His judgment no longer. He sent the cruel Assyrians against Israel. They drove the Israelites from their promised land to a strange country far away. They showed no mercy to anyone—not even the old, the young, or the sick.

God was judging the sins of Jeroboam and all those who had followed him. The wicked Israelites never returned to their homeland. Instead, the Assyrians brought in foreigners from other lands, who mixed with the few remaining Israelites. This mixed race became known as the Samaritans.

God rejects those who refuse to fear and obey Him.

A. ANSWERS FROM THE BIBLE

Trouble in Israel

Jehu's family reigned longer than any other family of kings in the Northern Kingdom. Just as the LORD had promised, four of Jehu's descendants sat on his throne.

During the reigns of Jehu and his son Jehoahaz, the LORD allowed the Syrians to take much of Israel's land. Finally Jehoahaz besought the LORD, and the LORD took pity on His people. He began to deliver them for a while, even though they did not turn to Him with all their hearts.

✎ Write true or false. *Correct each false statement on the lines after the sentence.*

2 Kings 13:1–7

_____false_____ 1. Jehoahaz was the son of Ahab. _____

Jehoahaz was the son of *Jehu.*

_____true_____ 2. Jehoahaz followed the sins of Jeroboam the son of Nebat. _____

_____true_____ 3. The LORD was angry against the Israelites and allowed the Syrians to oppress them.

_____false_____ 4. The LORD refused to help Jehoahaz when he besought Him. _____

The *LORD hearkened unto* Jehoahaz when he besought Him.

In the rewritten sentences for numbers 1–8, the corrections are in italics. The pupil's sentences may vary somewhat.

Lesson 14

Oral Review

1. What did Elisha throw into the bad water of Jericho? [11] **salt**
2. Who told Naaman where to go for healing? [12] **an Israelite maid**
3. What did the LORD do to the Syrian soldiers who tried to capture Elisha? [12] **At Elisha's request, He smote them with blindness.**
4. What fraction of a bushel equals about one seah? [12] **1/4 bushel**
5. How did the LORD reward Jehu for destroying Ahab's house and the Baal worshipers? [13] **He promised that four generations of Jehu's descendants would reign over Israel.**
6. What idols did Jehu leave in Israel? [13] **the golden calves that Jeroboam had made at Bethel and Dan**
7. What did the LORD want His people to trust in rather than in chariots? [13] **He wanted them to trust in Him.**
8. What are the five Books of Poetry? (Be sure you know the correct order and spelling.) [1, 11] **Job, Psalms, Proverbs, Ecclesiastes, Song of Solomon**

90   Chapter Three   Israel's Downfall

_____   true   _____   5. The Israelites had only a small army left. _____

_____

God's Mercy Toward Israel

2 Kings 13:10, 11, 22–25

Joash became king after his father, Jehoahaz. As you saw in Lesson 12, he visited Elisha and was rebuked for striking the ground only three times.

_____   false   _____   6. Joash (sometimes called Jehoash) the son of Jehoahaz did that which was right in the

sight of the LORD.   _Joash (sometimes called Jehoash) the son of Jehoahaz_

did that which was evil in the sight of the LORD. _____

_____   true   _____   7. The LORD had mercy on Israel because He remembered His covenant with Abraham,

Isaac, and Jacob. _____

_____

_____   true   _____   8. Joash smote Syria three times and regained some of Israel's cities. _____

_____

2 Kings 14:23–29

The next king was Jeroboam the son of Joash. (Sometimes he is called Jeroboam II because he was the second Jeroboam to reign in Israel.) During his reign, the LORD continued to have mercy on Israel, and they regained more of their land.

9. Jeroboam II did _____ evil _____ in the sight of the LORD, and departed not from the

sins of _____ Jeroboam _____ the son of Nebat.

10. In spite of Jeroboam II's sin, God allowed him to restore some of Israel's land. This fulfilled a prophecy

of _____ Jonah _____, the son of Amittai. (This was the same prophet who preached at Nineveh.)

Prophets of Judgment and Love

Because of God's mercy, Israel was rich and happy during the reign of Jeroboam II. But instead of thanking God and turning back to Him, the people continued in their sin. God was grieved and angry. Soon He would need to bring judgment upon His people. But first He sent more prophets to warn them and to plead with them to repent.

11. Amos was from Tekoa, a town in Judah. Amaziah, the priest of the golden calf at Bethel, wanted Amos

to return to Judah and prophesy there. But Amos answered: "I was no _____ prophet _____,

neither was I a prophet's _____ son _____; but . . . the _____ LORD _____ said unto

me, Go, prophesy unto my people _____ Israel _____" (Amos 7:14, 15).

12. Amos also said that Amaziah's family would suffer and be destroyed and that Israel would surely go

into _____ captivity _____ (Amos 7:17).

13. About the same time that Amos warned Israel of coming judgment, Hosea preached about God's love

for them. Hosea's wife was not faithful to him. But God told Hosea to love her anyway, "according to

- *Joash* is a shortened form of *Jehoash*. The Bible uses both forms to name two different kings. One Joash (Jehoash) was saved by his aunt and was anointed king of Judah when he was seven years old. The other Joash (Jehoash) was a grandson of Jehu, and became king of Israel after his father, Jehoahaz, died.

- Two different men named Jeroboam reigned over Israel. The first Jeroboam, who set up the golden calves at Bethel and Dan, was the son of Nebat. The second Jeroboam, often called Jeroboam II, was the great-grandson of Jehu.

In This Lesson

Scope: 2 Kings 13; 14:23–29; 15:8–31; 17; Amos 7:10–17; Hosea 3:1; 14:1

Main Events
- Jehoahaz loses much land to the Syrians and finally cries to the LORD for help.
- Joash smites the Syrians three times, according to the prophecy of Elisha.
- Jeroboam II enjoys a prosperous reign, but the Israelites continue doing evil.
- God sends prophets with messages of judgment and love.

- Zachariah is the fourth and last descendant of Jehu to reign.
- The nation of Israel is taken into captivity and scattered by the Assyrians. Their land is repopulated, and the mixed race of the Samaritans develops.

Objectives
- The students should know
  —why God allowed the Syrians to take some of the Israelites' land. (Israel had sinned, and God was angry with them.)
  —that Joash defeated the Syrians three times, just as Elisha had prophesied.

the _____love_____ of the LORD toward the _____children_____ of

_____Israel_____ ” (Hosea 3:1).

14. Hosea cried out: "O Israel, _____return_____ unto the LORD thy God; for thou hast fallen by

thine _____iniquity_____ ” (Hosea 14:1).

The Last Kings of Israel

The Israelites refused to listen to the prophets that God sent. They continued in the sins of Jeroboam the son of Nebat. Finally God allowed the Assyrians to carry them away as captives. Most of them never saw their homeland again. All references are from 2 Kings.

✎ *The names of the last six kings of Israel are given below. Choose a name for each blank. Some names are used more than once.*

| Hoshea | Menahem | Pekah | Pekahiah | Shallum | Zachariah |

Answer		
Zachariah	15.	Fourth and last descendant of Jehu to reign (15:8–12)
Shallum	16.	Killed Zachariah and reigned one month (15:10, 13)
Menahem	17.	Killed Shallum and reigned ten years (15:14, 17)
Menahem	18.	Paid a tribute of silver to the king of Assyria (15:19, 20)
Pekahiah	19.	Killed by Pekah (15:23–25)
Pekah	20.	During this king's reign, the king of Assyria conquered a number of Israel's cities and carried some Israelites away as captives (15:29)
Hoshea	21.	Killed Pekah (15:30)
Hoshea	22.	In the ninth year of this king's reign, the king of Assyria conquered Samaria and carried the Israelites away to other lands (17:6).

B. BIBLE WORD STUDY

✎ *Match these definitions with the Bible words on the right. All references are from 2 Kings unless marked otherwise.*

f	1. To stir up or arouse (13:3)	a.	affliction
b	2. To have earnestly asked; begged (13:4)	b.	besought
g	3. To interfere in the affairs of others (14:10)	c.	confirm
a	4. Something that causes suffering or pain (14:26)	d.	exact
i	5. To kill (15:14)	e.	iniquity
c	6. To verify, support, or strengthen (15:19)	f.	kindle
d	7. To demand and get by force (15:20)	g.	meddle
e	8. Sin (Hosea 14:1)	h.	prophesy
h	9. To give God's message to people (Amos 7:15)	i.	slay

—why God sent prophets to speak to the Israelites. (He loved His chosen people.)

—why the Israelites were taken into captivity. (They continued to refuse to obey God, and He could withhold His judgment no longer.)

Truths to Instill

• "The Lord is . . . not willing that any should perish, but that all should come to repentance" (2 Peter 3:9). God sent many prophets to Israel and Judah. The Lord's long-suffering and His desire to see all men come to the truth have extended the day of grace to our day.

• "He, that being often reproved hardeneth his neck, shall suddenly be destroyed, and that without remedy" (Proverbs 29:1). God's mercy is often mistaken for tolerance. Someday judgment will fall on all who refuse to repent and obey.

Challenge Problem

✎ *Determine how much silver Menahem took from each wealthy man to give to the king of Assyria (2 Kings 15:20).*

10. 1 shekel = about ⅖ ounce; 50 shekels = about __1 lb.__ pound(s) __4 oz.__ ounce(s)

            (about 565 g)

C. THINKING ABOUT BIBLE TRUTHS

The Judgment of God

When people or nations ignore God and disobey Him, they can expect God to bring judgment, or punishment, upon them. Such people cannot blame God for His judgment, because they deserve it. This was the case with the Israelites. For many generations they had forsaken God, served idols, and taken their own way. Now they had to reap the results of their sin.

✎ *Read these verses about judgment, and then answer the questions by filling in the blank or circling the letter of the correct answer.*

1. Read Amos 3:2. God punished the Israelites for their _____iniquities_____ when He sent the Assyrians to take them captive. What is a more common word that means the same as this word does? _____sins_____ (See "Bible Word Study" on page 91 if you need help.)

2. Read Ezekiel 18:30–32. Some people seem to enjoy seeing others get punished, but God is always grieved when He needs to bring judgment upon people.

   a. Verse 30 shows that if the Israelites had _____repented_____ and _____turned_____ from their transgressions (sins), God would have forgiven them instead of bringing judgment upon them.

   b. When the Israelites refused to turn from their sin, God needed to bring judgment upon them. Copy the part of verse 32 that shows how this made God feel. _____
"I have no pleasure in the death of him that dieth."

3. Read 2 Samuel 12:14. According to this verse, one reason God punished David was that his sin had given the enemies of God cause to blaspheme. This shows that

   a. God does not care if His people sin as long as no one finds out about it.

   b. No one knew about the sin that King David had committed until God punished him.

   ⓒ One reason God punished His people was to show their ungodly neighbors that He hates sin and will not tolerate it.

4. Read Revelation 20:12, 13. God sent judgment on the whole nation of Israel by allowing the Assyrians to defeat them. But at the final judgment, God will judge each person individually according to his _____works_____.

Avoid arousing premature feelings of guilt by keeping the discussion of this section focused on the Israelites rather than on the student's personal accountability to God.

D. LEARNING MORE ABOUT THE BIBLE

Where Did the Ten Tribes Go?

According to 2 Kings 17:6, the Assyrians carried the captive Israelites to Assyria and placed them in Halah, in Habor by the river of Gozan, and in the cities of the Medes (probably around Ecbatana).

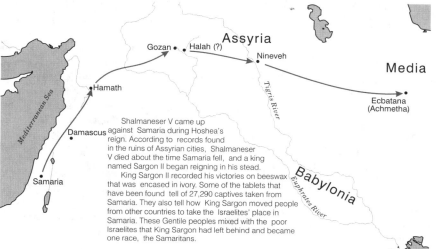

Shalmaneser V came up against Samaria during Hoshea's reign. According to records found in the ruins of Assyrian cities, Shalmaneser V died about the time Samaria fell, and a king named Sargon II began reigning in his stead.

King Sargon II recorded his victories on beeswax that was encased in ivory. Some of the tablets that have been found tell of 27,290 captives taken from Samaria. They also tell how King Sargon moved people from other countries to take the Israelites' place in Samaria. These Gentile peoples mixed with the poor Israelites that King Sargon had left behind and became one race, the Samaritans.

- The Samaritans and their religion could be studied in more detail. Their early days are described in 2 Kings 17:24–41. Students could use Bible dictionaries and concordances to find additional information about them.

Many stories not based on fact have arisen about the ten "lost" tribes of Israel. The Bible indicates that many descendants of the ten tribes mixed with other races and lost their identity. The rest may have kept their Hebrew identity by associating with the tribes of Judah and Benjamin. The Bible verses below mention some Israelites from the ten tribes who remained faithful to God and kept their identity.

1. Josiah reigned in Judah about one hundred years after Assyria took Israel captive. In his days, some from the tribes of _____Manasseh_____ and _____Ephraim_____ and of all the remnant of Israel gave money to help repair the temple (2 Chronicles 34:9).

2. Individuals from four tribes are mentioned in the New Testament. Tell which tribe each of these were from.

   a. Jesus: _____Juda (Judah)_____ (Hebrews 7:14)
   b. Paul: _____Benjamin_____ (Philippians 3:5)
   c. Barnabas: _____Levi_____ (Acts 4:36)
   d. Anna: _____Aser (Asher)_____ (Luke 2:36)

3. James wrote to "the _____twelve_____ tribes which are scattered abroad" (James 1:1). Perhaps some other Jews of that time could trace their lineage back to other tribes besides the four listed above.

94

Chapter Three Review

A. ORAL REVIEW

✎ *Be sure you know the answers to these questions. Answer as many as you can from memory. If you need help, you may check the reference or lesson given in brackets.*

Why >>

1. Why did the Syrians flee and leave their goods in their tents outside Samaria? [2 Kings 7:6]
2. Why was Elisha angry with King Joash? [2 Kings 13:18, 19]

How >>

3. How did Elisha heal the waters of Jericho? [2 Kings 2:21]
4. How many men were fed with twenty loaves of barley bread and some ears of grain? [2 Kings 4:43]
5. How was Gehazi punished for his covetousness? [2 Kings 5:20–27]
6. How did Elisha recover an axe head from the Jordan River? [2 Kings 6:6]
7. How was Elijah's prophecy concerning Jezebel fulfilled? [2 Kings 9:32–37]
8. How did Jehu get rid of the Baal worshipers? [2 Kings 10:19, 25]
9. How did the LORD reward Jehu for destroying Ahab's house and the Baal worshipers? [2 Kings 10:30]
10. How many times did Joash, the grandson of Jehu, smite the Syrians? [2 Kings 13:25]

Who

11. Who said, "The spirit of Elijah doth rest on Elisha"? [2 Kings 2:15] the sons of the prophets
12. Who told Naaman where to go for healing? [2 Kings 5:2, 3] an Israelite maid
13. Who went to a building site near the Jordan River with the sons of the prophets? [2 Kings 6:1–3] Elisha
14. Who killed Ahab's son Joram (Jehoram)? [2 Kings 9:24] Jehu
15. Who loved an unfaithful wife as a sign of God's love for the unfaithful Israelites? [Lesson 14] Hosea
16. Who was the fourth and last descendant of Jehu to reign? [2 Kings 15:8–12] Zachariah

1. God made them hear a noise of chariots, horses, and a great host.
2. Elisha wanted him to smite the ground with the arrows five or six times because it was a sign of smiting the Syrians.
3. He threw salt into it and healed it in the Name of the LORD.
4. one hundred
5. He was smitten with leprosy.
6. He threw a stick into the water, and the axe head floated.
7. The dogs ate most of her body.
8. He called them together to a sacrifice and had his men kill them.
9. He promised that four generations of Jehu's descendants would reign.
10. three

Chapter Three Review

This review is divided into two parts, an oral review and a written review. The oral review is intended for class discussion, but students could also use it for self-study.

If your students have memorized Elisha's miracles, you may want to have them list the miracles for the review and the test.

B. WRITTEN REVIEW

✎ *Write the answers to these questions. Do as many as you can from memory. If you need help, you may check the reference or lesson given in brackets.*

What

1. What request did Elisha make before Elijah was taken up to heaven? [2 Kings 2:9] _____
   "Let a double portion of thy spirit be upon me."

2. What happened to the Shunammite woman's son one day when he was out in the field with his father? [2 Kings 4:18–20, 35] _____
   He became sick. Then he died, but Elisha raised him back to life.

3. What miracle did the LORD perform through Elisha after Elisha's death? [2 Kings 13:21] _____
   He raised a dead man who touched Elisha's bones.

4. To what tool did Jeremiah compare God's Word? [Jeremiah 23:29] a hammer

5. What did the Moabite king offer to his god? [2 Kings 3:27] his oldest son

6. What did Elisha's servant see on the hills when God opened his eyes? [2 Kings 6:17] _____
   horses and chariots of fire

7. What happened to the man who doubted Elisha's predictions during the siege of Samaria? [2 Kings 7:17] _____
   The people trampled him, and he died.

8. What fraction of a bushel equals about one seah? [Lesson 12] ¼ bushel

9. What happened to Ahab's seventy sons? [2 Kings 10:6, 7] _____
   The men of Samaria killed them and sent their heads to Jehu.

10. What idols did Jehu leave in Israel? [2 Kings 10:29] _____
    the golden calves that Jeroboam had made at Bethel and Dan

11. What nation conquered Samaria and carried the Israelites away? [2 Kings 17:6] Assyria

12. What do these words mean? [Lessons 11–14]
    a. dearth: a famine
    b. sojourn: to stay for a short time
    c. affliction: something that causes suffering or pain
    d. avenge: to punish in return for a wrong
    e. iniquity: sin
    f. prophesy: to give God's message to people
    g. treachery: unfaithfulness to someone's trust or confidence

96   Chapter Three   Israel's Downfall

13. What are the five Books of Poetry? (Be sure to spell them correctly.) [Lessons 1, 11] _____

Job, Psalms, Proverbs, Ecclesiastes, Song of Solomon

When

14. When did the king of Israel make a feast for the Syrians in Samaria? [2 Kings 6:19–23] _____

when Elisha led the blinded soldiers to Samaria

15. When did Jehoahaz ask the LORD for help? [2 Kings 13:3, 4] _____

after the LORD allowed the Syrians to oppress Israel

Where

16. Where were lepers required to live? [Leviticus 13:46] outside the camp

17. Where did the LORD send Amos to prophesy? [Amos 7:15] to Israel

Where Is It Found?

✎ *Match the events on the right with the chapters that record them.*

  d   18. 2 Kings 2

  b   19. 2 Kings 5

  f   20. 2 Kings 9

  a   21. 2 Kings 10

  c   22. 2 Kings 13

  e   23. 2 Kings 17

a. The elders of Samaria kill Ahab's seventy sons. Jehu destroys the Baal worshipers and their temple.

b. Naaman is healed of his leprosy after he dips seven times in the Jordan.

c. Joash visits Elisha on his deathbed. He hits the ground three times with his arrows. Later he defeats the Syrians in battle three times.

d. God takes Elijah to heaven by a whirlwind. Elisha serves as prophet in Elijah's place.

e. The Assyrians conquer Samaria and take the Israelites captive.

f. A young prophet anoints Jehu king of Israel, and Jehu begins to destroy Ahab's wicked house.

97

Lesson 15. Israel's Neighbors

When Joshua led the Israelites into Canaan, the Canaanite tribes were living in the land. Joshua began to conquer the Canaanites, and by the time of Israel's kings, the Israelites had destroyed or subdued most of them. But around the edges of Israel lived people who worshiped other gods. Some were Canaanites whom the Israelites had never destroyed, and others were tribes who were related to the Israelites.

The LORD planned that His chosen people should live holy lives apart from these nations around them. Then He could bless them, and other nations could see the holiness and greatness of the LORD God of Israel.

Many heathen did learn to fear and respect the LORD and the Israelites. The people of Jericho were terrified when they heard how the LORD had dried up the Red Sea and how He had helped the Israelites in battle. The Queen of Sheba traveled a great distance to hear the wisdom of Solomon. Naaman the Syrian learned that the LORD is the only true God.

But sometimes, instead of showing their neighbors how to live right, the Israelites learned the evil ways of their neighbors. Then the LORD could no longer bless them. He allowed their neighbors to come up against them and defeat them.

God's people still live among ungodly people. God wants us to be holy examples to our neighbors rather than falling into their sins.

A. ANSWERS FROM THE BIBLE

✎ *You probably remember some Bible stories that involve Israel's neighbors. Fill in as many of these blanks as you can from memory. If you need help, read the verses given.*

1. Aaron and Hur held up Moses' hands while the Israelites fought against the _____Amalekites_____ (Exodus 17:8–11).

2. Eglon, the king of _____Moab_____, was killed by Ehud, a judge of Israel (Judges 3:15, 21).

3. The LORD used Gideon and three hundred men to deliver Israel from the _____Midianites_____ (Judges 7:7).

4. Samson began to deliver the Israelites out of the hands of the _____Philistines_____ (Judges 13:5, 24).

5. Ruth was from the land of _____Moab_____ (Ruth 1:4).

6. The idol Dagon, god of the _____Philistines_____, broke into pieces before the ark of the LORD (1 Samuel 5:1–4).

7. Nahash the _____Ammonite_____ threatened to pluck out the right eyes of the men of Jabesh-gilead (1 Samuel 11:1, 2).

8. The LORD told King Saul to utterly destroy the _____Amalekites_____, but he saved the king and the best animals (1 Samuel 15:3, 9).

Life in Bible Times

Lesson 15

Oral Review
1. Where did men in Bible times carry their tools and weapons? [5] **in their girdles (belts)**
2. What two marriage practices did the Old Testament Law permit that were not according to God's original plan for marriage? [10] **having more than one wife, and divorce**
3. What tool did Elisha recover from the Jordan River? [11] **an axe head**
4. How was Gehazi punished for his covetousness? [12] **He was smitten with leprosy.**
5. How was Elijah's prophecy concerning Jezebel fulfilled? [13] **The dogs ate most of her body.**
6. Who prophesied that Jeroboam II would regain some of Israel's land? [14] **Jonah**
7. What prophet brought a message of God's love for Israel? [14] **Hosea**
8. What country conquered Samaria and carried the Israelites away? [14] **Assyria**

9. David killed Goliath, a giant from the land of the _____ Philistines _____ (1 Samuel 17:49).

10. While hiding from Saul, David left his parents in the land of _____ Moab _____ (1 Samuel 22:3).

11. King _____ Solomon _____ bought cedar and fir trees from Hiram, king of Tyre, which was a city of Phoenicia (1 Kings 5:8–11).

12. The prophet _____ Elijah _____ was fed by a widow who lived at Zarephath, a city of the Phoenicians (1 Kings 17:9, 15).

13. Mesha, the king of _____ Moab _____, burned his oldest son as an offering to his god Chemosh (2 Kings 3:4, 5, 26, 27).

14. After being healed of leprosy, Naaman, a captain of the host of _____ Syria _____, promised to worship the LORD instead of the idol Rimmon (2 Kings 5:1, 17, 18).

Israel's Neighbors

✎ *Study the map "Israel's neighbors" to fill in the blanks below.*

1. Of Israel's neighbors, the _____ Midianites _____, the _____ Edomites _____, and the _____ Ishmaelites >> _____ were also descendants of Abraham.

2. The _____ Syrians _____ were descendants of Aram, the son of Shem.

3. The _____ Ammonites _____ and the _____ Moabites _____ were descendants of Lot.

4. The Law of Moses forbade the offering of children to _____ Molech _____, god of the Ammonites.

5. Jezebel encouraged the worship of Baal, god of the _____ Phoenicians _____.

6. The city of Tyre was known for its seafaring _____ traders _____.

7. The land called the Gaza Strip today once belonged to the _____ Philistines _____.

8. The lands of the _____ Ammonites _____, the _____ Moabites _____, and the _____ Edomites _____ are part of the modern country of Jordan.

9. The modern country of Lebanon is where _____ Phoenicia _____ once was.

Give at least partial credit for Arabians, but point out that some Arabians might not have been Abraham's descendants.

Life in Bible Times

In This Lesson

Main Points
- The Israelites' neighbors during the divided kingdom included Phoenicians, Philistines, Syrians, Ammonites, Moabites, Edomites, Amalekites, Midianites, and Arabians.
- God was concerned about Israel's relationship with her neighbors. He had commanded the Israelites to utterly destroy certain ones and to avoid close relations with the others. But sometimes the Israelites married heathen wives and began worshiping their idols.

Objectives
- The students should know
  —who the close neighbors of Israel were. (Phoenicians, Philistines, Amalekites, Midianites, Syrians, Ammonites, Moabites, Edomites, Arabians)
  —how the Israelites were affected by their evil neighbors. (Sometimes they followed the evil ways of their neighbors.)

Israel's Neighbors

(Note: The Amalekites, Midianites, and Arabians were nomads, who wandered from place to place.)

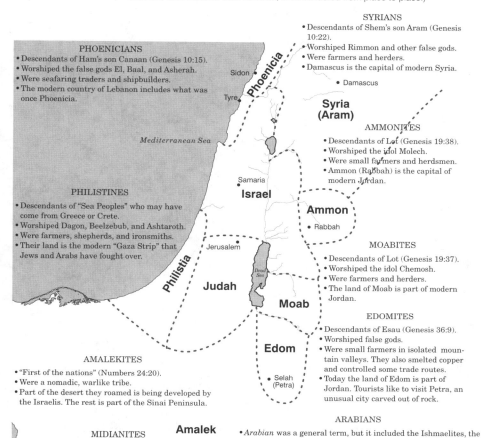

SYRIANS
- Descendants of Shem's son Aram (Genesis 10:22).
- Worshiped Rimmon and other false gods.
- Were farmers and herders.
- Damascus is the capital of modern Syria.

PHOENICIANS
- Descendants of Ham's son Canaan (Genesis 10:15).
- Worshiped the false gods El, Baal, and Asherah.
- Were seafaring traders and shipbuilders.
- The modern country of Lebanon includes what was once Phoenicia.

AMMONITES
- Descendants of Lot (Genesis 19:38).
- Worshiped the idol Molech.
- Were small farmers and herdsmen.
- Ammon (Rabbah) is the capital of modern Jordan.

PHILISTINES
- Descendants of "Sea Peoples" who may have come from Greece or Crete.
- Worshiped Dagon, Beelzebub, and Ashtaroth.
- Were farmers, shepherds, and ironsmiths.
- Their land is the modern "Gaza Strip" that Jews and Arabs have fought over.

MOABITES
- Descendants of Lot (Genesis 19:37).
- Worshiped the idol Chemosh.
- Were farmers and herders.
- The land of Moab is part of modern Jordan.

EDOMITES
- Descendants of Esau (Genesis 36:9).
- Worshiped false gods.
- Were small farmers in isolated mountain valleys. They also smelted copper and controlled some trade routes.
- Today the land of Edom is part of Jordan. Tourists like to visit Petra, an unusual city carved out of rock.

AMALEKITES
- "First of the nations" (Numbers 24:20).
- Were a nomadic, warlike tribe.
- Part of the desert they roamed is being developed by the Israelis. The rest is part of the Sinai Peninsula.

ARABIANS
- *Arabian* was a general term, but it included the Ishmaelites, the descendants of Abram and Hagar's son Ishmael (Genesis 17:20).
- Worshiped many false gods.
- Herded sheep, goats, and camels in the desert.
- Modern Arabs have become wealthy from the petroleum found in their deserts.

MIDIANITES
- Descendants of Abraham's son Midian (Genesis 25:2).
- Were nomadic herdsmen.
- The Bedouin, herdsmen with goats' hair tents, still roam the desert where the Midianites once lived.

- The maps in this lesson show approximate boundaries. Nations gained land when they won battles, and lost land when they were defeated.

Life in Bible Times

Truths to Instill
- The danger of evil associations. God also calls us to "come out from among them, and be . . . separate" (2 Corinthians 6:17).
- All men worship something. Israel's neighbors illustrate the tendency of man to degenerate from the true worship of a holy God to a perverted worship that gratifies man's carnal nature. A number of Israel's neighbors were descendants of Abraham and Lot, who worshiped the LORD.

- Many of the lands and peoples mentioned in the Bible can still be identified today. A brief discussion of modern nations in the Middle East might help students grasp the reality of Bible events. The struggle between modern Jews and Arabs dates back to Ishmael and Isaac. Some cities, such as Jerusalem and Damascus, are still located at the same places and are still called by their ancient names. The valley where David met Goliath is just as real a place as your school playground.

100 Chapter Three   Israel's Downfall

B. BIBLE STUDY BOOKS

✎ *Look up the italicized word in a concordance, and find a reference that gives the needed information. Fill in the blanks and write the references.*   (References may vary slightly.)

1. *Jethro,* Moses' father-in-law, was a priest of _____Midian_____. Reference: _____Exodus 3:1_____ or Exodus 18:1

2. Moses sent messengers from *Kadesh* to the king of _____Edom_____, but this king refused to allow the Israelites to pass through his land. Reference: __Numbers 20:14 or Judges 11:17__

3. *Balak,* king of _____Moab_____, sent messengers to ask Balaam to curse Israel. Reference: _____Numbers 22:4, 5_____

4. *Shamgar* slew six hundred _____Philistines_____ with an ox goad. Reference: _____Judges 3:31_____

5. A certain soldier in the _____Syrian_____ army drew a bow at a *venture* and fatally wounded King Ahab. Reference: __1 Kings 22:34, 35 or 2 Chronicles 18:33, 34__

✎ *Fill in each blank on the map with the correct name from the list.*

Ammon
Edom
Israel
Judah
Moab
Philistia
Phoenicia
Syria

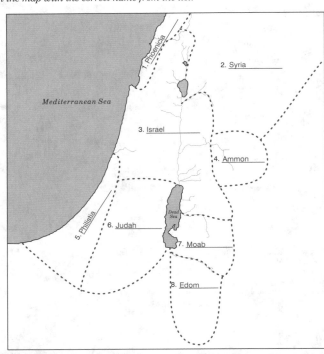

1. Phoenicia
Mediterranean Sea
2. Syria
3. Israel
4. Ammon
5. Philistia
Dead Sea
6. Judah
7. Moab
8. Edom

Life in Bible Times

You may want your students to color this map. Have them lightly shade each country with a different color. Color the bodies of water blue, and the deserts in the south and west light brown.

CHAPTER FOUR

David's Family Reigns Over Judah

Thou wilt keep him in perfect peace,
whose mind is stayed on thee:
because he trusteth in thee.
Trust ye in the LORD for ever:
for in the LORD JEHOVAH
is everlasting strength.
Isaiah 26:3, 4

TIME LINE—Chapter Four

The Kings of Judah

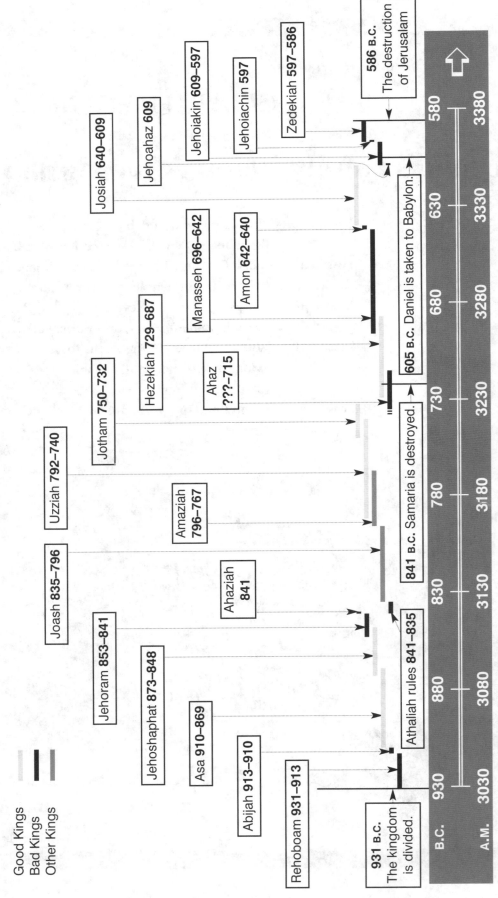

Good Kings
Bad Kings
Other Kings

Rehoboam **931–913**

931 B.C.
The kingdom
is divided.

Abijah **913–910**

Asa **910–869**

Jehoshaphat **873–848**

Jehoram **853–841**

Athaliah rules **841–835**

Ahaziah
841

Joash **835–796**

Amaziah
796–767

Uzziah **792–740**

Jotham **750–732**

841 B.C. Samaria is destroyed.

Ahaz
???–715

Hezekiah **729–687**

Manasseh **696–642**

Amon **642–640**

Josiah **640–609**

605 B.C. Daniel is taken to Babylon.

Jehoahaz **609**

Jehoiakin **609–597**

Jehoiachin **597**

Zedekiah **597–586**

586 B.C.
The destruction
of Jerusalem

B.C. 930   880   830   780   730   680   630   580
A.M. 3030   3080   3130   3180   3230   3280   3330   3380

NOTES:
* All dates in the text boxes are B.C.
* See the time lines in Chapters 2 and 3 to compare these kings with those of the Northern Kingdom of Israel.
* All dates are approximate. Those on this time line should be reasonably accurate, but there is some variation of opinion among chronologists about this period.

103

Lesson 16. The Kingdom of Judah

(Rehoboam, Abijah, Asa, and Jehoshaphat)

In Chapters 2 and 3, you studied the history of the ten northern tribes, who rebelled against Solomon's son Rehoboam. This lesson goes back to the time of Rehoboam and takes up the story of the southern kingdom of Judah.

You have learned that all the northern kings followed Jeroboam in his worship of the golden calves. The Bible compares many of the southern kings with David, the first king of their long-lasting dynasty. Some kings of Judah "walked in the ways of the kings of Israel" instead of following David's good example (2 Chronicles 28:1, 2). Others "did that which was right in the sight of the LORD, but not with a perfect heart" (2 Chronicles 25:2). Only a few of Judah's kings "did that which was right in the sight of the LORD, according to all that David [their] father had done" (2 Chronicles 29:2).

The righteous kings helped to restore true worship at Jerusalem. Because of them, God allowed the people of Judah to live in their land more than one hundred years longer than the northern tribes. But the wicked kings of Judah also affected the course of the nation. Eventually Judah as a whole became so wicked that God sent them into captivity too.

Yet even in captivity, the influence of David and his righteous descendants still lingered. Prophets such as Jeremiah, Ezekiel, and Daniel instructed and encouraged the few who had remained faithful to God. After seventy years, some Jews returned to their homeland, and eventually Jesus came through David's family.

Judah's kings, both good and bad, helped set the course of the kingdom. Our obedience or disobedience to God's Word also influences many homes, churches, and individuals.

God blesses those who set a good example for others to follow.

A. ANSWERS FROM THE BIBLE

King Rehoboam

The kingdom of Israel reached its highest point of glory and power during Solomon's reign. Rehoboam inherited a glorious kingdom, but he could not keep it. God had told Solomon that because of his sin, He would take most of the kingdom away from his son.

2 Chronicles 10:3–5, 16

1. Why did the northern tribes refuse to accept Rehoboam as their king? _____

     Rehoboam refused to listen to their request that their yoke be made lighter.

Rehoboam gathered his army to fight against the northern tribes. But when the prophet Shemaiah told him that the LORD did not approve of his plans, Rehoboam returned to Jerusalem. Apparently the two sides fought later, because the Bible says that there was war between Rehoboam and Jeroboam all their days (1 Kings 14:30).

2 Chronicles 11:11–14

2. The tribes of _____Judah_____ and _____Benjamin_____ supported Rehoboam.

3. Many priests and _____Levites_____ also came to Rehoboam from the Northern Kingdom.

For three years, Rehoboam and his people served the LORD. But after he had established his kingdom, he forsook the Law of God (2 Chronicles 11:17; 12:1).

Lesson 16

Oral Review

The numbers in brackets tell which lessons are being reviewed.

1. Why did the prophet Nathan pronounce judgment on David? [3] **David had committed adultery and murder.**

2. How did Solomon become the wisest man? [4] **He asked God for wisdom.**

3. What did the ten northern tribes ask of Rehoboam? [6] **They asked him to make their burdens lighter.**

4. Why did Jeroboam make golden calves at Bethel and Dan? [6] **He wanted to keep the northern tribes from returning to Jerusalem.**

5. Where did Elijah stay during the years of drought? (Give two places.) [9] **near the Brook Cherith, and with a widow at Zarephath**

6. What did Elisha's servant see on the hills when God opened his eyes? [12] **horses and chariots of fire**

7. Who was the ancestor of the Israelites, the Ishmaelites, the Edomites, and the Midianites? [15] **Abraham**

8. What country was Ruth from? [15] **Moab**

104   Chapter Four   David's Family Reigns Over Judah

2 Chronicles 12:1–9

4. What punishment did the LORD send when Rehoboam forsook Him? _____

   Shishak king of Egypt came up against the cities of Judah.

5. What did Rehoboam and the princes of Israel do and say when Shemaiah told them they had sinned?

   They humbled themselves and said, "The LORD is righteous."

6. King Shishak took away the _____treasures_____ of the LORD's house, the treasures of the

   _____king's_____ house, and the shields of _____gold_____ that Solomon had made.

King Abijah

Rehoboam's son Abijah (called Abijam in 1 Kings) became the next king of Judah. In Abijah's day, the ten northern tribes continued to make war with Judah.

2 Chronicles 13

7. Circle the letters of *three* things for which Abijah criticized Jeroboam and the Israelites (13:8, 9).

   (a.) They had rebelled against the kingdom of David.

   (b.) They had set up the golden calves for gods.

   c. They had stolen treasures from the temple.

   (d.) They had cast out the priests of the LORD.

8. Why did Abijah's men win the battle? (13:14–16) _____

   The men of Judah cried unto the LORD, and the LORD delivered Israel into their hands.

9. Abijah trusted in the LORD during a battle, but he did not serve the LORD with all his heart as his

   great-grandfather David had. Whose sins did Abijah walk in? (1 Kings 15:3) _____his father's_____
   (Rehoboam's)

King Asa

King Asa, Abijah's son, started out well. The Bible says he "did that which was right in the eyes of the LORD, as did David his father" (1 Kings 15:11). But he became less and less faithful as he grew older.

✎ *Fill in the blanks to tell the good things Asa did. (All references are from 2 Chronicles.)*

10. Asa took away the _____altars_____ of the strange gods, broke down the

    _____images_____, and cut down the _____groves_____ (14:3).

11. Asa commanded Judah to seek the _____LORD_____ _____God_____ of their

    fathers and to do the _____law_____ and the _____commandment_____ (14:4).

12. How did Asa show that he trusted in the LORD when a huge army of Ethiopians came against him?

    (14:9–12) He cried unto the LORD for help (and said that God could easily help, whether the enemy
    was many or few).

13. When Asa heard the words of _____Oded_____ the prophet, he was encouraged to put

    away more idols and to repair the _____altar_____ of the LORD (15:8).

14. Asa removed Maacah, his wicked (grand)mother, from being _____queen_____ (15:16).

    (Maacah was Abijah's mother [2 Chronicles 11:21], so she was Asa's grandmother. The Bible some-

    times uses the terms *mother* and *father* to refer to an ancestor.)

This verse also mentions the removal of the high places, but 2 Chronicles 15:17 indicates that Asa did not take all of them away.

See note on page 113.

In This Lesson

Scope: 2 Chronicles 10–20

Main Events

• After the ten tribes rebel, Rehoboam reigns over Judah and Benjamin. Many priests and Levites also support him.

• Rehoboam forsakes the LORD and is punished for his sin.

• Abijah trusts in God during a battle with Israel, but his heart is not perfect toward the LORD. He continues in the sins of Rehoboam his father.

• Asa does right in the eyes of the LORD, but he becomes less faithful near the end of his life.

• Jehoshaphat seeks the LORD and walks in God's commandments. However, God rebukes him for helping Ahab.

Objectives

• The students should know

—why the ten tribes of the Northern Kingdom set up their own kingdom instead of following Rehoboam. (Rehoboam refused to listen to their request that their yoke be made lighter.)

—that Rehoboam and Abijah largely forsook God.

—that Asa and Jehoshaphat started out as good kings, but they were less faithful as they grew older.

✎ *Fill in the blanks to tell how Asa failed. All references are from 2 Chronicles.*

15. Asa made a _____league_____ with the king of Syria (16:2, 3).

16. What did Asa do when Hanani the prophet rebuked him for seeking help from the Syrians? (16:7–10)
    __He became angry and put Hanani into prison (and oppressed some of the people).__

17. Instead of seeking healing from the LORD, Asa sought only the help of _____physicians_____ (16:12).

King Jehoshaphat

Like his father Asa, King Jehoshaphat did what was right when he began to reign. Like Asa, he made some serious mistakes and was rebuked by a prophet. Jehoshaphat's worst mistake was his friendship with wicked King Ahab. The house of Ahab brought many problems to Judah after Jehoshaphat's death.

In spite of his failures, Jehoshaphat was one of Judah's best kings. The Bible says that he "sought the LORD with all his heart" (2 Chronicles 22:9).

✎ *Match the sentence beginnings with the correct endings. All references are from 2 Chronicles.*

__a__ 18. When Jehoshaphat sought the LORD and walked in His commandments, . . . (17:3–6)

__g__ 19. In the third year of Jehoshaphat, . . . (17:7–9)

__e__ 20. Because Jehoshaphat feared the LORD, . . . (17:10, 11)

__b__ 21. When Jehoshaphat became wealthy and secure, . . . (18:3)

__d__ 22. As part of the peace made between Israel and Judah, . . . (21:5, 6)

__f__ 23. After Jehoshaphat returned from helping King Ahab, . . . (19:1–3)

__c__ 24. When the Moabites and Ammonites came to fight against Jehoshaphat, . . . (20:3, 20–24)

a. the LORD established his kingdom and gave him great riches.

b. he made peace with Ahab, king of Israel.

c. he proclaimed a fast, and the LORD delivered Judah when they began to sing and praise the LORD.

d. Jehoshaphat's son Jehoram married King Ahab's daughter.

e. the fear of the LORD fell on the surrounding nations, and the Philistines and Arabians brought Jehoshaphat presents.

f. Jehu the prophet rebuked him.

g. he sent out princes, Levites, and priests to teach the people from the Law of the LORD.

B. BIBLE WORD STUDY

✎ *Write a word or phrase from the verse given to match each definition. All references are from 2 Chronicles.*

__strong holds (strongholds)__ 1. Fortresses (11:11)

__victual__ 2. Food (11:11)

__consecrate__ 3. To set aside for a sacred purpose (13:9)

__abominable__ 4. Causing disgust; loathsome (15:8)

__league__ 5. An agreement between two or more parties (16:3)

__seer__ 6. A prophet (16:7)

Note from page 112

- Maacah was Rehoboam's favorite wife and the grandmother of Asa (2 Chronicles 11:21–23). Apparently she held her position as queen mother after her son Abijah's death.

  Maacah is called the daughter of Absalom in 2 Chronicles 11:21, but in 13:2 she is called "Michaiah the daughter of Uriel." Perhaps she was the daughter of Uriel and the granddaughter of Absalom. If this is correct, she may have been named after her great-grandmother Maacah, David's wife and Absalom's mother (2 Samuel 3:3). This first Maacah was a princess from Geshur (2 Samuel 3:3). It is possible that she left an evil influence that affected generations of David's descendants.

- *Victual* is pronounced *VIHT uhl.*

—what God expected of the kings that ruled His people. (to be a godly example and to lead the Israelites in obedience to Him)

Truths to Instill

- The need for careful obedience. If the kings of Judah had carefully obeyed God's instructions about idol worship (Leviticus 26), God's blessing, rather than judgment, could have rested upon them.

- God is no respecter of persons. King Asa, who removed his grandmother from office because of her idol worship, set a good example of impartiality. But later God rebuked both Asa and Jehoshaphat for their sin, even though they were more righteous than many of the other kings (James 2:1–9).

_____Baalim_____   7. The plural of *Baal* (17:3) (Baal *was a Canaanite word meaning "lord." The heathen gave this title to a number of their idol-gods.*)

_____tribute_____   8. A forced payment made by a weak nation to a strong ruler or nation (17:11)

✎ *Use a concordance to complete this exercise.*

9. Because of Jeroboam's idolatry, many righteous priests and Levites in Israel left their *suburbs* and possessions and moved to Judah (2 Chronicles 11:14). Their suburbs were the lands surrounding their towns. Use a concordance to find a reference in Numbers that describes the suburbs. Give the reference, and then tell how the Levites used their suburbs. _____

  Numbers 35:2–7 (The answer does not need to include all of these verses.)

  The Levites kept their cattle, goods, and beasts in their suburbs.

C. THINKING ABOUT BIBLE TRUTHS

God's Plan for Godly Kings

Long before Israel had a king, God knew that sometime they would demand one. When He gave the Law to Moses, He included some instructions for the future kings of His people.

Perhaps God had planned to set up a king over the Israelites someday, and they sinned by asking for one before the right time. Or He may have given them these instructions because He knew that they would insist on having a king, even though that was not His plan for them. God has always been concerned that the leaders of His people would lead them in the right way.

Deuteronomy 17:14–20

1. God gave the Israelites specific instructions about the king that they would set up over themselves. Which *two* items below tell what the king was to be?

   (a.) an Israelite   b. a priest   c. a stranger   (d.) someone chosen by God

2. Verses 16 and 17 list a number of things that the king was not to do. Most of the Hebrew kings disobeyed at least one or two of these commands, and some kings, including Solomon, disobeyed all of them. Circle the letters of the *four* things that the king was *not* allowed to do.

   (a.) have as many wives as he wanted   (d.) become as rich as possible
   (b.) send people to Egypt to buy horses for himself   (e.) own many horses
   c. have slaves and servants to do his work

3. Each king was to write his own copy of the Law and to read it regularly. This would help him to remember that

   a. the work of a scribe was very difficult and time-consuming.
   (b.) he was just as responsible to keep God's commandments as the rest of the Israelites were.
   c. he was more important than any other person in his kingdom.

2 Samuel 23:3

4. These words were spoken by King David. Many kings seemed to think that they could do anything they wanted to do. However, according to this verse, God expected the kings to

(a.) be fair to the people whom they ruled over.

b. work for a living like everyone else in the country.

c. let people who disobeyed the laws go free without punishment.

What Do You Think?

5. Which of the following statements *best* describes what God expected of the king?

a. God wanted the king to fearlessly deliver the Israelites from their enemies.

b. God wanted the king to make the Israelites obey the Laws of God.

(c.) God wanted the king to be a godly example and to lead the Israelites in obedience to Him.

D. LEARNING MORE ABOUT THE BIBLE

Old Testament Books

✎ *Review the Old Testament books and their divisions. (See Lesson 1 if you need help.) You will need to know the order and spelling of the Major Prophets for the Chapter 4 Test.*

Doctors in Bible Times

1. When King Asa's feet became diseased, he sought the help of doctors. Why did this displease God? (2 Chronicles 16:12) _____

   He did not seek the LORD's help.

2. What promise about health did God give the Israelites in Exodus 15:26? _____

   He promised to keep them from the diseases He had brought upon the Egyptians, if they followed Him.

3. Who healed a woman who had spent all her living on doctor bills, and yet had not been cured? (Luke 8:43–48) _____ Jesus _____

4. a. Which of Paul's helpers was a doctor? (Colossians 4:14) _____ Luke _____

   b. Which two books of the Bible did this doctor write? (Use a Bible dictionary.) _____

      Luke, Acts

Make sure that the students understand the difference between b and c. It was not enough to make others do what was right. The king was responsible to lead out in doing right by being obedient himself. While a was part of a king's job too, c was the most important.

Review the Old Testament books and their divisions together in class as needed. The students will need to know the order and spelling of the Major Prophets for the Chapter 4 Test.

108

Lesson 17. Judah Corrupted by the House of Ahab

(Jehoram, Ahaziah, Joash, and Amaziah)

Joash had an unusual childhood. He was born into King David's royal family, yet his grandfather Jehoram and his father Ahaziah were both evil kings. They were influenced by Joash's great-grandmother, wicked Queen Jezebel, and his grandmother, wicked Queen Athaliah.

But Joash probably did not remember much of his family. His grandfather Jehoram died about the time he was born. While he was just a baby, Jehu killed his father along with the rest of Ahab and Jezebel's family. When his wicked grandmother, Athaliah, heard about this, she killed all of Joash's brothers. She tried to kill him too, but his kind aunt Jehosheba rescued him. Jehosheba hid Joash in an out-of-the-way room in the temple.

For six years Jehosheba and her husband, the good priest Jehoiada, concealed Joash from his grandmother. Then at seven years of age, Joash was crowned king of Israel!

Think about a seven-year-old boy you know. Can you imagine him being the leader of your country?

As long as Joash's good uncle Jehoiada lived, Joash was a good king. Jehoiada helped him make good decisions. The temple was repaired. The people of Judah served God and were happy. But Jehoiada grew old and died, and then Joash had to make decisions of his own.

After his uncle's death, Joash listened to evil men and turned away from serving God. This grieved the family of his good uncle and aunt who had saved his life and helped him all these years. Zechariah—Jehoiada's son and Joash's cousin—spoke against Joash's sin. But instead of repenting, Joash and his men became angry. They stoned Zechariah until he died. "Thus Joash the king remembered not the kindness which Jehoiada his father had done to him, but slew his son" (2 Chronicles 24:22).

The people of Judah were shocked and greatly disappointed. God was grieved. He let the Syrian army smite Joash. Soon afterward, Joash's own servants killed him on his bed.

Why did Joash turn away from God after doing so much good? We do not know for sure, but it seems that he had never learned to make good decisions on his own. While he was young, Jehoiada and Jehosheba made important decisions wisely for him. But after Jehoiada's death, Joash had to choose his own course. His failure to make right decisions cost him his life.

God wants us to choose the right way, even if those who have taught us the truth are no longer with us.

A. ANSWERS FROM THE BIBLE

Jehoram—Ahab's Son-in-Law

Jehoram was the son of good King Jehoshaphat. His father probably taught him to worship the LORD on the Sabbath and to study God's Law. No doubt Jehoram helped his father on many good projects. But his father, Jehoshaphat, made the serious mistake of developing a friendship with King Ahab. This friendship may be one reason Jehoram married Athaliah, the wicked daughter of Ahab and Jezebel. Soon Jehoram was following the house of Ahab rather than his own father.

Jehoram made no effort to do what was right. Shortly after his father died, King Jehoram killed all his brothers. He worshiped idols, and he walked in the ways of the kings of Israel.

Lesson 17

Oral Review

1. When did Saul throw a javelin at David? [2] **while David was playing his harp**
2. What words does the Bible use again and again to describe Jeroboam? [7] **"He made Israel to sin."**
3. What did Ahab sell himself to do? [8] **wickedness in the sight of the LORD**
4. How was Elijah's prophecy concerning Jezebel fulfilled? [13] **The dogs ate most of her body.**
5. How many times did Joash, the grandson of Jehu, smite the Syrians? [14] **three** (Remind the students that this Joash is not the same king that they will study in this lesson.)
6. Who remained loyal to Rehoboam after some of the tribes rebelled? [16] **the tribes of Judah and Benjamin, and many priests and Levites**
7. What did Asa do to Maacah, his wicked grandmother? [16] **He removed her from being queen.**
8. What good king was a friend to Ahab? [16] **Jehoshaphat**

Lesson 17.   Judah Corrupted by the House of Ahab   **109**

When God saw Jehoram's sin, He had to punish him. Evil deeds do not escape punishment. No matter how good Jehoram's father had been, Jehoram had to suffer for his own wrong choices. God judges people without respect of persons.

2 Chronicles 21:1–7, 12–20

1. Jehoshaphat gave the kingdom to Jehoram, his oldest son. What evil thing did Jehoram do to his father's family soon after he became king?_____

   He killed all his brothers (and many other princes of Judah).

2. Jehoram lived like the wicked kings of Israel because he had married the daughter of _Ahab (Jezebel)_.

3. The prophet Elijah sent Jehoram a letter of warning. The letter said that because of Jehoram's wickedness, the LORD would smite his people, his _____children_____, his _____wives_____, and all his goods with a great plague.

4. The letter also said that Jehoram would be afflicted with a great _____sickness (disease)_____.

5. The Philistines and Arabians took away all except the youngest of Jehoram's _____sons_____.

6. Jehoram died without being _____desired_____ by his people. They were not sorry that he died.

Ahaziah's Short Reign

✎ *Circle the letter of the best ending.*

2 Chronicles 22

7. Ahaziah, king of Judah after Jehoram,
   a. was more righteous than his father.
   b. was helped by a band of Arabians.
   (c.) was Jehoram's youngest son.

8. The Bible says that Ahaziah walked in the ways of the house of Ahab because
   (a.) his evil mother influenced him.
   b. his father and grandfather had both been wicked.
   c. everyone else in Judah had forsaken the LORD.

9. Ahaziah reigned one year. Then Jehu's men killed him while he was
   a. at the palace, sleeping in his bed.
   (b.) in Israel, visiting his uncle, King Jehoram.
   c. at Ramoth-gilead, fighting King Hazael.

10. When King Ahaziah's mother, Athaliah, learned of his death, she tried to
   (a.) kill all the royal descendants of David.
   b. make war with Jehu for killing her son.
   c. give the throne to her favorite grandson.

11. Jehoshabeath (Jehosheba), King Ahaziah's sister,
   a. restrained Athaliah from doing such evil deeds.
   (b.) rescued Ahaziah's youngest son from death.
   c. killed Athaliah and reigned over Judah.

In This Lesson

Scope: 2 Chronicles 21–25

Main Events

- Jehoram reigns after the death of his father, Jehoshaphat. He marries the daughter of Ahab, kills his brothers, and walks in the ways of Ahab.
- Ahaziah becomes king of Judah. Through his association with his uncle, King Joram of Israel, he is killed by Jehu.
- Ahaziah's mother, Athaliah, tries to destroy all the royal seed of Judah so that she herself can reign.
- Young Joash is hidden by his aunt Jehosheba.
- When Joash is seven years old, he is crowned king by his uncle Jehoiada, the high priest.
- Joash is a good king as long as Jehoiada advises him, but after Jehoiada's death, Joash worships idols.
- Amaziah begins to serve the LORD, but after he defeats the Edomites in battle, he worships their gods.

Ahab's daughter Athaliah was an evil counselor to her husband Jehoram during his eight-year reign and to her son Ahaziah during his one-year reign. After Ahaziah was killed, Athaliah seized the throne for herself. Like her mother, Jezebel, she worshiped Baal. She tried to destroy all those who had a rightful claim to the throne of David. But the LORD had promised to establish David's kingdom forever. Although God allowed most of Ahaziah's sons and relatives to be killed, He made sure one son was spared. Many years later, Jesus was born into Joash's family line.

Joash—a Boy Crowned King

Jehosheba hid baby Joash in a room in the temple. When Joash was seven years old, Jehoiada anointed him king. The people of Judah killed Athaliah and destroyed the temple of Baal. They also killed the priest of Baal.

Note: *Joash* is a shortened form of *Jehoash*. The Bible uses both forms to name two different kings. Be sure to notice the difference: Jehoahaz's son Jehoash (Joash) was a king of Israel; Jehoram's son Joash (Jehoash) was a king of Judah. (See the chart of the kings of Israel and Judah in Lesson 7.)

2 Chronicles 24:1–10

12. How long did Joash do right in the sight of the LORD? _____

    all the days of Jehoiada the priest

13. Why did the house of the LORD need repair? _____

    The sons of Athaliah had broken it up.

14. How was money collected to pay for the temple repairs? _____

    A chest was set at the gate of the temple for the people's offerings.

2 Chronicles 24:15–25

15. Who encouraged Joash to worship idols after Jehoiada's death? _____

    the princes of Judah

16. Who rebuked Joash for his sin?   Zechariah, the son of Jehoiada

17. What was done to Zechariah at Joash's command? _____

    He was stoned to death.

18. God had promised that if the Israelites were faithful, He would help small numbers of them to defeat large armies (Leviticus 26:8). How did the LORD reverse His promise because of Joash's sin? _____

    God allowed a small number of men from Syria to defeat a very great army of Judah.

19. Because of his evil deeds, Joash was afflicted with great _____ diseases _____.

20. Joash's own _____ servants _____ conspired against him and killed him on his _____ bed _____.

Amaziah's Imperfect Heart

Like his father Joash, Amaziah started out right. But like his father, Amaziah failed to continue serving only the LORD, and he was also killed by conspirators.

• The royal descendants must have been very few during Joash's childhood. His grandfather Jehoram had killed all his own brothers and many other princes (2 Chronicles 21:4). As a judgment, God allowed Judah's enemies to kill all of Jehoram's sons except Ahaziah, the youngest (21:17; 22:1). A year after Jehoram's death, Jehu killed Ahaziah, some sons of Ahaziah's brothers, and other princes of Judah (22:8, 9). When Athaliah heard this, she killed "all the seed royal of the house of Judah" except baby Joash (22:10, 11). All this took place within about nine years of Jehoshaphat's death. What a terrible price Jehoshaphat paid for his friendship with Ahab! How hard Satan tried to cut off David's line! Yet God's hand can be seen through it all, removing much of Jezebel's influence while sparing a remnant to fulfill His promise.

Objectives

• The students should know
  —how Jehoshaphat's friendship with the house of Ahab caused problems for Judah. (Jehoshaphat's son Jehoram married Ahab's daughter Athaliah, who influenced her husband to follow the ways of Ahab, which brought God's punishment.)
  —why Athaliah tried to kill all her grandchildren. (She wanted to reign over Judah.)
  —how Joash was protected from his grandmother's evil plan. (His aunt Jehosheba rescued him and hid him.)
  —why Joash started to serve idols. (He listened to evil men.)
  —what the duties of a king were. (See Part C.)

Truths to Instill

• Evil associations bring harmful results. The results of Jehoshaphat's friendship with Ahab are shown in this lesson. Jehoram's marriage to Athaliah led him down the path of sin. Ahaziah's continued association with his mother's wicked family cost him his life, and the lives of his sons.

✎ *Number the events in the order they are recorded.*

2 Chronicles 25:1–9

21. __3__ Amaziah gathers 300,000 soldiers from Judah.

__1__ Amaziah begins to reign and does right in the LORD's sight, but not with a perfect heart.

__4__ Amaziah hires 100,000 soldiers from Israel.

__5__ A man of God tells Amaziah to send the Israelite soldiers back home.

__2__ Amaziah kills the murderers of his father.

2 Chronicles 25:10–16

22. __5__ Amaziah tells the prophet to stop giving him advice.

__3__ Amaziah begins worshiping the gods of the Edomites.

__4__ The LORD sends a prophet to rebuke Amaziah for his sin.

__2__ Because they have been sent back home, the Israelite soldiers take revenge on the cities of Judah.

__1__ Amaziah's army smites the Edomites (children of Seir).

2 Chronicles 25:17–27

23. __2__ Joash tells Amaziah to stay at home and stop meddling with trouble.

__3__ Amaziah insists on fighting against Israel.

__1__ Amaziah challenges Joash, the king of Israel, to battle.

__5__ Amaziah is killed by men who conspire against him.

__4__ The men of Judah are badly defeated by the men of Israel.

B. BIBLE WORD STUDY

✎ *Match these definitions with the Bible words or phrases on the right. All references are from 2 Chronicles.*

__c__ 1. A center of worship on a hill or mountain (21:11)   a. burning

__a__ 2. A fire in honor of a good king (21:19)   b. counselor

__b__ 3. A person who gives advice or guidance (22:3)   c. high place

__e__ 4. Act of bowing to show respect or honor (24:17)   d. incense

__f__ 5. Goods taken during a battle (24:23)   e. obeisance

__d__ 6. Perfume that is burned as a sacrifice (25:14)   f. spoil

✎ *Use a Bible dictionary to complete this exercise.*

Some Bible names sound strange to people who speak English, but many of them have beautiful meanings. The names that Jehoshaphat gave to his sons show that he wanted them to serve the Lord (Jehovah) as he had done (2 Chronicles 21:2). Instead, Jehoram followed his wife's wickedness and killed all his brothers.

- We need to do what is right, no matter who is with us. Joash did many good things while Jehoiada lived, but after his death he readily took another course.
- It is vital to have sound character (*moral or ethical strength; integrity; fortitude*). Joash had weak character. When the princes offered their support (obviously the wrong kind), Joash willingly accepted it and began worshiping idols.

Answers may vary slightly.

7. Find the meanings of the names of Jehoshaphat's sons. Some of them have been done for you. Notice that two of the names are the same.

a. Jehoram: ___Jehovah is exalted.___

b. Azariah: ___Jehovah has helped.___

c. Jehiel: ___May God live!___

d. Zechariah: ___Jehovah has remembered___

e. Azariah: ___Jehovah has helped.___

f. Michael: ___Who is like God?___

g. Shephatiah: ___Jehovah has judged___

C. THINKING ABOUT BIBLE TRUTHS

The King's Duties

You might think that a king had an easy life, but this is not true. Kings had many responsibilities. Those who tried to live a life of ease and pleasure did not prosper. It was the kings who worked hard and fulfilled their responsibilities who were successful.

1. Read 1 Kings 3:28. The king was expected to be wise so that he could _____judge_____ the people. If he was foolish or unfair, the people would no longer _____fear_____ him, and they might even look for another king.

2. Read 2 Kings 9:6. The Israelites considered the king to be anointed of God. Since God appointed him, he was
   (a.) responsible directly to God in everything he did.
   b. responsible to the people he ruled over, to do what they wanted him to do.
   c. more godly than the people that he ruled over.

3. Read 1 Kings 20:13, 14. The king was responsible to _____order_____ the battle. In other words, he was to direct it and lead his army. This often put the king in a dangerous place during a battle. It also made him responsible if the battle was lost.

4. Read 2 Chronicles 14:6, 7. The king was responsible to keep his country as safe as possible from invaders. In these verses King Asa built _____fenced_____ (fortified) cities in Judah, which he protected with _____walls_____, _____towers_____, _____gates_____, and _____bars_____. These cities gave the Israelites some safety from their enemies.

Lesson 17.   Judah Corrupted by the House of Ahab   **113**

What Do You Think?

5. The king was responsible to care for the needs of his people. In return, they respected and supported him. But if a king became selfish and took advantage of his people, the people turned against him. A good king needed

a. much money so that he could meet his obligations.

b. a large army to help him protect his country.

(c.) to think of the welfare of his people before his own happiness.

D. LEARNING MORE ABOUT THE BIBLE

The Results of Mixed Marriages

 Asa, king of Judah, worshiped God.

 Omri, king of Israel, worshiped the golden calves Jeroboam had set up.

 Ethbaal, king of Phoenicia, worshiped Baal.

Son

 King Jehoshaphat worshiped God, but he made friends with Ahab.

Son

Son

Daughter

The LORD had commanded His people to marry wives from only their own nation. But some of the kings tried to make friends with heathen kings by marrying their daughters. This brought bad results. The marriages shown here illustrate what often happened.

 King Ahab and his wife Jezebel worshiped Baal.

Daughter

 King Jehoram and his wife Athaliah worshiped Baal.

Son

 King Ahaziah worshiped Baal. His mother killed all but one of his sons.

1. Why did God not want the Israelites to marry people of other nations? (Deuteronomy 7:3, 4) _____

    He knew this would cause His people to turn to other gods.

2. What false god did Jezebel cause Ahab to worship? _____ Baal _____

114 Chapter Four David's Family Reigns Over Judah

3. What mixed marriage was probably a result of Jehoshaphat's friendship with Ahab? _____

   __Jehoram's marriage to Athaliah_____

4. a. Who was Ahaziah's grandmother on his mother's side? _____ Jezebel _____

   b. Who was Ahaziah's grandfather on his father's side? _____ Jehoshaphat _____

   c. Did Ahaziah follow his good or his wicked grandparents? _He followed his wicked grandparents._

5. What two men helped remove some of the influence that Jezebel and Athaliah brought into Israel and Judah? (2 Chronicles 22:8; 23:14) _____ Jehu, Jehoiada _____

115

Lesson 18. Prosperity, Sin, and Revival

(Uzziah, Jotham, Ahaz, and Hezekiah)

Some of Judah's kings had good parents, yet they chose evil ways. But Hezekiah, who had a wicked father, chose to do right.

During Hezekiah's long reign, the people of Judah turned back to the LORD. After years of idolatry, treachery, and defeat, they prospered once more under God's mighty hand.

Hezekiah led the people in ridding Jerusalem of its idols. He opened the doors of the temple, and he commanded the priests and the Levites to purify themselves. The priests lit the lamps in the holy place and offered sacrifices on the altar. Hezekiah commanded great feasts to be held in Jerusalem according to the Law given by Moses. God was pleased, and His people rejoiced.

Not everything was pleasant, however. Before Hezekiah began to reign, the Assyrians had demanded tribute from Judah. But Hezekiah knew that God could take care of His people, so he stopped paying tribute. This made the Assyrians angry, and several years later they sent a large army against Judah. Hezekiah and his people faced a time of trouble.

Some people think that God always spares His people from trouble, but this is not true. God often calls His people to serve Him in times of trouble. Jesus was arrested and killed by His enemies, and so were most of His disciples. Many of the early Christians were killed for their faith in Jesus. Four hundred years ago faithful Christians called Anabaptists suffered severe persecution in Europe. In more recent times, Christians have been persecuted in communist and Muslim countries.

When Hezekiah and the people of Judah saw the Assyrians coming against them, they turned to God for help. The proud Assyrians wrote a threatening letter to King Hezekiah. The men who brought the letter spoke loud, boastful words. But Hezekiah told his people not to talk back. He took the letter and spread it out before the LORD. God's promise of help calmed and strengthened him.

That night the angel of the LORD smote thousands of soldiers in the Assyrian camp. The remaining Assyrians departed in shame, and the siege around Jerusalem was lifted.

God stays with his people and helps them through troublesome times.

A. ANSWERS FROM THE BIBLE

Uzziah—the King Who Tried to Burn Incense

King Uzziah of Judah, the son of Amaziah, was a good king. He reigned for many years and prospered while he served God. However, he was not content to be only a king. He wanted to burn incense as a priest too. God needed to punish him for his disobedience. King Uzziah learned his lesson, but things were never the same again.

✎ *Write* true *or* false. *Correct each false statement on the lines after the sentence.*

2 Chronicles 26:1–6, 15–23

__false__   1. Uzziah reigned sixty-two years in Jerusalem. _____

   __Uzziah reigned *fifty-two* years in Jerusalem.__ _____

• Uzziah is called Azariah in 2 Kings 15.

In the rewritten sentences for numbers 1–6, the corrections are in italics. The pupil's sentences may vary somewhat.

Lesson 18

Oral Review

1. What idols did Jehu leave in Israel? [13] **the golden calves that Jeroboam had made at Bethel and Dan**

2. What country conquered Samaria and carried the Israelites away? [14] **Assyria**

3. Who was the ancestor of the Moabites and the Ammonites? [15] **Lot**

4. Why was God displeased when Asa sought help from physicians? [16] **Asa did not seek the LORD's healing.**

5. Why did God want the Hebrew kings to have their own copy of the Law? [16] **God wanted the kings to remember that they also were responsible to keep the Law. (so that they would fear God and remain humble)**

6. What were some results of Jehoram's marriage to Athaliah? [17] *Examples:* **Jehoram did evil as did Ahab's house. Athaliah was Ahaziah's wicked counselor. Athaliah killed most of the royal descendants and reigned wickedly.**

7. What did Joash do after his uncle Jehoiada's death? [17] **He turned away from the LORD and served idols.**

116   Chapter Four   David's Family Reigns Over Judah

_____true_____   2. Uzziah sought the LORD, and the LORD helped him prosper. _____

_____false_____   3. God helped the Philistines defeat Uzziah. _____
      God helped *Uzziah* defeat the *Philistines.*

_____true_____   4. People in distant lands heard how God had marvelously helped Uzziah. _____

_____false_____   5. Uzziah humbly worshiped God all his life according to the Law. _____
      Uzziah *became proud and tried to burn incense to the LORD.*

_____true_____   6. The LORD smote Uzziah with leprosy. _____

Jotham—a Good, Prosperous King

7. Why did Jotham start judging the people while his father was still living? (2 Chronicles 26:21) _____
    Jotham judged the people after the LORD smote his father with leprosy. _____

8. Judah prospered during Jotham's reign. Why did God allow Jotham to become mighty? (2 Chronicles 27:6) _____
    Jotham prepared his ways before the LORD his God. _____

9. How did the people of Judah live during the prosperous reign of righteous Jotham? (2 Chronicles 27:2)
    corruptly _____

King Ahaz—Looking the Wrong Way for Help

Ahaz, the son of good King Jotham, was a very wicked king. Like Jehoram and Ahaziah, he walked in the ways of the kings of Israel. Because of his sin, the LORD delivered Judah into the hands of their enemies. The prosperity they had enjoyed during Uzziah's and Jotham's reigns was lost.

2 Chronicles 28

10. Ahaz made molten images for _____Baalim_____, burned incense to false gods, and burned his _____children_____ in the fire, after the _____abominations_____ of the heathen.

11. Because of Ahaz's sin, the LORD delivered Judah into the hands of Syria and Israel. How many men of Judah did Pekah's army kill in one day? _____120,000_____

12. a. What did the Israelites do to another 200,000 of the children of Judah? _____
    They carried them captive. _____

   b. Why did the Israelites let them return home? (28:8–11) _____
    The prophet Oded told the Israelites that the LORD was angry with them too. _____

13. Where did King Ahaz look for help? (28:16) to the kings of Assyria _____

8. What false gods did Amaziah begin to worship after he had defeated the Edomites? [17] **the gods of the Edomites**

In This Lesson

Scope: 2 Chronicles 26–32 and parallel passages in 2 Kings 20 and Isaiah 36–38

Main Events
- Uzziah and Jotham have basically good and prosperous reigns, but Ahaz turns to idolatry.
- Hezekiah restores true worship and cleanses the land of idolatry.
- The Assyrians threaten Israel, but God saves Jerusalem by destroying much of the Assyrian army in one night.
- Hezekiah faces death, but God grants him another fifteen years of life.

Objectives
- The students should know
  —how the reigns of Uzziah and Jotham were different from the reign of Ahaz. (See Part A, numbers 1–15.)
  —how God delivered Hezekiah from the Assyrians. (The angel of the LORD killed 185,000 Assyrian soldiers during the night.)

14. What was the result of his request? (28:20) _____

   The king of Assyria distressed him instead of helping him.

15. Where did King Ahaz turn for help next? (28:22, 23) _____

   to the gods of Damascus

King Hezekiah—Looking the Right Way for Help

Quite surprisingly, wicked King Ahaz had a good son. Perhaps Hezekiah had a godly mother or a good teacher who taught him the right way. Whatever the case, Hezekiah helped to bring the greatest revival since the time of Solomon.

✎ *Match. All references are from 2 Chronicles.*

b	16. (29:3–5)	a. Hezekiah invites all Israel and Judah to keep the Passover. This is the greatest Passover since the time of Solomon.
d	17. (29:20–25)	b. Hezekiah opens the temple and commands the priests and Levites to cleanse it.
a	18. (30:1, 26)	c. The worshipers of God utterly destroy all the images, high places, and altars throughout Judah and Israel.
c	19. (31:1)	d. Hezekiah and the people offer sacrifices and songs of praise to the Lord.

20. How did the people show that they found joy in keeping the Passover? (30:23) _____

   They decided to keep it another week.

Hezekiah and the Assyrians

While Hezekiah reigned, the little kingdom of Judah was all that was left of Israel. The Northern Kingdom (under Samaria) had already fallen to the Assyrians. So had Syria, Ammon, Moab, and Edom. Now the Assyrians were at the gates of Jerusalem and planned to take it too.

The Assyrians said that Hezekiah did not have a chance. They thought it was foolish for Hezekiah to even try to resist them. However, they did not know the Lord. They did not know, as Hezekiah knew, that God was much stronger than they. God answered Hezekiah's prayers and marvelously delivered Judah.

✎ *Match. All references are from the Book of Isaiah.*

c	21. (36:1)	a. The angel of the Lord kills 185,000 Assyrian soldiers during the night.
d	22. (37:14–20)	b. The prophet Isaiah gives an answer from the Lord.
b	23. (37:21–23)	c. Sennacherib, king of the Assyrians, comes up against the cities of Judah.
a	24. (37:36)	d. Hezekiah spreads Sennacherib's letter before the Lord and prays.

—that the fall of Samaria took place during the early years of Hezekiah's reign.

—which prophets prophesied during this period. (Isaiah and Micah prophesied in Judah. Amos and Hosea prophesied in Israel.)

Truths to Instill

- Some of Judah's kings had good parents and some did not. Nevertheless, each king was responsible for his own actions. In the same way, we are all responsible for our own lives. We cannot depend on the fact that our parents were good, nor can we blame them for our failures if they lived in sin (Ezekiel 18).

- If we have godly parents, we should appreciate this blessing. We also admire the courage and zeal of men like Hezekiah, who sought after righteousness in spite of his father's poor influence.

- It is a blessing to have the Lord to turn to in times of trouble. In facing the Assyrians, Hezekiah met one of the world's most ruthless and cruel armies. The Assyrians conquered by terror, at times torturing and dismembering their captives. Facing such threats, Hezekiah depended entirely on the Lord.

118   Chapter Four   David's Family Reigns Over Judah

Hezekiah's Cure

✎ *Number these events in the correct order.*

2 Kings 20:1–6

25. __3__ Hezekiah prays and weeps.

    __2__ Isaiah tells Hezekiah to prepare to die.

    __1__ Hezekiah becomes sick unto death.

    __4__ Isaiah returns with a new message.

2 Kings 20:7–11

26. __1__ Isaiah calls for figs to be put on Hezekiah's boil.

    __4__ The shadow moves ten degrees back on the sundial.

    __2__ Isaiah gives Hezekiah a choice of signs.

    __3__ Isaiah cries unto the LORD.

Extra Activity

✎ *Read 2 Chronicles 32:1–23 and Isaiah 37:36–38, and then write the story of Hezekiah and the Assyrians in your own words. Your story should have between 100 and 250 words.*

> *This is individual work. Be sure the stories include the main points.*

B. BIBLE WORD STUDY

✎ *Match these definitions with the Bible words on the right. All references are from 2 Chronicles unless marked otherwise.*

__b__ 1. A sundial (2 Kings 20:11)

__e__ 2. A farmer (26:10)

__d__ 3. A coat of armor made of small, overlapping pieces of metal (26:14)

__c__ 4. A large war machine used to shoot arrows or heavy stones (26:15)

__g__ 5. To set apart for holy service; consecrate (29:5)

__f__ 6. A feast reminding the Israelites that the LORD passed over them when He killed the oldest sons of the Egyptians (30:1)

__a__ 7. Holy beings who dwell in God's presence; golden figures of these beings placed above the ark within the temple (Isaiah 37:16)

a. cherubim
b. dial
c. engine
d. habergeon
e. husbandman
f. Passover
g. sanctify

✎ *Use the tables of measure in the back of this book to complete these exercises.*

8. One talent equals about __75 (34 kg)__ pounds (2 Chronicles 27:5).

9. The *measures* of 2 Chronicles 27:5 were *cors*. One cor equals about __8 (282 l)__ bushels.

> *The answers for numbers 8 and 9 will be used in numbers 2 and 3 of Part D.*

C. THINKING ABOUT BIBLE TRUTHS

The Message of the Prophets

Isaiah and Micah lived during the same time. They prophesied in Judah while Amos and Hosea were prophesying in Israel.

1. a. Isaiah prophesied during the reigns of _____Uzziah_____, _____Jotham_____, _____Ahaz_____, and _____Hezekiah_____ (Isaiah 1:1).

   b. Micah prophesied during the reigns of _____Jotham_____, _____Ahaz_____, and _____Hezekiah_____ (Micah 1:1).

2. Isaiah saw a vision of God's glory in the year that King _____Uzziah_____ died (Isaiah 6:1).

3. a. Isaiah brought the LORD's message to King Ahaz and told him to ask for a sign. But wicked Ahaz wearied God by replying, "I will _____not_____ _____ask_____" (Isaiah 7:10–13).

   b. God gave a sign anyway. He said a virgin would have a son, and would call his name _____Immanuel_____ (Isaiah 7:14).

   c. What does this name mean? (Matthew 1:23) _God with us_

4. The New Testament quotes many verses from the Book of Isaiah. Here are two quotations Paul gives in Romans.

   a. Isaiah (Esaias) was very bold and said, "I [God] was found of them that _____sought_____ _____me_____ _____not_____" (Romans 10:20). This was a prophecy that the Gentiles would believe in Jesus.

   b. Isaiah rebuked Israel for rejecting God. He told them, "All day long I [God] have stretched forth my hands unto a _____disobedient_____ and gainsaying people" (Romans 10:21).

   c. Use a concordance to find the reference in Isaiah for the two verses quoted above. (Paul did not quote the verses word for word, so you may need to look up several words to find the reference.) Reference in Isaiah: _____Isaiah 65:1, 2_____

5. During the reigns of good kings, some people offered sacrifices to the LORD, yet did not please Him. What three simple, important things does Micah say God requires? (Micah 6:6–8)

   a. _to do justly_

   b. _to love mercy_

   c. _to walk humbly with thy God_

120   Chapter Four   David's Family Reigns Over Judah

D. LEARNING MORE ABOUT THE BIBLE

What Did King Uzziah Enjoy?

King Uzziah loved husbandry (2 Chronicles 26:10). He ordered the digging of many wells. He had great herds of cattle. He employed husbandmen and vinedressers.

1. What would we call Uzziah today? _____

   a farmer

Jotham—the Tribute Collector

King Uzziah's son Jotham was a good king. He served the LORD and repaired the temple. He fought the Ammonites and made them pay him a tribute of one hundred talents of silver, ten thousand measures (cors) of wheat, and ten thousand measures (cors) of barley every year for three years.

2. About how many pounds of silver did the Ammonites pay each year? (See exercises 8 and 9 in "Bible Word Study.") _____ 7,500 lb. (3,400 kg)

3. a. About how many bushels of wheat did they pay each year? 80,000 bushels (2,820,000 l)

   b. About how many bushels of barley? 80,000 bushels (2,820,000 l)

Hezekiah's Extra Years

Soon after God delivered King Hezekiah from the Assyrians, Hezekiah became seriously ill. God sent the prophet Isaiah to tell him that he was going to die. Hezekiah did not want to die yet, so he prayed to God, and God gave him fifteen extra years of life. During those fifteen years, he entertained company from Babylon.

4. What did Hezekiah show his visitors from Babylon? (2 Kings 20:14, 15) _____

   all the treasures of his house

5. What did God say the Babylonians would do? (2 Kings 20:16–18) They would take away the treasures from Hezekiah's house, and they would carry his sons (descendants) to Babylon.

121

Lesson 19. Wicked Manasseh; Righteous Josiah

(Manasseh, Amon, and Josiah)

Josiah grew up in a wicked home, just as his great-grandfather Hezekiah had. His grandfather Manasseh and his father Amon were two of Judah's most wicked kings. When Josiah was eight years old, some enemies killed his father, and Josiah became king. At sixteen years of age, Josiah began to "seek after the God of David his father." Four years later he began to clean up the temple and to prepare to keep the feasts of the LORD.

Josiah was one of the best and most respected kings of Judah. Far and wide, people felt the effects of his honorable reign. Idolatrous priests fled as Josiah's men broke down their temples and destroyed their false gods. Righteous men and women worshiped the LORD at a great Passover feast. Children were taught the Law of Moses. Some of these children, including Daniel and his three friends, remained faithful to God even after Josiah's death.

While Josiah's men were cleaning up the temple, a priest called Hilkiah found an old scroll. It was the scroll of the Law of God, given by Moses. When Josiah read the scroll, he tore his clothes and called to God for help. He saw that his people had broken many of God's commands for many years.

This is the answer God gave to King Josiah: "Because thine heart was tender, and thou didst humble thyself before God . . . and didst rend thy clothes, and weep before me; I have even heard thee also. . . . I will gather thee to thy fathers, and thou shalt be gathered to thy grave in peace" (2 Chronicles 34:27, 28).

Even though the future looked dark for Judah, God promised Josiah peace while he lived. Terrible punishments awaited his people, but Josiah would die an honorable death and go to live forever with God.

God promises blessings for those who obey Him with tender hearts.

A. ANSWERS FROM THE BIBLE

Manasseh—the Wicked King Who Repented

Manasseh, the son of righteous Hezekiah, was probably the most wicked king of Judah. He also reigned longer than any other king of Judah or Israel. He did evil as Ahab did, and he made Judah sin worse than the heathen. He filled Jerusalem with the blood of innocent people and even sacrificed his children to an idol.

The LORD could not tolerate such wickedness. He pronounced judgment upon His people.

✎ *Most of these sentence endings are correct. Draw a line through the one ending for each number that is not correct.*

2 Chronicles 33:1–10

1. Manasseh was

   a. the son of righteous Hezekiah.

   b. twelve years old when he became king.

   c. ~~king in Samaria~~.

   d. king for fifty-five years.

Lesson 19

Oral Review

1. Why did God bless Jehoshaphat with riches and honor? [16] **He sought the LORD and walked in His commandments.**

2. What do the words *consecrate* and *tribute* mean? [16] *consecrate:* **to set aside for a sacred purpose;** *tribute:* **a forced payment made by a weak nation to a strong ruler or nation**

3. Who was Ahaziah's wicked counselor? [17] **his mother, Athaliah**

4. Why did God not want the Israelites to marry people of other nations? [17] **He knew this would cause His people to turn to other gods.**

5. Who paid large amounts of tribute to Jotham? [18] **the Ammonites**

6. Where did Ahaz look for help? (Give two sources.) [18] **to the kings of Assyria and to the gods of Damascus**

7. Where did Hezekiah look for help when the Assyrians came against Judah? [18] **to the LORD**

8. What are the five books of the Major Prophets? (Be sure you know the correct order and spelling.) [1, 16] **Isaiah, Jeremiah, Lamentations, Ezekiel, Daniel**

122   Chapter Four   David's Family Reigns Over Judah

2. Manasseh

   a. made altars for Baal.

   b. tore down the high places that Hezekiah had built.

   c. ~~worshiped the host of heaven (the sun, moon, and stars).~~

   d. made groves (for the worship of the idol Asherah).

3. Manasseh

   a. ~~built altars to the LORD in a heathen temple.~~

   b. burned his children in sacrifice to a false god.

   c. used enchantments and witchcraft.

   d. dealt with familiar spirits and wizards.

4. Manasseh

   a. made his people do worse than the heathen.

   b. ~~oppressed the ten northern tribes of Israel.~~

   c. refused to listen to the warnings from the LORD.

   d. killed many innocent people in Jerusalem (2 Kings 21:16).

2 Kings 21:10–15

5. Because of Manasseh's extreme wickedness, the LORD said he would

   a. bring such evil on Jerusalem that people's ears would tingle.

   b. wipe Jerusalem as a man wipes a dish and turns it upside down.

   c. forsake the remnant of His inheritance.

   d. ~~cause even the stones in Israel to cry out.~~

Manasseh refused to hear the prophets of the LORD, but the LORD had another way of speaking to Manasseh. He sent the Assyrians, who cruelly bound Manasseh and carried him away as a captive. In his severe affliction, Manasseh prayed to the LORD, and the LORD returned him to his throne. Then Manasseh knew that the LORD is the true God.

2 Chronicles 33:11–20

6. King Manasseh

   a. was bound by the Assyrians and carried to Babylon.

   b. humbled himself and sought the LORD in his affliction.

   c. ~~cried out to Baal and his other gods for deliverance.~~

   d. was heard by God when he humbly prayed, even though he had sinned terribly.

7. After Manasseh returned to Jerusalem, he

   a. removed his idol and the heathen altars from the temple.

   b. ~~worshiped only a few idols at the high places.~~

   c. repaired the LORD's altar and offered sacrifices to Him.

   d. commanded the people to serve the LORD God of Israel.

- King Manasseh's Assyrian captivity is mentioned in the Assyrian records. According to the chronology generally accepted, it took place around 678 B.C., or about the eighteenth year of his reign. However, the evil of his early reign overshadowed the good that he did later.

- It is doubtful that the people of Judah did much more than offer lip service to God during the reforms of Manasseh, because they very quickly returned to their old ways when Amon was king. The same seems to have been true after Josiah died. It is no wonder that God did not withhold His judgment on them.

In This Lesson

Scope: 2 Chronicles 33–35 and parallel passages in 2 Kings 21–23

Main Events

- King Manasseh leads Judah into gross sin and idolatry.
- Manasseh repents after the Assyrians take him captive. The LORD returns him to his throne, and Manasseh makes some reforms.
- King Amon returns to the worship of all of Manasseh's images.

- King Josiah seeks the LORD with all his heart. He zealously purges the land of idolatry and keeps the greatest Passover since the days of Samuel.

Objectives

- The students should know
  - what happened to Manasseh to bring him to repent of his evil ways. (The Assyrians cruelly bound Manasseh and carried him away captive.)
  - that Amon also was a very wicked king.
  - that King Josiah sought after the LORD with all his heart.

The Bible says that the people of Judah sacrificed to God after Manasseh's repentance, but the reformation lasted only as long as Manasseh lived. This seems to indicate that the people of Judah had not repented of their sinful ways as Manasseh had. As soon as he died, they went back to idolatry.

Amon—the Wicked Son of a Repentant Father

Amon followed his father Manasseh's sinful ways, but he did not repent as his father had done.

2 Chronicles 33:20–25

8. What evil did Amon do in the sight of the LORD? _____

   He sacrificed to all the carved images that Manasseh had made.

9. What happened to Amon after he had reigned two years? _____

   His servants conspired against him and killed him in his own house.

King Josiah—the Last Good King of Judah

Josiah's father was very wicked, yet Josiah became one of Judah's best kings. We do not know who taught Josiah to love God. Josiah was about six years old when his grandfather Manasseh died, so perhaps Manasseh taught Josiah some things about the true God. Or perhaps his mother or some other good person told him about God. Whatever the case, Josiah rejected the sins of his father and served the LORD with all his heart.

2 Chronicles 34:1–3

10. Josiah began reigning when he was _____eight_____ years old.

11. In the eighth year of his reign, he began to __seek after the God of David his father__.

12. In the twelfth year, he began to purge _____Judah_____ and _____Jerusalem_____ from idolatry.

Josiah Overthrows Idolatry

King Josiah hated idol worship. He removed every idol, image, altar, and priest that had anything to do with false gods. He burned the wooden images and ground the stone idols to powder. He defiled the places of heathen worship with dead bodies and ashes so that no one would want to use them again. Josiah despised even the graves of the wicked. He opened their tombs and burned their bones on the very altars where they had worshiped. Then he demolished the altars and burned the surrounding areas. Nor did he stop at his own country, but he did the same in Israel. No king before or after him so thoroughly cleansed Judah and Israel.

2 Kings 23:4–20

13. Josiah removed the vessels made for Baal and other idols from the house of the LORD, _____burned_____

   them in the fields outside Jerusalem, and carried the ashes to _____Bethel_____ (23:4).

14. Josiah put down the idolatrous _____priests_____ (23:5). According to verse 20, he killed them.

15. He brought out the grove from the temple, _____burned_____ it at the brook Kidron, and

   stamped it into fine _____powder_____ (23:6).

16. He _____defiled_____ the valley where his grandfather Manasseh and other wicked men had

   sacrificed their children (23:10).

17. Josiah destroyed and defiled the high places near Jerusalem that King _____Solomon_____

   had made for his heathen wives (23:13, 14).

- Most scholars believe the Hebrew word often translated *grove* in the King James Bible refers to a wooden image or pillar associated with the idol Asherah. This would explain how it could be placed in the temple.

—what King Josiah did to purify the land of its sin, and why this was not enough to turn away the wrath of God. (See Part A, numbers 13–26, and Part C, number 3.)

Truths to Instill

- God desires that even the vilest sinner repent. During the first part of his reign, Manasseh was probably the most wicked king in Judah's history. He took Judah so low into sin that even Josiah's great revival could not turn away God's fierce judgment upon the nation (2 Kings 23:26; 24:3, 4). God did not even record Manasseh's repentance in 2 Kings. Yet 2 Chronicles 33:13 tells us that God heard his prayer when he humbled himself and made supplication to Him. Truly "thou, O LORD, art a God full of compassion, and gracious, longsuffering, and plenteous in mercy and truth" (Psalm 86:15).

- God's Word has power to cleanse and restore. Where men wholeheartedly seek to know God's will, the Word illuminates their darkened understanding and restores men in the ways of godliness and the beauty of holiness. God's Word revives!

18. a. Josiah traveled to _____Bethel_____ to destroy the altar and the idols that _____Jeroboam_____ the son of Nebat had made (23:15).

    b. While destroying this high place, Josiah took the _____bones_____ of the wicked priests out of their tombs and burned them on the altar (23:16).

    c. This fulfilled the prophecy of a man of God from Judah, who had warned King _____Jeroboam_____ about three hundred years before Josiah's time (1 Kings 13:1, 2).

19. Josiah also destroyed the other high places in the cities of _____Samaria_____ that the kings of Israel had made (2 Kings 23:19).

Josiah Finds the Book of the Law

While Josiah was growing up, he did not have a Bible as you have. He did not even have a copy of the Law of Moses. God's Word had evidently been lost during the long reign of Manasseh. But during all those years, God had preserved a copy of His Law in the temple.

This scroll was found in the eighteenth year of Josiah's reign. Josiah listened intently as Shaphan the scribe read it to him for the first time. But as he listened, he tore his clothes and wept. He knew that his people had not kept God's Law, and that the LORD must be very angry with them.

2 Chronicles 34:14–33

20. a. Who found the book of the Law? (34:14, 15) __Hilkiah the priest__

    b. Where did he find the book? __in the house of the LORD__

21. God's Word reveals sin and tells man how to be cleansed. What *three* things did Josiah do after hearing God's Law that showed his sorrow for his nation's sin? (34:27) _____
    __He humbled himself, rent his clothes, and wept.__

22. Josiah sent men to inquire of the LORD, and the prophetess Huldah gave them God's message. What did the LORD say He would do to the inhabitants of Judah? (34:23–26) _____
    __He would bring evil (all the curses in the Book of the Law) upon them.__

23. What did the LORD promise Josiah as a reward for his faithfulness? (34:28) _____
    __Josiah would not see the evil in his lifetime.__

2 Chronicles 35:1, 18

Like his great-grandfather Hezekiah, Josiah decided to observe the Passover. Josiah's Passover was even greater than the one King Hezekiah had kept.

24. The Bible says that the Passover Josiah kept was the greatest one since the time of the prophet _____Samuel_____.

Josiah Dies From Battle Wounds

2 Chronicles 35:20–27

25. What happened to Josiah when he went out against Necho, king of Egypt? _____
    __The archers wounded Josiah, and he died.__

- Although Josiah's revival did not turn away God's judgment or completely reform Judah, it had far-reaching effects. From this revival arose great men of faith who encouraged and taught the Jews during their captivity. Jeremiah began prophesying during Josiah's reign and continued to prophesy until after Jerusalem was destroyed. Daniel was taken captive to Babylon only three years after Josiah's death, and Ezekiel was taken a few years later. No doubt Josiah's zeal for God influenced all these prophets and many other faithful Jews.

- God's Spirit will not always strive with men. His forbearance with sin has a limit. Judah's wickedness during the reigns of Manasseh and Amon was so great that God's judgment could not be withheld. Even though Manasseh repented and righteous Josiah brought great reforms, they did not cure Judah's great wickedness.

- There is always a way to do right. Even in the midst of an extremely wicked nation, Josiah sought after God and received His help. No matter how wrong others around us may be, we can still find a way to serve God.

26. After Josiah's death, all _____Judah_____ and _____Jerusalem_____ mourned for him.

The prophet _____Jeremiah_____ also lamented for him.

King Josiah turned to the LORD with all his heart, soul, and might (2 Kings 23:25). He tried to obey all God's commands, and he encouraged his people to do the same. Josiah's revival helped to strengthen God's faithful people for the trials they would soon face. However, Josiah's revival was not enough to turn God from the judgment He had foretold during Manasseh's reign. Even though the people of Judah obeyed Josiah, they apparently did not turn to the LORD in complete repentance. Less than five years after Josiah's death, the Babylonians invaded Judah, taking Daniel and others captive.

B. BIBLE WORD STUDY

✎ *Write a word or phrase from the verse given to match each definition. All references except the first three are from 2 Chronicles.*

_____tingle_____	1. To sting or prickle with astonishment or terror (2 Kings 21:12)
_____defiled_____	2. Made unclean or unfit for use (2 Kings 23:10)
__sepulchres (sepulchers)__	3. Tombs; graves (2 Kings 23:16)
_____abominations_____	4. Things that cause abhorrence or great disgust (33:2)
_____host of heaven_____	5. The sun, moon, and stars (33:5)
_____supplication_____	6. A humble prayer or request (33:13)
_____purge_____	7. To purify by removing sin, filth, and uncleanness (34:3)
_____artificers_____	8. Skilled workers; craftsmen (34:11)
_____archers_____	9. Persons who shoot arrows (35:23)

• *Artificers* is pronounced *ar TIHF ih surz.*

C. THINKING ABOUT BIBLE TRUTHS

Manasseh's Sin

The good kings encouraged Judah to live right, but the evil kings caused Judah to sin. Yet each person still had to decide for himself whether to serve the LORD or not. Some men and women were faithful even when the king worshiped idols. Others did not serve God with their whole heart even when the king worshiped the LORD.

1. How did Manasseh's wickedness affect the people of Judah? (2 Chronicles 33:9) _____

   He made them sin worse than the heathen.

2. What did Manasseh command his people to do after he repented? (2 Chronicles 33:16) _____

   He commanded Judah to serve the LORD God of Israel.

3. Josiah destroyed idolatry in Judah, but he could not completely change the evil course of Judah. Read 2 Kings 23:25–27 and 2 Kings 24:3, 4. Why did the LORD deliver Judah into the hands of their enemies soon after Josiah's death? _____

   The LORD needed to punish Judah for the sins of Manasseh.

Review of the Kings of Judah

The chart "The Kings of Judah" on the next page lists some of their righteous deeds and their sins. This chart helps to show the course of the kingdom of Judah. Notice the cycles of good and evil kings. The numbers in parentheses following each king's name give the chapters in 2 Chronicles that record his reign. The last four kings will be covered in Lesson 21.

✎ *Use the following chart, the chart in Lesson 7, and your Bible to answer these questions.*

4. How many descendants of David reigned over Judah after Solomon's death? (Include the four who reigned after Josiah.) _____nineteen_____

5. List six of the best kings of Judah. (Omit the kings who began worshiping idols when they were old.)
_____Asa_____, _____Jehoshaphat_____, _____Uzziah_____, _____Jotham_____, _____Hezekiah_____, _____Josiah_____

6. List five of the worst kings of Judah. (Do not include the four who reigned after Josiah.)
_____Jehoram_____, _____Ahaziah_____, _____Ahaz_____, _____Manasseh_____, _____Amon_____

Because Manasseh was extremely wicked during the first part of his reign, he is usually remembered as an evil king, even though he repented. See 2 Kings 24:3, 4.

7. The "high places" were places of worship on hills or mountains. Sometimes the people sacrificed to the LORD at these altars. But often the high places were centers of idol worship.

a. List six kings from the chart who were at least partly good, and yet who failed to remove the high places. _____Asa_____, _____Jehoshaphat_____, _____Joash_____, _____Amaziah_____, _____Uzziah_____, _____Jotham_____

b. The six kings you listed stopped the worship of idols. To whom did the people offer sacrifices at the high places during times of reform? (2 Chronicles 33:17) _unto the LORD their God only_

c. Read Deuteronomy 12:10–14. God knew that if His people offered sacrifices to Him in many places, they would soon worship idols there too. Where did God tell His people to offer their sacrifices? _in the place that He would choose (at the temple)_

The Kings of Judah

King (The numbers in parentheses give the chapters from 2 Chronicles.)	Righteous Deeds	Sins
Rehoboam (10–12) (mostly bad)	• Followed God for a short time	• Rudely refused to lighten Israel's burdens • Turned away from God
Abijah (13) (mostly bad)	• Rebuked Jeroboam for making the golden calves	• Walked in his father's sins
Asa (14–16) (mostly good)	• Commanded Judah to seek the LORD and obey the Law • Restored true worship • Cried to God for help • Removed Queen Maacah	• Failed to remove the high places • Hired Syrian soldiers • Oppressed Hanani and others • Failed to seek healing from the LORD
Jehoshaphat (17–20) (mostly good)	• Sought the LORD • Walked in the ways of David • Sent out good teachers and judges • Cried to God for help	• Failed to remove the high places • Helped Ahab and Ahaziah
Jehoram (21) (wicked)		• Married Athaliah • Killed his brothers • Walked in the ways of Ahab
Ahaziah (22) (wicked)		• Followed Athaliah's counsel • Did evil like Ahab's house
Queen Athaliah usurped the throne and ruled six years. Her reign was very wicked.		
Joash (23, 24) (partly good)	• Did right all the days of Jehoiada • Repaired the temple	• Failed to remove the high places • Served idols • Killed Zechariah
Amaziah (25) (partly good)	• Did right (but not with a perfect heart) • Obeyed the prophet who told him to send the Israelite soldiers home.	• Failed to remove the high places • Worshiped the gods of Edom • Refused to listen to a prophet
Uzziah (26) (mostly good)	• Did right in God's sight • Sought God through Zechariah • Defeated Judah's enemies with God's help	• Failed to remove the high places • Tried to burn incense in the temple
Jotham (27) (good)	• Did right in God's sight • Repaired the temple • Defeated Judah's enemies	• Failed to remove the high places • The people did corruptly in spite of Jotham's righteousness.
Ahaz (28) (wicked)		• Sinned like the kings of Israel • Worshiped Baal and other false gods • Sacrificed his children • Closed the temple
Hezekiah (29–32) (one of the best)	• Repaired the temple and restored true worship • Kept the greatest Passover since Solomon's time • Removed the high places • Destroyed heathen altars throughout Judah and Israel • Prayed to God for help • Repented of his pride	• Became proud • Showed his wealth to the Babylonians • Was more concerned about peace in his lifetime than he was about his descendants
Manasseh (33) (very wicked in the first part of his reign)	• After the LORD punished him, he humbled himself greatly, worshiped the LORD, and tried to reform Judah.	• Made Judah do worse than the heathen • Worshiped Baal and other false gods • Worshiped the host of heaven • Placed altars to idols and an image in the courts of God's temple • Sacrificed his children to false gods • Practiced witchcraft • Killed very many innocent people in Jerusalem
Amon (33) (wicked)		• Worshiped all the images Manasseh had made
Josiah (34, 35) (one of the best)	• Zealously destroyed idolatry throughout Judah and Israel • Removed the high places • Repaired the temple and restored true worship • Honored the Book of the Law • Kept the greatest Passover since Samuel's days • Turned to God with all his heart, soul, and might	• (No serious sins are given, but Josiah foolishly fought against the king of Egypt.)
Jehoahaz Jehoiakim Jehoiachin Zedekiah (36) (all wicked)		• These last four kings all did evil in God's sight. • Jehoiakim burned Jeremiah's scroll. • Zedekiah broke a covenant he had sworn in God's Name.

128   Chapter Four   David's Family Reigns Over Judah

D. LEARNING MORE ABOUT THE BIBLE

The World in Josiah's Time

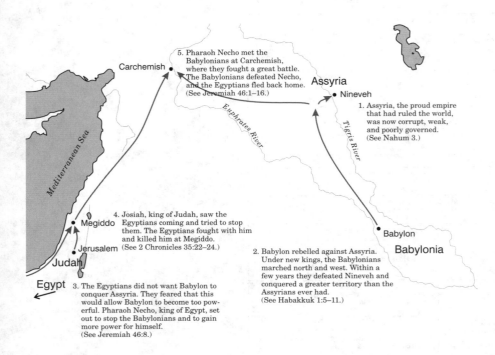

5. Pharaoh Necho met the Babylonians at Carchemish, where they fought a great battle. The Babylonians defeated Necho, and the Egyptians fled back home. (See Jeremiah 46:1–16.)

1. Assyria, the proud empire that had ruled the world, was now corrupt, weak, and poorly governed. (See Nahum 3.)

4. Josiah, king of Judah, saw the Egyptians coming and tried to stop them. The Egyptians fought with him and killed him at Megiddo. (See 2 Chronicles 35:22–24.)

2. Babylon rebelled against Assyria. Under new kings, the Babylonians marched north and west. Within a few years they defeated Nineveh and conquered a greater territory than the Assyrians ever had. (See Habakkuk 1:5–11.)

3. The Egyptians did not want Babylon to conquer Assyria. They feared that this would allow Babylon to become too powerful. Pharaoh Necho, king of Egypt, set out to stop the Babylonians and to gain more power for himself. (See Jeremiah 46:8.)

✎ *Study the map to answer these questions. (The paragraph numbers above give the general order of events.)*

1. Which nation became the most powerful in the region soon after Josiah's death: Egypt, Babylon, or Assyria? _____ Babylon _____

2. Who killed King Josiah? the Egyptians _____

3. Who defeated the Egyptians? the Babylonians _____

4. Why was it easy for Babylon to rebel against Assyria? _____
   Assyria was corrupt, weak, and poorly governed. _____

129

Chapter Four Review

A. ORAL REVIEW

✎ *Be sure you know the answers to these questions. Answer as many as you can from memory. If you need help, you may check the reference or lesson given in brackets.*

Why >>

1. Why was God displeased when Asa sought help from physicians? [2 Chronicles 16:12]
2. Why did God bless Jehoshaphat with riches and honor? [2 Chronicles 17:4, 5]
3. Why did Amaziah tell the Israelite soldiers whom he had hired to return home? [2 Chronicles 25:7]
4. Why did God not want the Israelites to marry people of other nations? [Deuteronomy 7:3, 4]

How >>

5. How did Joash and Jehoiada collect money to repair the temple? [2 Chronicles 24:8–10]
6. How can we know that the people enjoyed Hezekiah's Passover feast? [2 Chronicles 30:23]
7. How many Assyrians were killed by the angel of the LORD? [Isaiah 37:36]
8. How did God show Hezekiah that he would recover from his sickness? [2 Kings 20:11]
9. How many bushels equal about one cor? [Lesson 18]

Who >>

10. Who remained loyal to Rehoboam after some of the tribes rebelled? [2 Chronicles 11:12, 13]
11. Whose sins did Abijah walk in? [1 Kings 15:3]
12. Who was Jehoram's wife? [2 Chronicles 21:6]
13. Who saved Joash's life when he was a very young boy? [2 Chronicles 22:11]
14. Who paid large amounts of tribute to Jotham? [2 Chronicles 27:5]
15. Who prophesied in Judah about the same time as Isaiah? [Lesson 18]
16. Who killed the idolatrous priests in Judah and Israel and burned their bones? [2 Kings 23:20]
17. Who kept the greatest Passover since the time of Samuel? [2 Chronicles 35:18]

B. WRITTEN REVIEW

✎ *Write the answers to these questions. Do as many as you can from memory. If you need help, you may check the reference or lesson given in brackets.*

What

1. What good king was a friend to Ahab? [2 Chronicles 19:2] Jehoshaphat

2. What did Athaliah do when she learned of her son's death? [2 Chronicles 22:10]
   She tried to kill all the royal descendants of David.

3. What did Joash do after his uncle Jehoiada's death? [2 Chronicles 24:17, 18]
   He turned away from the LORD and served idols.

1. Asa did not seek the LORD's healing.
2. Jehoshaphat sought the LORD and walked in His commandments.
3. A man of God told him that the LORD was not with Israel.
4. He knew this would cause His people to turn to other gods.
5. They placed a money chest at the gate of the temple for the people's offerings.
6. They decided to keep the feast for seven extra days.
7. 185,000
8. The shadow moved back ten degrees on the sundial.
9. 8
10. the tribes of Judah and Benjamin, and many priests and Levites
11. his father's (Rehoboam's)
12. Ahab's daughter, Athaliah
13. Jehosheba
14. the Ammonites
15. Micah
16. Josiah
17. Josiah and his people

Chapter Four Review

This review is divided into two parts, an oral review and a written review. The oral review is intended for class discussion, but students could also use it for self-study.

If your students have memorized the names of the kings of Judah, you may want to review them together in class. For the test, you may cover the king's names on the chart in Lesson 19 and make copies of it, and then have your students fill in the names.

4. What false gods did Amaziah begin to worship after he had defeated the Edomites? [2 Chronicles 25:14]
   the gods of the children of Seir, the Edomites

5. What mistake did good King Uzziah make? [2 Chronicles 26:16]
   He went into the temple to burn incense.

6. What king caused the people of Judah to do worse than the heathen? [2 Chronicles 33:9]
   Manasseh

7. What cruel, wicked thing did Manasseh do to some of his children? [2 Chronicles 33:6]
   He burned them in sacrifice to a false god.

8. What did Manasseh do when he was taken captive and afflicted by the Assyrians? [2 Chronicles 33:12, 13]   He humbled himself and prayed to the LORD.

9. What did the priest find in the temple during Josiah's reign? [2 Chronicles 34:14]
   the Book of the Law of the LORD

10. What three things did Josiah do when the Book of the Law was first read to him? [2 Chronicles 34:27]
    He humbled himself, rent his clothes, and wept.

11. What happened to Josiah when he went out against the king of Egypt? [2 Chronicles 35:20–24]
    The archers wounded him, and he died.

12. What do the following words mean? [Lessons 16, 17, 19]

    consecrate: to set aside for a sacred purpose

    tribute: a forced payment made by a weak nation to a strong ruler or nation

    high place: a center of worship on a hill or mountain

    supplication: a humble prayer or request

13. What six kings in the following list were mostly good? What five are remembered for their wickedness? Asa, Jehoshaphat, Jehoram, Ahaziah, Uzziah, Jotham, Ahaz, Hezekiah, Manasseh, Amon, Josiah [Lesson 19 chart]

    Mostly good: Asa, Jehoshaphat, Uzziah, Jotham, Hezekiah, Josiah

    Remembered as wicked: Jehoram, Ahaziah, Ahaz, Manasseh, Amon

14. What are the five books of the Major Prophets? (Be sure to use the correct order and spelling.) [Lessons 1, 16] Isaiah, Jeremiah, Lamentations, Ezekiel, Daniel

Where

15. Where did Ahaz look for help? (Give two sources.) [2 Chronicles 28:16, 23]
    to the kings of Assyria and to the gods of Damascus

Where Is It Found?

<u> e </u> 16. 2 Chronicles 10–13

<u> h </u> 17. 2 Chronicles 14–16

<u> b </u> 18. 2 Chronicles 17–20

<u> f </u> 19. 2 Chronicles 21–25

<u> g </u> 20. 2 Chronicles 26–28

<u> a </u> 21. 2 Chronicles 29–32

<u> d </u> 22. 2 Chronicles 33–35

<u> c </u> 23. 2 Chronicles 36

a. the reign of Hezekiah

b. the reign of Jehoshaphat

c. the reigns of Jehoahaz, Jehoiakim, Jehoiachin, and Zedekiah

d. the reigns of Manasseh, Amon, and Josiah

e. the reigns of Rehoboam and Abijah

f. the reigns of Jehoram, Ahaziah, Joash, and Amaziah

g. the reigns of Uzziah, Jotham, and Ahaz

h. the reign of Asa

132

Lesson 20. Foods and Mealtime Customs

When God drove Adam and Eve out of the Garden, He gave them a big assignment: "In the sweat of thy face shalt thou eat bread, till thou return unto the ground" (Genesis 3:19). From that time on, men and women had to work for the food they ate.

People in Bible times ate some of the same foods we do. They baked bread, made cheese, and drank milk. Honey, vegetables, and fresh fruits such as grapes and melons made their diet a healthy one. They also enjoyed raisins and dried figs. But the Jews of Bible times never had potatoes, sweet corn, pork sausages, tomato juice, strawberries, ice cream, or chocolate chip cookies.

The Bible tells us about some of the foods and mealtime customs of people who lived long ago.

- Additional information on foods and mealtime customs can be found in *Manners and Customs of Bible Lands* or in Bible dictionaries.

A. ANSWERS FROM THE BIBLE

1. People in Bible times ate two main meals a day. Jesus called these meals _____dinner_____ and _____supper_____ (Luke 14:12). The first meal was a breakfast served sometime during the morning; the second meal was served in the evening.

2. Before they ate, the people prayed and gave thanks to God. Before feeding a multitude, _____Jesus_____ blessed the food (Matthew 14:19). While on a ship, _____Paul_____ thanked God for their food in the presence of the sailors and the other passengers (Acts 27:35).

3. The most important food was _____bread_____ (Genesis 3:19). Sometimes it was made of _____barley_____ (Judges 7:13), but the best kind was made of _____wheat_____ (Psalm 147:14).

4. Travelers were permitted to pluck kernels of _____corn_____ (grain) from a field and eat them raw (Matthew 12:1). Sometimes grain was _____parched_____, or roasted, before it was eaten (Leviticus 23:14).

5. Milk from cows, sheep, and _____goats_____ (Proverbs 27:27) was used to make _____cheese_____ (1 Samuel 17:18) and _____butter_____ (Proverbs 30:33). Curdled sour milk was often eaten, since milk could not be kept fresh.

6. Poor families ate _____flesh_____, or meat (1 Kings 19:21), only on special occasions. Meats served could be _____fish_____ (Matthew 7:10), beef, mutton, goat, _____venison_____ (Genesis 27:31), or fowl such as _____quail_____ (Exodus 16:13).

7. Rich people ate meat more frequently. King Solomon's household used thirty _____oxen_____ and a hundred _____sheep_____ every day, besides fatted fowl and several kinds of venison (1 Kings 4:23).

Life in Bible Times

Lesson 20

Oral Review

1. What trouble did David reap, even though he repented of his sin? [3] **He reaped much fighting and death in his own family.**
2. What request did Elisha make before Elijah was taken up to heaven? [11] **"Let a double portion of thy spirit be upon me."**
3. What did Athaliah do when she learned of her son's death? [17] **She tried to kill all the royal descendants of David.**
4. What were the high places? [17] **centers of worship on hills or mountains**
5. What mistake did good King Uzziah make? [18] **He went into the temple to burn incense.**
6. Who kept the Passover for an extra week? [18] **Hezekiah and his people**
7. How did God punish Manasseh for his evil deeds? [19] **God sent the Assyrians, who bound Manasseh and took him captive.**
8. Who kept the greatest Passover since the time of Samuel? [19] **Josiah and his people**

8. The Law of God forbade the eating of certain animals that were considered _____unclean_____ (Leviticus 11:8). The Israelites were required to carefully separate the meat from the _____blood_____ (Deuteronomy 12:16).

9. Daniel and his friends ate _____pulse_____ (vegetables) rather than the food King Nebuchadnezzar served (Daniel 1:12).

10. People of Bible times used their fingers rather than spoons, forks, or knives to eat their meals. The Pharisees thought it very important to _____wash_____ their hands before each meal (Matthew 15:2). Note, however, that the Pharisees required a ceremonial washing that God's Law did not require. Washing before eating is good, but the Pharisees seemed more concerned about enforcing their own rules than about true cleanliness.

11. People in Bible times used seasoning with their food. Job asked, "Can that which is unsavoury be eaten without _____salt_____?" (Job 6:6).

Common people sat on the ground to eat. Their "table" was a rug spread out before them.

12. Wealthy people and people attending special meals lay on couches to eat. While Jesus ate at Simon's house, a woman washed His _____feet_____ (Luke 7:38).

13. Using thin pieces of bread, the whole family dipped foods like soup out of one pot. Soup was often made of beans, ___lentiles (lentils)___ (Genesis 25:34), or other _____herbs_____ [vegetables] (2 Kings 4:39).

14. A number of fruits grew in Canaan. These included _____grapes_____, _____pomegranates_____, and _____figs_____ (Numbers 13:23).

15. Oil from _____olive_____ berries was used for frying food (Deuteronomy 8:8). This oil was also used in lamps, as medicine, for anointing, and for various other purposes.

Life in Bible Times

In This Lesson

Main Points
- People in Bible times ate a variety of food. This included bread, grain kernels, dairy products, some meats, vegetables, soups, fruit, and nuts.
- A number of mealtime customs of Bible times are studied in this lesson, including the two regular meals each day, thanking God for food, eating without utensils, and sitting on the floor or lying on low couches to eat.
- The Law of Moses forbade the eating of blood or of unclean animals.

Truths to Instill
- God has provided a variety of food for our nourishment, but He expects us to work for it.
- We should thank God for our food and eat it to His glory (Romans 14:6).
- Jesus taught that the thoughts and deeds that come from a person's heart are more important than which foods he eats. The New Testament permits the eating of any kind of meat, but it forbids the eating of blood (Acts 15:28, 29).

✎ *Unscramble the letters of these foods. If you need help, you may use the references.*

16. OHYEN _____honey_____ : The most common sweetener used in Bible times (Psalm 19:10)

17. PERGA CUJIE _____grape juice_____ : This was sometimes boiled until thick to spread on bread or to use as a drink mix. (Genesis 40:11)

18. FISG _____figs_____ : These were eaten either fresh or dried (Jeremiah 24:1)

19. SISIARN _____raisins_____ : A handy dried food for travelers (2 Samuel 16:1)

20. LOMNADS _____almonds_____ : Tasty nuts eaten in Bible times (Genesis 43:11)

21. GESG and HISF ___eggs___ , ___fish___ : Less common foods, eaten in certain places or when available (Luke 11:11, 12)

B. BIBLE STUDY BOOKS

✎ *Use a concordance to find Bible verses that mention these foods or seasonings. Only one reference is needed for each number.*

1. broth _____ Judges __6__ : 19, 20 Isaiah 65:4

2. cucumbers and melons _____ Numbers __11__ : __5__

3. leeks, onions, and garlick (garlic) _____ Numbers __11__ : __5__

4. locusts _____ Leviticus __11__ : __22__ Matthew 3:4; Mark 1:6

5. millet (a type of grain) _____ Ezekiel __4__ : __9__

6. mint, anise, and cummin (seasonings) _____ Matthew __23__ : __23__

7. mustard _____ Matthew __13__ : __31__ 17:20; Mark 4:31 Luke 13:19; 17:6

8. nuts (probably pistachios and walnuts) _____ Genesis __43__ : __11__ Song of Solomon 6:11

CHAPTER FIVE

Judah Taken Captive

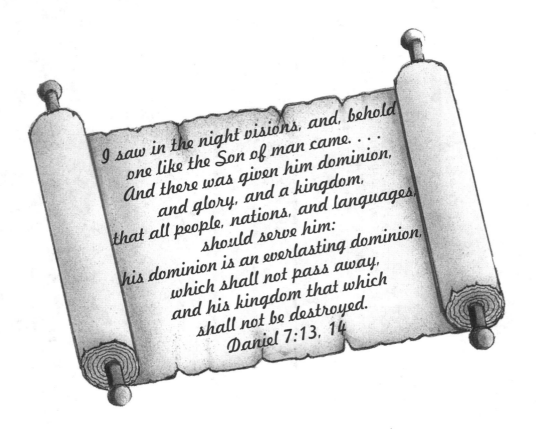

I saw in the night visions, and, behold, one like the Son of man came. . . . And there was given him dominion, and glory, and a kingdom, that all people, nations, and languages, should serve him: his dominion is an everlasting dominion, which shall not pass away, and his kingdom that which shall not be destroyed.

Daniel 7:13, 14

TIME LINE—Chapter Five

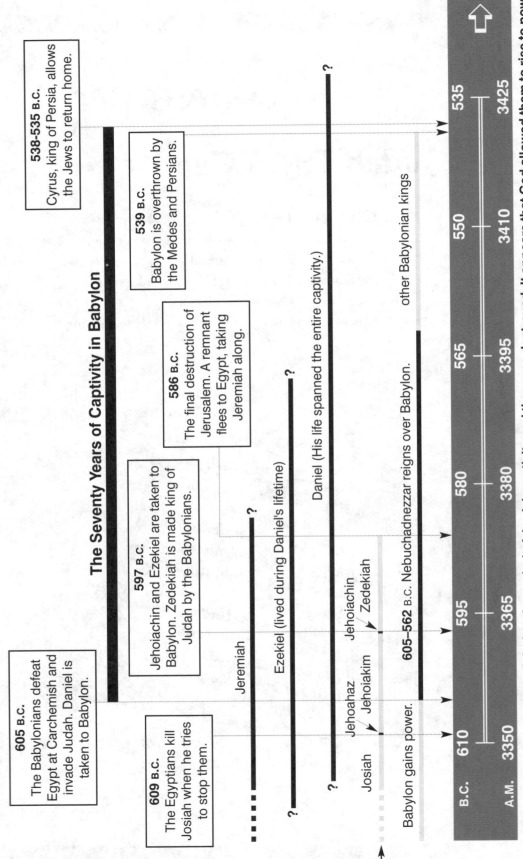

The Seventy Years of Captivity in Babylon

605 B.C.
The Babylonians defeat Egypt at Carchemish and invade Judah. Daniel is taken to Babylon.

609 B.C.
The Egyptians kill Josiah when he tries to stop them.

597 B.C.
Jehoiachin and Ezekiel are taken to Babylon. Zedekiah is made king of Judah by the Babylonians.

586 B.C.
The final destruction of Jerusalem. A remnant flees to Egypt, taking Jeremiah along.

539 B.C.
Babylon is overthrown by the Medes and Persians.

538-535 B.C.
Cyrus, king of Persia, allows the Jews to return home.

Jeremiah

Ezekiel (lived during Daniel's lifetime)

Daniel (His life spanned the entire captivity.)

Josiah

Jehoahaz
Jehoiakim

Jehoiachin
Zedekiah

other Babylonian kings

605–562 B.C. Nebuchadnezzar reigns over Babylon.

Babylon gains power.

| B.C. | 610 | | 595 | | 580 | | 565 | | 550 | | 535 |
| A.M. | 3350 | | 3365 | | 3380 | | 3395 | | 3410 | | 3425 |

NOTE: Babylon prospered during the period of Jewish captivity and then was destroyed. It appears that God allowed them to rise to power for the specific purpose of sheltering His people during their chastisement. The Babylonians did not destroy the Jewish culture as the Assyrians might have if they had conquered Judah. God, in His mercy, raised up the Babylonians to punish His people so that a remnant would be able to return to Canaan.

137

Lesson 21. The Last Kings of Judah

As early as the time of Moses, God had warned the Israelites not to disobey Him by living like the wicked Canaanites. He said that if they defiled the land with sin, the land would spew them out as it had the Canaanites before them (Leviticus 18:26–28).

But the people of Judah did not always listen to God's warnings. Some of them worshiped Canaanite idols. They built high places on hills, where they thought they would be closer to their gods (1 Kings 14:22, 23). There they offered sacrifices and incense to idols. Idol worship involved many sinful practices that God had strictly forbidden. King Manasseh even offered up his children to the idol Molech.

Because of Judah's terrible wickedness, God needed to punish them, just as He had punished the Northern Kingdom. He allowed the Jews' enemies to destroy the land of Judah and carry them away captive. Just as God had warned them nearly a thousand years before, the land was spewing them out because they had done abominable things.

God still loved His chosen people. He remembered the promises He had made to Abraham. But God is also just and holy, and always does right. When His chosen people disobeyed, He brought punishment upon them. They had worshiped as the heathen did, and now they needed to suffer with the heathen.

After the Jews became captives, they began to understand how wrong it is to worship idols and how important it is to obey God. The Jews who returned to Judah after seventy years of captivity did not always love the LORD with all their hearts. But never again do we read of them building high places or worshiping idols.

God demands obedience from His people.

- A number of themes from this lesson could be expanded and used for extra study or for devotional topics. Examples: "The Law of Sowing and Reaping," "The Goodness and Severity of God," "The Sure Word of Prophecy," and "God Is No Respecter of Persons."

A. ANSWERS FROM THE BIBLE

A Time to Weep

Josiah was the last righteous king of Judah. After him four other kings ruled, but none of them followed God.

Just before Josiah's death, the Babylonian king Nabopolassar had attacked and destroyed Nineveh, the capital of Assyria. The great Assyrian Empire, which had conquered the Northern Kingdom of Israel about one hundred years before, had come to an end.

Nabopolassar sent his son Nebuchadnezzar westward to fight the Egyptians, who were also trying to gain lands that Assyria had controlled. King Josiah evidently thought he should stop these Egyptians. Even though Pharaoh warned him to leave them alone, Josiah opposed them anyway and was killed.

Nebuchadnezzar won a great victory over the Egyptians at the city of Carchemish. Now Babylon ruled the entire region. Judah faced new challenges that its ungodly kings were unprepared to meet.

King Jehoahaz

2 Kings 23:31–34

After Josiah was killed, the people of the land made his son Jehoahaz king.

1. How long did King Jehoahaz reign? __three months__

- The Middle East was in turmoil during this period. The Babylonians and the Egyptians were both trying to take advantage of the fall of Assyria to build a world empire for themselves. For a few years the Egyptians controlled Canaan, but the Babylonians defeated them at Carchemish about 605 B.C. After that, Judah had to deal with Babylonia rather than Egypt or Assyria.

Lesson 21

Oral Review

The numbers in brackets tell which lessons are being reviewed.

1. What covenant did God make with David? [3] **God promised to establish David's throne forever.**
2. Which two dynasties in the Northern Kingdom of Israel lasted for more than two generations? [7] **Omri's and Jehu's**
3. How did the LORD reward Jehu for destroying Ahab's house and the Baal worshipers? [13] **He promised that four generations of Jehu's descendants would reign over Israel.**
4. How did God show Hezekiah that he would recover from his sickness? [18] **The shadow on the sundial moved back ten degrees.**
5. Which king caused the people of Judah to do worse than the heathen? [19] **Manasseh**
6. Which six kings in this list were mostly good? Which five were known for their wickedness? Asa, Jehoshaphat, Jehoram, Ahaziah, Uzziah, Jotham, Ahaz, Hezekiah, Manasseh, Amon, Josiah. [19] *mostly good:* **Asa, Jehoshaphat, Uzziah, Jotham, Hezekiah, Josiah;** *known for wickedness:* **Jehoram, Ahaziah, Ahaz, Manasseh, Amon**

2. During this time, Pharaoh Necho of Egypt controlled Judah. Name two things from these verses that show this is true. (Any two of these. Answers may vary slightly.)

   a. —He took Jehoahaz away captive.   —He required Judah to pay a tribute.

   b. —He made Jehoiakim king in the place of Jehoahaz.

Jeremiah 22:10–12
During the reigns of the last four kings of Judah, Jeremiah the prophet gave God's message to the people. In this passage he prophesied about Shallum, which is another name for Jehoahaz.

3. What did Jeremiah prophesy would happen to Jehoahaz?

   He would not return to Judah, but would die in the place where he had been led captive.

4. Which verse in 2 Kings 23:31–34 shows that Jeremiah's prophecy came true?   verse 34

King Jehoiakim

2 Kings 23:34–37
When Pharaoh of Egypt took King Jehoahaz captive, he made Jehoiakim king instead.

5. What was Jehoiakim's name before Pharaoh changed it?   Eliakim

6. How was Jehoiakim related to Jehoahaz? (Compare verses 30 and 34.)

   Jehoahaz and Jehoiakim were brothers.

7. Like Jehoahaz, Jehoiakim did   evil   in the sight of the LORD.

Daniel 1:1–6
The Babylonians did not want Egypt to become a world power. Since Judah was under the control of Egypt at this time, it was one of the countries that they conquered while they were trying to gain control over Egypt.

8. What happened in the third year of Jehoiakim's reign? (1:1)

   Nebuchadnezzar besieged Jerusalem.

9. What did Nebuchadnezzar do with some of the vessels from God's temple?

   He took them to Shinar (Babylon) and placed them in the house of his god.

10. At this time, Nebuchadnezzar also took some captives to Babylon.

    a. From what special class of people did he take captives? (1:3)

       He took captives from the king's seed (descendants) and the princes.

    b. What four boys were among this group of captives?

       Daniel (Belteshazzar), Hananiah (Shadrach), Mishael (Meshach), and Azariah (Abednego)

Jeremiah 22:13–19
Jeremiah also prophesied about King Jehoiakim.

11. The people of Judah had mourned when King Josiah died. How would they respond differently when his son Jehoiakim died (1:18)?

    They would not lament for Jehoiakim.

7. What was the most important food in Bible times? [20] **bread**
8. What was the most common sweetener in Bible times? [20] **honey**

In This Lesson

Scope: 2 Kings 23:31–25:30; 2 Chronicles 36; Jeremiah 22; Daniel 1:1–6

Main Events
• After King Josiah dies, Jehoahaz reigns for three months. The Egyptians take him captive and put Jehoiakim on the throne.

• King Jehoiakim becomes subject to the Babylonians, who take Daniel and other captives to Babylon. Jehoiakim rebels and the Babylonians come to suppress the rebellion. Jehoiakim dies an ignoble death.

• Jehoiachin reigns for three months and then surrenders. The Babylonians take him and ten thousand other Jews captive to Babylon.

• King Zedekiah promises to serve the Babylonians, but he soon rebels. God allows the Babylonians to destroy Jerusalem and take most of the remaining Jews captive.

12. From verses 15–17, find at least two reasons why the people did not like Jehoiakim. _____

     (Answers may vary slightly.) His eyes and his heart were covetous.

     He shed innocent blood and oppressed the people.

2 Kings 24:1, 7

13. What did Jehoiakim do after he had served Nebuchadnezzar for three years? _____

     Jehoiakim rebelled against Nebuchadnezzar.

14. Pharaoh Necho had controlled Judah at the beginning of Jehoiakim's reign, but who was in complete

     control when Jehoiakim died eleven years later? (24:7) _the king of Babylon (Nebuchadnezzar)_

2 Chronicles 36:5, 6

15. How did Nebuchadnezzar punish Jehoiakim for his rebellion? _____

     Nebuchadnezzar bound Jehoiakim to carry him to Babylon.

   Jeremiah had prophesied that King Jehoiakim's body would be thrown outside Jerusalem. King Jehoiakim was evidently taken out of his fetters, killed, and thrown outside Jerusalem (Jeremiah 22:19). Then his son Jehoiachin became king. (The last syllable of Jehoiachin's name is pronounced *kin*, not *chin*.)

King Jehoiachin

2 Kings 24:8

16. How long did Jehoiachin reign? __three months__

Jeremiah 22:24–30

   Jeremiah prophesied about Jehoiachin (Jeremiah called him Coniah).

17. Who would capture Jehoiachin? _____Nebuchadnezzar_____

18. Who would be taken captive with him? _his mother_

19. Where would he die? _in a foreign country (Babylon)_

20. Would any of his descendants sit on the throne of David? ____no____

   All these prophecies came true. When the Babylonians attacked Jerusalem, young King Jehoiachin surrendered and went out to meet them. His mother went with him. The Babylonians looted the city and took captive Jehoiachin, his mother, and ten thousand other Jews (2 Kings 24:11–16). In Babylon, Jehoiachin sat in prison for thirty-seven years. Then a new king gave him freedom and allowed him to eat at his table. But neither Jehoiachin nor his mother ever returned to Judah (Jeremiah 52:31–34).

King Zedekiah

   After removing Jehoiachin, the Babylonians crowned Zedekiah king of Judah. Zedekiah was Josiah's son, Jehoahaz and Jehoiakim's brother, and Jehoiachin's uncle. Zedekiah was the third son of King Josiah to reign over Judah.

2 Chronicles 36:11–13

21. How did Nebuchadnezzar try to make sure King Zedekiah would not rebel against him? _____

     Nebuchadnezzar made Zedekiah swear by God (to be loyal to him).

22. How long did Zedekiah reign? __eleven years__

Objectives
- The students should know
  —that Judah quickly apostatized after King Josiah's death, and within five years the first captives were taken to Babylon.
  —what happened to each of the four kings they studied in this lesson. (See Part A.)

Truths to Instill
- God is faithful in warning men. His judgment is usually preceded by many warnings and much long-suffering (Jeremiah 7:25–28). (However, we dare not presume on God's long-suffering. Ananias and Sapphira died suddenly for their deliberate deceit.)
- God's Word never fails. Jeremiah's prophecies about Judah's kings came to pass in every detail. Jesus will fulfill God's promise of an everlasting kingdom for David's seed, even though David's dynasty at Jerusalem ended with Zedekiah.
- God is holy. His judgments "are true and righteous altogether" (Psalm 19:9). If they seem severe to us, it is because of our limited understanding. (See Romans 11:33.)

140 Chapter Five Judah Taken Captive

The Fall of Jerusalem

In spite of his promise, Zedekiah rebelled against Babylon. King Nebuchadnezzar sent an army against Judah. For two years the Babylonians surrounded Jerusalem, not letting people go in or out. The Jews became very hungry, but they did not turn to God. Finally the Babylonians broke through the city walls. Zedekiah fled through a secret gate, but the Babylonians caught him. Nebuchadnezzar and his men forced Zedekiah to watch while his sons were killed, and then they put out his eyes and took him to Babylon (2 Kings 25:1–7).

2 Chronicles 36:17–20

23. The Chaldees (Babylonians) had no _____compassion_____ on young men, maidens, or old men.

They _____burned_____ the house of God and the palaces, and broke down the

___wall___ of Jerusalem. They took those who had escaped the sword to Babylon.

B. BIBLE WORD STUDY

✎ *Write words from the verses given to match these definitions.*

___pertained___ 1. Belonged to (2 Kings 24:7)

___fetters___ 2. Rings or bands chained together and placed around the ankles to restrain a prisoner (2 Chronicles 36:6)

___sore___ 3. Bitterly; greatly (Jeremiah 22:10)

___covetousness___ 4. A greedy desire for what belongs to someone else (Jeremiah 22:17)

___oppression___ 5. Cruel and unfair rule (Jeremiah 22:17)

___lament___ 6. Mourn; show great sorrow (Jeremiah 22:18)

___signet___ 7. A ring or other instrument having the special design of its owner, which, when pressed into soft clay, left his personal mark (Jeremiah 22:24)

✎ *Use the tables of measure in the back of this book to complete this exercise.*

8. How many pounds of silver and gold did Pharaoh Necho collect from Judah as tribute? (2 Kings 23:33)

a. __7,500__ pounds of silver b. __75__ pounds of gold
(3,400 kg)   (34 kg)

C. THINKING ABOUT BIBLE TRUTHS

Why Did God Judge His People?   (Some answers in this section may vary.)

God gave many reasons for allowing His people to be taken captive. Jeremiah 7 lists some of these reasons.

1. List the sins of Judah that God mentioned in Jeremiah 7:9. _____

 stealing, murder, adultery, swearing falsely, burning incense to Baal, walking after other gods

2. In spite of their sins, what did the people trust in? (7:4, 14) _____

 They trusted in (lying words about) the temple of the LORD.

Lesson 21. The Last Kings of Judah   **141**

3. What did the people of Judah refuse to do? (7:23, 24) _____

   They refused to obey God's voice and walk in His ways.

4. What expression did God use to describe how urgently He had sent His prophets? (7:25, 26) _____

   God sent His prophets, "daily rising up early and sending them."

Was This the End of David's Kingdom?

God had promised that David's kingdom would be established forever (2 Samuel 7:16). Did God break His promise when He allowed the Babylonians to conquer Judah? No, God never breaks His promises. God had planned something better for David's family than an earthly kingdom. Shortly before the Babylonians captured Zedekiah, the last descendant of David to reign at Jerusalem, Jeremiah foretold how God would fulfill His promise to David.

5. Read Jeremiah 33:15–17 and Luke 1:30–33. How did God fulfill His promise that David's kingdom

   would be established forever? _____

   Jesus, who was born into David's family, will reign forever.

IMPORTANT: Discuss this question in class to be sure the students understand how Jesus is the fulfillment of God's promise to David. This is one of the most important points in this course.

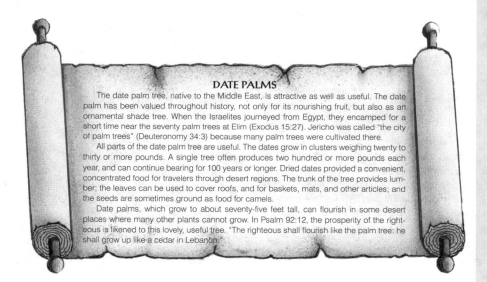

DATE PALMS

The date palm tree, native to the Middle East, is attractive as well as useful. The date palm has been valued throughout history, not only for its nourishing fruit, but also as an ornamental shade tree. When the Israelites journeyed from Egypt, they encamped for a short time near the seventy palm trees at Elim (Exodus 15:27). Jericho was called "the city of palm trees" (Deuteronomy 34:3) because many palm trees were cultivated there.

All parts of the date palm tree are useful. The dates grow in clusters weighing twenty to thirty or more pounds. A single tree often produces two hundred or more pounds each year, and can continue bearing for 100 years or longer. Dried dates provided a convenient, concentrated food for travelers through desert regions. The trunk of the tree provides lumber; the leaves can be used to cover roofs, and for baskets, mats, and other articles; and the seeds are sometimes ground as food for camels.

Date palms, which grow to about seventy-five feet tall, can flourish in some desert places where many other plants cannot grow. In Psalm 92:12, the prosperity of the righteous is likened to this lovely, useful tree. "The righteous shall flourish like the palm tree: he shall grow up like a cedar in Lebanon."

D. LEARNING MORE ABOUT THE BIBLE

Old Testament Books

✎ *Review the Old Testament books and their divisions. (See Lesson 1 if you need help.) You will need to know the order and spelling of the Minor Prophets for the Chapter Five Test.*

Review the Old Testament books and their divisions together in class as needed. The students will need to know the order and spelling of the Minor Prophets for the Chapter Five Test.

Jeremiah prophesied during the reigns of the last four kings of Judah. These kings did not like Jeremiah or his message. They made life difficult for him. But Jeremiah continued to give God's message.

Jeremiah, like the date palms of the Middle East, faced many hard times before his life bore fruit. At times Jeremiah may have felt he was not accomplishing anything, because the kings of Judah would not listen to him. But his life was not in vain. God still speaks to us through Jeremiah's writings. His life is still bearing fruit more than two thousand years after his death.

✎ *Write each sentence in the correct blank to show the order of some major events during Jeremiah's lifetime. (Notice that the events start at the bottom.)*

Jeremiah weeps when Josiah is killed.
The Babylonians capture Zedekiah and destroy Jerusalem.
The Babylonians take captives, including Daniel.
The Babylonians take captives, including Jehoiachin.

Jeremiah begins to prophesy.
The remnant of the Jews take Jeremiah to Egypt.
Josiah keeps a great Passover.

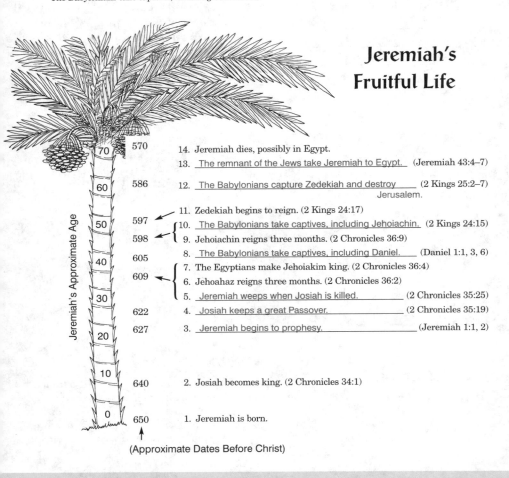

Jeremiah's Fruitful Life

70 — 570 — 14. Jeremiah dies, possibly in Egypt.
13. <u>The remnant of the Jews take Jeremiah to Egypt.</u> (Jeremiah 43:4–7)

60 — 586 — 12. <u>The Babylonians capture Zedekiah and destroy</u> (2 Kings 25:2–7)
Jerusalem.

11. Zedekiah begins to reign. (2 Kings 24:17)
50 — 597 — 10. <u>The Babylonians take captives, including Jehoiachin.</u> (2 Kings 24:15)
598 — 9. Jehoiachin reigns three months. (2 Chronicles 36:9)

605 — 8. <u>The Babylonians take captives, including Daniel.</u> (Daniel 1:1, 3, 6)

40 — 7. The Egyptians make Jehoiakim king. (2 Chronicles 36:4)
609 — 6. Jehoahaz reigns three months. (2 Chronicles 36:2)

30 — 5. <u>Jeremiah weeps when Josiah is killed.</u> (2 Chronicles 35:25)

622 — 4. <u>Josiah keeps a great Passover.</u> (2 Chronicles 35:19)

627 — 3. <u>Jeremiah begins to prophesy.</u> (Jeremiah 1:1, 2)
20

10
640 — 2. Josiah becomes king. (2 Chronicles 34:1)

0
650 — 1. Jeremiah is born.

↑
(Approximate Dates Before Christ)

Jeremiah's Approximate Age

143

Lesson 22. Jeremiah—the Strong, Weeping Prophet

Because God loves His people, He warns them that they will be punished if they disobey Him. Today God warns people through the Bible. Long ago He warned them through the messages of the prophets. Jeremiah faithfully gave God's message, but the people did not listen to his warnings.

Warnings do no good if people do not take them seriously. In 1845, a snow-capped volcano called Ruiz (roo EETH), erupted in the highlands of Colombia. When hot gases and molten rock burst from its crater, its snow melted, and great streams of mud rushed down its slopes to destroy the valley below. Someone from the valley wrote about this disaster, which was permitted "by the Holy Will of the Highest," and recorded it in a church record book in one of the villages "so that . . . their successors would not forget."

But people did forget. More than a hundred years passed. The old people who had talked about the mud flow died, and their grandchildren forgot what they had said. Then, early in 1985, the Ruiz volcano started rumbling again. Clouds of steam rose from its crater, and tremors began to shake the earth.

In spite of these warnings from the volcano, no one became very alarmed. Some people considered leaving their homes, but their friends told them to just stay calm. All summer the warning rumbles continued, becoming worse and worse. On November 10 the tremors intensified, and a strong smell of sulfur hung in the air. People grew uneasy, but the radio kept telling everyone not to worry. It played cheerful music until the lights suddenly went out at 11:00 P.M. on November 13. In the darkness, people scrambled to flee as a river of mud and ashes 130 feet (40 meters) high descended upon them. In one town, twenty thousand people were buried alive, along with their houses and everything they owned.

Many people treat the Bible as the residents of Colombia treated the warnings of the Ruiz volcano. They read the warnings of the prophets and learn what happened to the Israelites, but they keep right on disobeying God. When a man such as Jeremiah urges them to repent, they make fun of him.

But what God says *will* happen. God saves only those who heed His warnings and obey Him.

A. ANSWERS FROM THE BIBLE

God Calls Jeremiah

Jeremiah was only a young man when God called him to prophesy. He said, "Ah, LORD GOD! behold, I cannot speak: for I am a child" (Jeremiah 1:6). But God did not change His mind because of Jeremiah's excuse.

Other prophets shared Jeremiah's fears. Being a prophet was not easy. Some prophets were thrown into prison or even stoned to death.

Jeremiah 1:17–19

1. God said He would make Jeremiah a defensed ____city____, an ____iron____ ____pillar____, and __brasen (brazen)__ walls.

2. God said: "I am with thee . . . to ____deliver____ ____thee____."

Jeremiah's Message Is Rejected

Jeremiah was born into a priest's family in the village of Anathoth. His name in Hebrew is *Yirmeyahu*, which means "Jehovah will rise" or "Jehovah will lift up."

Lesson 22

Oral Review

The chart "Jeremiah's Fruitful Life" in Lesson 21 would provide a good review for this lesson. Point out that Jeremiah was probably born during Manasseh's reign, that he prophesied during the reigns of Josiah and the last four kings of Judah, and that he was taken to Egypt after the destruction of Jerusalem.

1. To what tool did Jeremiah compare God's Word? [11] **a hammer**
2. Which good king was a friend to Ahab? [16] **Jehoshaphat**
3. Who prophesied in Judah about the same time as Isaiah? [18] **Micah**
4. Who kept the greatest Passover since the time of Samuel? [19] **Josiah and his people**
5. Who were the last four kings of Judah? [21] **Jehoahaz, Jehoiakim, Jehoiachin, and Zedekiah**
6. Who removed Jehoahaz from his throne and made Jehoiakim king? [21] **Pharaoh Necho**
7. Which king of Judah broke a covenant he had made with Nebuchadnezzar? [21] **Zedekiah**
8. How did God fulfill His promise that David's kingdom would be established forever? [21] **Jesus, who will reign forever, was born into David's family.**

3. What did the men from his hometown threaten to do to him if he did not stop prophesying? (Jeremiah 11:21) __They threatened to kill him.__

4. Did Jeremiah's family support him? (Jeremiah 12:6) ___no___

Jeremiah 19:14–20:2

5. Where did Jeremiah go to prophesy after he returned from prophesying at Tophet? _____ __into the court of the LORD's house (temple)__

6. What priest did not like Jeremiah's message? _____Pashur_____

7. What did he do to Jeremiah? __He smote Jeremiah and put him in the stocks.__

8. What did Jeremiah say would happen to the priest? (Jeremiah 20:6) _____ __He would be taken to Babylon and would die there.__

Jeremiah 36:20–23, 32

In the fourth year of Jehoiakim's reign, Jeremiah spoke God's words to Baruch, who wrote them in a scroll. Jeremiah sent Baruch to read this scroll to the people who had gathered at the temple. When King Jehoiakim heard about the scroll, he asked for it.

9. What wicked thing did Jehoiakim do when the scroll was read to him? _____ __Jehoiakim cut the scroll with his penknife and threw it into the fire.__

10. How was Jeremiah like an iron pillar when he heard about Jehoiakim's deed? _____ __He (with Baruch's help) rewrote the scroll and added many more words.__

Jeremiah Endures Suffering

Jeremiah 37:11–21

When King Zedekiah and the princes of Judah rebelled, the Chaldeans (Babylonians) came to fight against Jerusalem. Then Pharaoh's army came to help Zedekiah, and the Babylonians drew back for a short time to fight the Egyptians. During this time Jeremiah decided to leave Jerusalem and go to the land of Benjamin, the tribe just north of Jerusalem. But when he arrived there, he was captured and falsely accused.

11. What did a captain falsely accuse Jeremiah of trying to do? _____ __He accused Jeremiah of falling away (deserting) to the Chaldeans.__

12. The princes were (a) ____wroth____ with Jeremiah. They (b) ____smote____ him and put him in (c) ____prison____ in Jonathan the scribe's (d) ____house____.

13. After Jeremiah had remained there (a) ____many____ days, King (b) ____Zedekiah____ sent and took him out. The king asked him secretly whether he had any word from the (c) ____LORD____. Jeremiah told the king that he would be delivered (d) ____into____ the hand of the king of Babylon.

In This Lesson

Scope: Selected passages from the books of Jeremiah and Lamentations

Main Events

• God calls Jeremiah to preach, to be an iron pillar for truth in the midst of apostasy.

• Jeremiah is persecuted by his hometown and family, rejected by his religious peers, arrested, beaten, and accused of treason.

• Through these trials, Jeremiah preaches God's unpopular message. He weeps as he watches the destruction of Jerusalem, and he is finally taken to Egypt by fellow Jews.

Objectives

• The students should know
  —why Jeremiah's message was so unpopular. (Jeremiah's message told of God's judgment on sin and called the Jews to repent.)
  —that the Babylonians were kinder to Jeremiah than his own people were.
  —that the prophecies of Jeremiah came true, even though they were ridiculed by almost everyone who heard them.

14. Jeremiah asked the king not to make him go back to the house of (a) __Jonathan (the scribe)__, lest

he (b) _____die_____ there.

15. The king allowed Jeremiah to stay in the (a) _____court_____ of the prison. Each day he

was given a (b) __piece of bread_____.

Even while Jeremiah was in prison, he did not stop giving people God's message. He told them they should not fight the Babylonians, as the princes wanted to do. The princes went to King Zedekiah and asked him to kill Jeremiah. Zedekiah allowed the princes to put Jeremiah into a dungeon.

Jeremiah 38:6–13

16. How was Jeremiah put into the dungeon? _____

___The men lowered Jeremiah into the dungeon with cords._____

17. What was in the bottom of the dungeon? _____mire_____

18. Who went to the king to try to help Jeremiah? _____Ebed-melech_____

19. How many men helped to get Jeremiah out? _____thirty_____

Jeremiah Is Taken to Egypt

After a two-year siege, the Babylonians broke through the wall and entered Jerusalem. They set Jeremiah free. Just as Jeremiah had said, they took King Zedekiah captive, along with many other Jews.

The king of Babylon appointed Gedaliah, a Jew who was kind to Jeremiah, as governor over the ruined cities of Judah. But Gedaliah was murdered, and the remaining Jews became fearful and wanted to flee to Egypt. They asked Jeremiah what they should do.

20. What was God's message to them? (Jeremiah 42:19) _____

___"Go ye not into Egypt."_____

The fearful Jews disobeyed God's word and went to Egypt anyway. They took Jeremiah with them, even though he did not want to go. He continued to warn them that God would punish them for their sins.

Jeremiah 44:15–17, 27

✎ *Write* true *or* false. *Correct each false statement on the lines after the sentence.*

____true____ 21. The Jews continued to worship idols after they arrived in Egypt. _____

_____

____false___ 22. The Jews obeyed the words that Jeremiah spoke to them in the Name of the LORD.

___The Jews *did not obey* the words that Jeremiah spoke to them in the Name of the___

___LORD._____

____true____ 23. The LORD said that He would bring evil upon His people rather than good. _____

_____

In the rewritten sentence for number 22, the correction is in italics. The pupil's sentence may vary somewhat.

The Bible does not tell how Jeremiah died. According to one tradition, the Jews in Egypt stoned him to death after they grew tired of his preaching. Another tradition says that he escaped to Babylon and died there in peace.

Truths to Instill

• God's message, even when it is unpopular and unheeded, is always true. God will judge unrepentant sinners according to His Word, just as surely as Jeremiah's prophecies were fulfilled.

• Jeremiah stood like an iron pillar, unmoved by opposition from all sides. Yet he keenly felt this rejection, and he is known as the weeping prophet. See Jeremiah's words after he was beaten and put in the stocks (Jeremiah 20:7–18). Also read Lamentations 3.

B. BIBLE WORD STUDY

✎ *Match each word in italics with its meaning on the right. All references are from Jeremiah.*

<u>h</u>   1. "Be not *dismayed* at their faces" (1:17).

<u>d</u>   2. "They have dealt *treacherously* with thee" (12:6).

<u>a</u>   3. "Pashur smote Jeremiah . . . and put him in the *stocks*" (20:2).

<u>e</u>   4. "He cut it with the *penknife*, and cast it into the fire" (36:23).

<u>c</u>   5. "I fall not away to the *Chaldeans*" (37:14).

<u>b</u>   6. "Ebed-melech . . . took thence old *cast clouts*" (38:11).

<u>g</u>   7. "O ye *remnant* of Judah; Go ye not into Egypt" (42:19).

<u>f</u>   8. "We will certainly . . . burn incense unto the *queen of heaven*" (44:17).

a. a frame with holes used to confine the feet (or hands) of prisoners

b. worn-out clothes

c. a race of people who moved into Babylonia and ruled the empire

d. unfaithfully, deceitfully

e. a tool used by scribes to sharpen reed pens

f. a heathen goddess

g. a small group of people who are left after the rest are destroyed

h. filled with fear or confusion

C. THINKING ABOUT BIBLE TRUTHS

More Lessons From Jeremiah

1. God used a number of object lessons to teach Jeremiah and the children of Judah spiritual truths. One day God sent Jeremiah to a potter's house (Jeremiah 18:1–6).

    a. What was wrong with the first vessel the potter made? _____
       It was marred (spoiled).

    b. What did the potter do with the first vessel? _____
       He made it into another vessel.

    c. What did God want Judah to learn from this object lesson? (Consider the question God asked in verse 6.)   God's people are in His hands as clay in a potter's hand, and He can do with them as He sees best.

2. Jeremiah stood like an iron pillar against the wicked Jews, yet he still loved them. What did he say he would do if the people did not listen to his warnings? (Jeremiah 13:15–17) _____
    He said he would weep for them.

3. Jeremiah lived to see the severe judgments that the LORD brought upon Judah. He probably wrote the Book of Lamentations, which is five poems of mourning, soon after the destruction of Jerusalem.

    a. What did the enemies of Judah do when they saw that Jerusalem was destroyed? (Lamentations 2:15, 16)   They mocked the Jews and were glad.

• The Book of Lamentations was probably written by Jeremiah. (The text itself does not specifically give the author. In the Hebrew, his name is not included in the title. It was added there when the book was translated into Greek.) Each chapter of Lamentations is a poem. In the original language, each verse in chapters 1, 2, and 4 begins with a different Hebrew letter, in alphabetical order. Chapter 3 has three verses for each of the twenty-two Hebrew letters. Chapter 5 has twenty-two verses, but they do not follow the alphabetical pattern.

Lesson 22. Jeremiah—the Strong, Weeping Prophet   **147**

b. God preserved the Old Testament so that we can learn from the Israelites' mistakes. What are some lessons we should learn as we read about God's judgment on His people? (Lamentations 2:17 may give you some ideas.) _____

(Sample answers) God's Word is always true. God will not always have mercy and pity on
sinners. God judges those who have sinned, even if they are His special people.
_____

c. Why could Jeremiah have hope for his people, even after they had been defeated and taken into captivity? (Lamentations 3:21–25) __(Sample Answers) The Lord's mercies are new every__
morning. The Lord is faithful, even though His people are not. The Lord is good to them who
wait for Him and seek Him.

D. LEARNING MORE ABOUT THE BIBLE

Jeremiah's Friends

Jeremiah never married. Because of the stern messages God asked him to deliver, he had few friends. Some Jews considered him a traitor because he told them not to fight against the Babylonians. Some probably thought he was foolish for risking his life by giving unpopular messages. But a few godly people stood with Jeremiah and helped him.

✎ *In your own words, tell how each of these four friends helped Jeremiah.*
(Answers may vary.)

1. Ebed-melech (Jeremiah 38:7–13)_____

Ebed-melech rescued Jeremiah from the dungeon.
_____
_____

2. Ahikam (Jeremiah 26:24) _____

Ahikam defended Jeremiah when the people wanted to kill him.
_____
_____

3. Baruch (Jeremiah 36:4) _____

Baruch wrote the words of Jeremiah on a scroll.
_____
_____

4. Gedaliah (Jeremiah 39:14) _____

Gedaliah took Jeremiah home and was kind to him.
_____
_____

148 Chapter Five   Judah Taken Captive

Jeremiah—Prophet of Doom

✎ *Through Jeremiah, God sent warnings to many other nations. Read the verses listed below to learn who received messages from Jeremiah, and write the correct names in the blanks on the map.*

1. Jeremiah 46:2   4. Jeremiah 49:1   7. Jeremiah 49:28
2. Jeremiah 47:1   5. Jeremiah 48:1   8. Jeremiah 50:1
3. Jeremiah 49:23   6. Jeremiah 49:7   9. Jeremiah 49:34

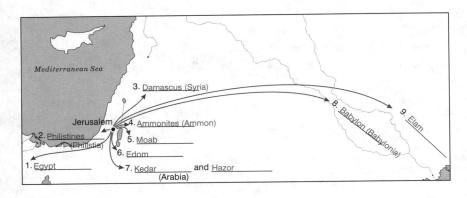

Note: If you have time in class, you may want to read the first part of the warning God sent to Babylon through Jeremiah (Jeremiah 50:1–5). This foretold the downfall of Babylon and the deliverance of the Jews.

149

Lesson 23. Daniel—Faithful Away From Home

For the Jews it must have seemed as if the land of Judah was being destroyed completely. First Pharaoh Necho took King Jehoahaz captive to Egypt. Then Nebuchadnezzar carried away some princes and royal descendants, including Daniel, to Babylon. About eight years later, Nebuchadnezzar took ten thousand more captives to his country, including King Jehoiachin and the well-to-do, important people of Judah. Eleven years later, the Babylonians came again and took King Zedekiah. They burned Jerusalem and carried the rest of its people captive to Babylon. Only a few Jews were left in Judah, and most of them fled to Egypt, where they mingled with the ungodly. God's people were confused, scattered, and discouraged.

The captives who were led to Babylon faced troublesome times. They had to work hard to make a living in a new land. If they trusted in the LORD, their captors made fun of them. "Look at your God!" they said. "He could not save you. Why do you keep trusting Him?" (But it was not the LORD's fault that Judah had fallen. It was because of the people's sins.)

The Jews in Babylon no longer had a temple. Their priests had no place in which to offer sacrifices. Yet God did not leave the captive Jews without good examples to follow. Daniel and his friends were faithful to God in spite of their troubles. Because of their faithfulness, even the king and other high officials had to recognize that the God whom they served was greater than all other gods.

God wants faithful people who leave good examples for others to follow.

A. ANSWERS FROM THE BIBLE

Daniel's New Home

Daniel's long trip was different from trips we make today. He never returned home. He left his family, his language, and his way of life behind him. In Babylon he made new friends and became well-liked. He learned the Babylonian language, and under Nebuchadnezzar he became governor of the province of Babylon. Belshazzar, a later king, made him the third-highest official of the empire. King Darius the Mede made him the head over 120 district governors.

Daniel 1

1. How many years of training did Daniel and his friends receive before going in to see the king?   three

2. Find the meanings of the names *Daniel* and *Belteshazzar* in a Bible dictionary.

   a. Daniel: "God is my judge."

   b. Belteshazzar: Belteshazzar: "Bel protect his life."

   c. Why would Nebuchadnezzar want his servant's name to include Bel, the name of one of his gods, rather than El, one of the names of Judah's God?

      (Answers may vary.) Nebuchadnezzar thought his gods were more important and more powerful than Judah's God.

3. The king of Babylon did not eat according to the Law of God, and his meat might have been offered to his gods. Why did Daniel purpose not to eat the king's meat or to drink his wine?

   Daniel did not want to defile himself by disobeying God's Law.

Part A in this lesson requires a lot of reading. You may need to give the students more time for this assignment or do some of it together in class. Another option would be to divide the class in half and assign half the stories to each group. If you do this, be sure to discuss the stories sufficiently so that all the students have some knowledge of each of the stories.

Lesson 23

Oral Review

1. What does the LORD look at rather than just the outward appearance of a person? [1] **the person's heart**

2. Why did God not want the Israelites to marry people of other nations? [17] **He knew this would cause His people to turn to other gods.**

3. Whom did Nebuchadnezzar take captive in the third year of Jehoiakim's reign? [21] **some of the king's children and princes, including Daniel and his three friends**

4. How long did Jehoahaz and Jehoiachin reign over Judah? [21] **They each reigned three months.**

5. Which king burned Jeremiah's scroll? [22] **Jehoiakim**

6. What three things did God say Jeremiah would be as strong as? [22] **a defensed city, an iron pillar, and brazen walls**

7. What message did Jeremiah give to the remnant of the Jews when they wanted to go to Egypt? [22] **"Go ye not into Egypt."**

8. Why could Jeremiah have hope for his people even after they were taken captive? [22] **The LORD is merciful; He is faithful, even when**

150   Chapter Five   Judah Taken Captive

4. How did Daniel's friends feel about the God of Israel? (Daniel 3:17, 18) _____

   They knew God could deliver them from the king, and they were determined not to worship any

   other gods.

5. How did Daniel show his respect for Jerusalem, his childhood home? (Daniel 6:10) _____

   He faced Jerusalem when he prayed to God.

Daniel's Long Trip

Nebuchadnezzar, the king of Babylon, began to control the land of Judah when Daniel was still young. Nebuchadnezzar wanted young men from all his conquered lands to stand before him.

The king ordered his servant, Ashpenaz, to look for boys who were well-mannered, intelligent, and healthy. Daniel was among the boys chosen from Judah.

For many days the Jewish boys traveled through Syria, down the wide Euphrates River, and then across the green plains of Babylon.

In Babylon the boys were given new names. They were taught the Babylonian language and educated in Babylonian ideas and ways. Ashpenaz took care of them. He gave them fine clothing and set rich foods before them.

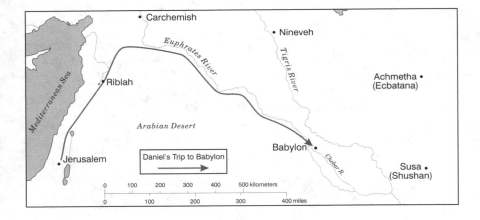

His people fail; He is good to them who wait for Him and seek Him.

In This Lesson

Scope: The Book of Daniel

Main Events
- Daniel is taken captive to Babylon as a youth. He is taught Babylonian culture.
- Daniel refuses to defile himself with the king's food.
- Daniel interprets dreams for the Babylonian rulers.
- Daniel's three friends are cast into a fiery furnace.
- Daniel is cast into a den of lions.
- Daniel has visions of future kingdoms.

Objectives
- The students should know
  —the basic facts about Daniel that are covered in this lesson.
  —that Daniel stood for what was right no matter what the cost.
  —that Daniel held high government positions under King Nebuchadnezzar and King Darius.

Truths to Instill
- A person without principle, no matter how well he may have been taught, will yield to temptation

Lesson 23. Daniel—Faithful Away From Home **151**

Stories From the Book of Daniel

✎ *The first half of the Book of Daniel contains a number of stories. Using these chapters as a guide, number the events of each story in the order they are recorded.*

Daniel 1

This first story took place very soon after Daniel and his friends arrived in Babylon.

6. **The Jewish Youths and the King's Meat**

_1_ Daniel is given a new name.

_3_ The prince of the eunuchs is worried.

_5 (or 6)_ The Jewish youths look the healthiest.

_4_ A vegetable diet is tested for ten days.

_6 (or 5)_ God blesses the Jewish youths for their faithfulness.

_2_ Daniel refuses to defile himself with the king's meat (food).

If you assign the stories in Extra Activity, numbers 6–11 could be skipped. Be sure to discuss the major points of all the stories in class, however, since the reviews and test include questions about the stories.

Daniel 2

This story took place after Daniel's education was completed. He was probably a young adult by this time.

7. **Nebuchadnezzar's Dream**

_1_ Nebuchadnezzar is troubled by a dream.

_7_ Nebuchadnezzar makes Daniel a great ruler.

_5_ Daniel explains the dream to Nebuchadnezzar.

_2_ The wise men of Babylon cannot interpret the dream.

_4_ God reveals the dream and its interpretation to Daniel.

_6_ Nebuchadnezzar declares that Daniel's God is a God of gods.

_3_ The king commands that all the wise men, including Daniel and his friends, be killed.

Daniel 3

This account probably took place soon after the previous one. It is possible that Nebuchadnezzar was inspired to make this image after he saw the image in his dream.

8. **The Jewish Youths and the Golden Image**

_3_ The king becomes angry.

_6_ A fourth man joins the three.

_2_ Three young men refuse to bow down.

_7_ The men's clothes do not smell burnt.

_5_ The three young men are cast into the fire.

_4_ The furnace is heated seven times hotter than usual.

_8_ Nebuchadnezzar commands that no one is to speak anything against God.

_1_ Nebuchadnezzar makes a golden image and commands everyone present to worship it.

rather than suffer for what is right. Examples of being true to principle can be seen in the following accounts.

—Daniel and his three friends refused to eat the king's meat.

—Daniel's three friends refused to bow to King Nebuchadnezzar's golden image.

—Daniel faithfully interpreted dreams, even when the interpretation might have brought the king's wrath upon him.

—Daniel steadfastly prayed, even when it meant being cast into the den of lions.

• "The most High ruleth in the kingdom of men" (Daniel 4:17).

—God used the Babylonians to punish the Jews for seventy years, and then He judged Babylon itself (Jeremiah 25:9–12).

—During the captivity, God placed Daniel and his friends in high positions where they could witness to heathen kings. Daniel's interpretations were direct messages from God.

—God demonstrated His mighty power by delivering Daniel and his friends, and by abasing Nebuchadnezzar. The heathen kings were forced to recognize the sovereignty of Israel's God.

• The visions in Daniel foretold the final triumph of God's eternal kingdom over all earthly kingdoms.

Daniel 4

This story seems to have taken place a number of years later, possibly near the end of King Nebuchadnezzar's reign.

9. Nebuchadnezzar's Second Dream and His Abasement

_4_ Daniel interprets the dream.

_1_ Nebuchadnezzar has a second dream.

_8_ Nebuchadnezzar becomes king again.

_3_ Nebuchadnezzar tells his dream to Daniel.

_5_ Nebuchadnezzar boasts about his great kingdom.

_2_ The wise men of Babylon cannot interpret the dream.

_7_ Nebuchadnezzar's understanding returns, and he blesses God.

_6_ Nebuchadnezzar lives like an animal for seven periods of time (possibly seven years).

Daniel 5

This story took place at the very end of the Babylonian Empire. Daniel was an old man by this time.

10. The Writing on the Wall

_7_ Daniel reads the writing.

_8_ King Belshazzar is slain.

_3_ A hand writes on the wall.

_1_ Belshazzar makes a great feast.

_4_ The king's knees shake with fear.

_6_ The queen tells the king about Daniel.

_5_ The wise men cannot read the writing.

_2_ Belshazzar calls for the temple vessels.

Daniel 6

This story took place after the fall of Babylon.

11. Daniel in the Lions' Den

_4_ Daniel is cast into the lions' den.

_1_ The princes are jealous of Daniel.

_3_ Daniel prays at his open window.

_2_ King Darius makes a foolish law.

_5_ The king cannot sleep and arises early.

_8_ Darius commands all men to fear God.

_6_ Daniel says: "God hath shut the lions' mouths."

_7_ Daniel's enemies are cast into the lions' den.

Extra Activity

✎ *Choose one of the stories above for an oral or written report. (Your teacher will tell you which kind it should be.) Different students in your class may want to pick different stories. Be sure to include details about the main points given above. Give the story in your own words, and conclude it with a lesson the story teaches.*

B. BIBLE WORD STUDY

✎ *Fill in the blanks with words from the verses given. All references are from the Book of Daniel.*

1. Daniel and his friends refuse to eat the king's food. They ask permission to eat _____pulse_____, or vegetables (1:12).

2. Chapters 2 to 7 of the Book of Daniel were written in the Aramaic language rather than in Hebrew, as most of the Old Testament was. Aramaic was the language of Aram, or Syria, and is called ___Syriack (Syriac)___ in Daniel 2:4.

3. A _____herald_____ is a man who makes important announcements (3:4).

4. A king's _____dominion_____ includes all the territory under his control (4:22).

5. _____Mene_____ means "numbered" and is closely related to *maneh*, a Bible unit of weight (5:25, 26).

6. _____Tekel_____ means "weighed" and is closely related to *shekel*, another Bible unit of weight (5:25, 27).

7. *Upharsin* (5:25) means "divided or split." It is a form of the Aramaic word _____Peres_____, used in Daniel 5:28.

C. THINKING ABOUT BIBLE TRUTHS

Lessons From the Life of Daniel

1. Daniel and his three friends served powerful kings who expected unquestioning obedience. Why did Daniel and his friends refuse to follow the kings' commands on a few occasions? _____
   (Answers may vary slightly.) Daniel and his friends knew that they must always obey God, even if that meant disobeying the king.

2. Nebuchadnezzar was proud of the great kingdom he had established (Daniel 4:30). What did God want him to recognize? (4:32) _____
   "The most High ruleth in the kingdom of men, and giveth it to whomsoever he will."

154   Chapter Five   Judah Taken Captive

3. Read Daniel 9:1–3. Daniel was a great prophet, and he also studied the writings of other true prophets. Nearly seventy years after he was taken captive, he remembered a promise God had made through Jeremiah.

   a. Jeremiah had said that Jerusalem would remain a desolation for how long?

      <u>seventy years</u>

   b. Use a concordance to find the reference for this prophecy: "For thus saith the LORD, That after seventy years be accomplished at Babylon I will visit you, and perform my good word toward you, in causing you to return to this place" (Jeremiah <u>29</u> : <u>10</u>).

   c. When the seventy years were nearly fulfilled, Daniel set his face unto the Lord God with <u>prayer</u>, supplications, <u>fasting</u>, <u>sackcloth</u>, and <u>ashes</u> (Daniel 9:3).

4. What did the people of Daniel's time think about him? (Daniel 4:9; 5:11; 6:4) <u>(Answers may vary.) They knew he had the spirit of the holy God, that he was wise, and that he was faithful.</u>

5. What did the angel of the LORD say about Daniel? (Daniel 9:23; 10:11, 19) <u>He was "greatly beloved."</u>

Always Pray

When King Darius signed the law that anyone who prayed
Be cast into the lions' den, then Daniel, undismayed,
Knelt down to pray three times each day, a window opened wide,
Although some jealous enemies were watching him outside
They hurried to the palace court in wicked, spiteful glee,
Demanding that this favored prince should pay the penalty.

Then King Darius grieved in vain; he neither ate nor slept.
The law unchanging had been signed; the order must he kept.
An angel locked the lions' jaws and stilled their savage roar,
While Daniel spent the night in peace upon the dungeon floor.

Pray when you're faced with obstacles; pray when the way is clear;
Pray when you feel you're being watched; pray when no one is near.
Pray when your day is going wrong, and when it seems all right;
Look to the Lord at early morn, at noontime, and at night.
Don't limit God because your faith is wavering or small,
But come to Him with every need, He'll surely hear your call.

—Ada L. Wine

D. LEARNING MORE ABOUT THE BIBLE

Daniel's Prophecy

The LORD revealed to Daniel many things that would happen in the future. Nebuchadnezzar's first vision had shown four world empires: the Babylonian, the Persian, the Greek, and the Roman. In chapters 7 and 8, Daniel recorded two visions he had that gave more details about these kingdoms.

✎ *Fill in the blanks on this chart to learn how Daniel saw these empires.*

Vision in Daniel 2	Vision in Daniel 7	Vision in Daniel 8	Identification
Head Of (1) gold (2:32)	Lion (7:4)		Babylon (2:38, 48)
Breast and Arms of (2) silver (2:32)	(3) bear (7:5)	(4) ram (8:3)	(5) Media and Persia (8:20)
Belly and Thighs of (6) brass (2:32)	(7) leopard (7:6)	Goat (8:5)	(8) Grecia (8:21)
Legs of (9) iron Feet of (10) iron and (11) clay (2:33)	Terrible and exceeding dreadful beast (7:7)		Not named in the Bible, but probably the Roman Empire.

12. What happened to the image in Nebuchadnezzar's vision? (Daniel 2:34, 35) _____

    It was broken into pieces by a stone cut out without hands.

13. In Daniel's vision in chapter 7, who became ruler over all people and nations after the other king-

    doms had been overthrown? (Compare Daniel 7:13, 14 with Revelation 11:15.) _____

    "one like the Son of man"—the Lord Jesus Christ

156

Lesson 24. The Jews in Babylon and Persia

After many generations of living in the Promised Land, the Jews found themselves far from home. In Babylon they were much farther from Canaan than they had been in Egypt. The hills of Zion, the winding road past the olive trees to Bethany, the open range down toward Beersheba where their flocks had roamed in happier times—all these things were nothing more than sad memories. The Jews no longer enjoyed singing the songs of Zion. On the Sabbath they gathered in the shade of willow trees along the river to weep.

Anna Huebert would have understood how those captive Jews felt. After her husband disappeared during World War II, she fled from her homeland in southern Russia. With her children and a few belongings, she left for Germany in a wagon.

From East Berlin Anna escaped with her family to West Germany. There they boarded a ship that took them to a pioneer Mennonite settlement in the jungles of eastern Brazil. Using sticks, vines, and leaves, Anna built a shelter for her family. Years later she moved with two of her married daughters to Canada.

Anna never forgot her homeland. She never forgot her parents and grandparents or the large church in the village of Gruenfeld, where she had once been a member. Until she died (at ninety-three years of age), Anna remembered the songs and Scripture verses she had learned as a child.

Anna never felt at home in the city of Kitchener, Ontario. At night, while the traffic rushed past her house and her neighbors played loud music, she had a hard time going to sleep. But when she slept, she was back in Gruenfeld, walking under the mulberry trees that grew along the wide, dusty village street. Anna never forgot her childhood.

The Jews in Babylon likewise never forgot their homeland. God did not want them to forget. He wanted them to remember that they were His people. He wanted them to remember His laws, His feasts and sacrifices, and the proper way to worship Him in His temple. God sent Ezekiel to the captive Jews to remind them.

Ezekiel used unusual stories and signs to speak to God's people. Thinking about God kept them from falling into the sins of the Babylonians. It kept them from getting too attached to the ungodly, foreign land in which they lived. And it kept the desire alive in their hearts to return someday to the Promised Land.

God blesses those who remember Him wherever they are.

A. ANSWERS FROM THE BIBLE

God's People in Exile

The Jews who were carried to Babylon lived through hard times. As captives they had few privileges. Perhaps what saddened them the most was to know that Jerusalem and the temple, now so far away, both lay in ruins.

1. What did the Jews do when they remembered their old home? (Psalm 137:1) _____

   They wept.

2. What did the people of Babylon want the Jews to do? (Psalm 137:2–4) _____

   They wanted the Jews to sing one of the songs of Zion.

Lesson 24

Oral Review

1. What were some results of Jehoram's marriage to Athaliah? [17] **Examples: Jehoram did evil as did Ahab's house. Athaliah was Ahaziah's wicked counselor. Athaliah killed most of the royal descendants and reigned wickedly.**

2. What did the Babylonians do to Jerusalem? [21] **They burned it and broke down its walls.**

3. What does the word *remnant* mean? [22] **a small group of people who are left after the rest are destroyed**

4. Why did Daniel refuse to eat the king's meat? [23] **He had purposed in his heart that he would not defile himself.**

5. What did God want Nebuchadnezzar to recognize about the Most High? [23] **"The most High ruleth in the kingdom of men, and giveth it to whomsoever he will."**

6. Who will rule over all people and nations after all earthly kingdoms are overthrown? [23] **Jesus**

7. How long did Jeremiah say the Jews' captivity would last? [23] **seventy years**

8. What are the twelve books of the Minor Prophets? (Be sure you know the correct order and spelling.) [1, 21] **Hosea, Joel, Amos, Obadiah, Jonah,**

Soon after the first Jews arrived in Babylon, some false prophets began telling the captives that they would soon be allowed to return to Judah. But Jeremiah prophesied that the captivity would last seventy years.

3. List at least four things that God told the Jews to do during their long captivity (Jeremiah 29:4–7).

  (Answers may vary slightly.) —build houses —plant gardens —marry and have children

  —seek the peace of their cities of captivity, and pray for them

The Prophet Ezekiel

Ezekiel was one of the captives taken to Babylon with King Jehoiachin eleven years before the destruction of Jerusalem (Ezekiel 40:1). Like Jeremiah, Ezekiel prophesied that God would punish His people for their sins.

The Jews in captivity no longer had a temple where they could offer sacrifices. Their priests and kings could no longer lead them as they had in Jerusalem. But those who desired to follow God could still hear His Word through faithful prophets such as Ezekiel.

The elders of Judah met at Ezekiel's house to hear his prophecies. Ezekiel had to rebuke certain of the elders for their sin, but quite likely some who listened to him sincerely wanted to hear God's Word. Eventually the Jews in exile began meeting in synagogues, where scribes read and explained the Scriptures. By New Testament times, almost every Jewish community had a synagogue.

4. a. Who met at Ezekiel's house to inquire of the Lord? (Ezekiel 14:1) _____

  some of the elders of Israel

  b. What did Ezekiel tell them they needed to do? (Ezekiel 14:6) _____

  to repent and turn from their idols

5. What was Jesus' custom on the Sabbath? (Luke 4:16) _____

  to go to the synagogue.

✎ *Write yes or no. (All references for numbers 6–13 are from Ezekiel.)*

____no____   6. Was Ezekiel still in the land of Judah when God first spoke to him? (1:2, 3)

____yes____   7. Did Ezekiel see any visions? (1:4–28)

____no____   8. Did God tell Ezekiel that the Israelites would obey his message? (3:4–7)

____no____   9. Was Ezekiel glad to see God punish the wicked Jews? (9:8)

____yes____   10. Did Ezekiel know Daniel? (14:12–14)

Ezekiel's Signs

God used the prophets in many different ways. He asked Ezekiel to do some strange things as object lessons to the Israelites.

11. How did Ezekiel show the Jews what would happen to Jerusalem? (4:1–3) _____

  He drew Jerusalem on a tile and then showed how it would be besieged.

12. a. How long did Ezekiel lie on his left side? (4:4, 5) _390 days

  b. How long did he lie on his right side? (4:6) _40 days

Micah, Nahum, Habakkuk, Zephaniah, Haggai, Zechariah, Malachi

In This Lesson

Scope: Selected Scripture passages that refer to the Jewish captivity during the Babylonian and Persian Empires

Main Events
• The Jews in Babylon remember their homeland.
• Jeremiah tells the Jews in Babylon to build houses, plant gardens, and raise families.
• Ezekiel prophesies in Babylon.

• Nebuchadnezzar becomes proud and loses his kingdom for a time. Later the Babylonians are conquered by the Persians.
• God uses King Cyrus to help the Jews return to their homeland.

Objectives
• The students should know
  —that God did not plan to destroy the people of Judah completely, but rather to teach them a lesson they would never forget.
  —that Ezekiel prophesied in Babylon while Jeremiah prophesied in Judah.

158   Chapter Five   Judah Taken Captive

13. a. What did Ezekiel do with his hair? (5:1–4)   <u>He cut it off, burned one-third of it, smote one-third</u>
     <u>of it with a knife, and scattered one-third of it in the wind.</u>

   b. What did his hair represent? (5:5)   <u>Jerusalem (the people of Jerusalem)</u>

   c. What did this sign mean? (5:12)   _____
      <u>A third of the people would die with the pestilence and famine, a third would be killed with the</u>
      <u>sword, and a third would be scattered.</u>

The Babylonian Empire

Nebuchadnezzar made the city of Babylon very beautiful. His wife had come from the cool mountains of Media (modern-day Iran). She became homesick in the hot lowlands of Babylon, so Nebuchadnezzar built "hanging gardens" for her, which looked like hills. Nebuchadnezzar was very proud of the city he had built. This chart shows the main events that affected both Babylon and Judah.

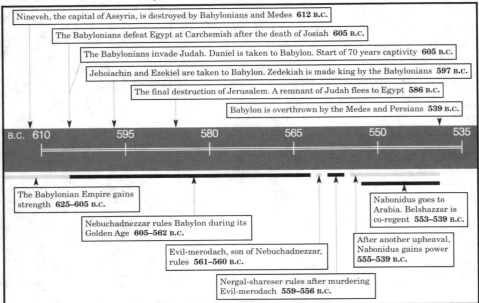

No questions are asked specifically about the timeline of the Babylonian Empire because the lesson seems long enough. However, you may want to use it to give the students a quick overview of the empire's history. Notice especially that it appears that God allowed the Babylonians to prosper specifically for the period that He used them to punish His people. The Assyrians were not a suitable instrument for this, because of their policies for dealing with captive populations. While the Babylonians also deported the population of Judah (as a last resort, it appears), they allowed them to keep their Jewish identity. When God was ready for His people to return home, He removed the Babylonians and placed His people in the hands of the Persians, who allowed them to return to the Promised Land.

14. What did Nebuchadnezzar say about Babylon? (Daniel 4:30)   _____
    <u>"Is not this great Babylon, that I have built?"</u>

15. How did God punish Nebuchadnezzar for his pride? (Daniel 4:31, 32)   _____
    <u>God took his kingdom away and made him live like an animal.</u>

As you can see from the time line above, Babylon's glory was short-lived. After Nebuchadnezzar's death, the throne passed from one man to another. Nebuchadnezzar's son Evil-merodach reigned briefly. Another man overthrew him and took the throne, but soon more fighting broke out. Eventually Nabonidus (possibly Nebuchadnezzar's son-in-law) came to the throne.

—that God works in the kingdoms of men. This is seen in the destruction of Babylon by a king who was very tolerant of other religious beliefs and who allowed the Jews to return to their homeland.

Truths to Instill

• The wages of sin are never pleasant. The Jews in captivity needed to learn a hard lesson about idol worship. While they still may not have had a proper worship of God (see Ezra, Nehemiah, and Malachi), the Jews as a whole did not worship idols after their captivity. But how much better it would have been for them had they obeyed God's commandments!

• "The most High ruleth in the kingdom of men" (Daniel 4:17). God used the Babylonians to punish the Jews, but when the seventy years of captivity were ended, He used Cyrus the Persian to send His people back home. Isaiah 45:1–13 is an amazing prophecy of what God would do through King Cyrus.

King Nabonidus thought the Babylonians should worship the god of his hometown. The Babylonians did not want to worship a different god, and King Nabonidus became very unpopular. He traveled into Arabia and lived there, leaving his son Belshazzar to rule for him in Babylon. The Babylonian Empire lasted only about ninety years—just long enough for God to use them to punish Judah for their sin.

16. What did Evil-merodach do after Jehoiachin had been in captivity for thirty-seven years? (2 Kings 25:27–30)   He took Jehoiachin out of prison, spoke kindly to him, set him on a throne, changed his prison garments, and gave him food every day.

17. What happened to Belshazzar? (Daniel 5:30)   He was killed (by the Medes and Persians).

18. Who took over the Babylonian kingdom that night? (Daniel 5:31)   Darius the Mede

The Medo-Persian Empire

About 559 B.C. a Persian ruler named Cyrus gained control over Babylon's neighbors, the Medes. With the Medes' help, Cyrus swiftly conquered other nations. In 539 B.C. one of his generals (perhaps Darius the Mede) took Babylon without a fight the same night Belshazzar saw the handwriting on the wall.

The Bible and other history sources are not clear on the relationship between Darius the Mede and Cyrus the Persian. Darius may have been appointed governor of the province of Babylon by King Cyrus. Whatever the case, we know that Cyrus the Persian was the most powerful ruler in the Medo-Persian Empire at this time.

King Cyrus treated the Babylonians differently than Nabonidus had done. He restored the worship of the Babylonian god and treated the people kindly. He was tolerant toward other conquered people as well, allowing them to keep their own customs and to worship their own gods. Perhaps he sensed that beyond his own religion and his own god there was a God he had not yet come to know.

19. How did the LORD use King Cyrus to help the Jews? (Ezra 1:1–3)   The LORD stirred him to make a decree that allowed the Jews to rebuild the temple at Jerusalem.

20. What had God spoken about Cyrus more than a hundred years before? (Isaiah 44:28)   "He is my shepherd, and shall perform all my pleasure: even saying to Jerusalem, Thou shalt be built; and to the temple, Thy foundation shall be laid."

King Cyrus and a later king, Darius the Persian, built up a vast empire. They reigned over many nations from India to southern Europe and northern Africa. The Persian kings spent much of their time in their capital cities of Shushan and Babylon. During the summer they moved to the cool mountain city of Ecbatana (also called Achmetha) in Media. Later they built the beautiful, costly city of Persepolis.

21. Ahasuerus (probably the king called Xerxes I by Greek historians) was a king of the Persian Empire. In his days, the Persian Empire stretched from _____ India _____ to _____ Ethiopia _____ (Esther 1:1).

22. In which city was Ahasuerus when the Bible speaks of him? (Esther 1:2)   Shushan

23. According to Ezra 6:2, what was kept in Achmetha?   a roll (scroll) with a record of Cyrus's decree

24. What Jew was a personal servant of King Artaxerxes of Persia? (Nehemiah 2:1–3)   Nehemiah

- Since most Biblical events after the fall of Jerusalem are dated by heathen kings, the chronology of this period must be based largely on secular history. By using the Scriptures, inscriptions from clay tablets and from monuments, and the writings of early Greek historians, a general history of the Babylonian and Persian Empires can be pieced together. Some questions remain, however. For example, Darius the Mede (Daniel 5:31) is not specifically mentioned in secular sources. (Many Bible scholars believe he is the same as Gobryas, governor of Babylon.)

The Bible does not claim to be a thorough world history book, but the history it does give is accurate, even when our understanding of those historical facts is imperfect. When modern man discredits the Scriptures, we must "let God be true, but every man a liar" (Romans 3:4).

160   Chapter Five   Judah Taken Captive

B. BIBLE WORD STUDY

✎ *Match these definitions with the Bible words on the right.*

____f____ 1. An official public announcement (Ezra 1:1)

____b____ 2. To give a duty or responsibility to someone (Ezra 1:2)

____h____ 3. A scroll; a piece of parchment or other writing material that may be rolled up (Ezra 6:2)

____d____ 4. Happiness; gladness; joy (Psalm 137:3)

____c____ 5. To become smaller or less (Jeremiah 29:6)

____a____ 6. An instrument used for weighing (Ezekiel 5:1)

____e____ 7. A disease that brings much suffering and death (Ezekiel 5:12)

____g____ 8. A remnant; remainder (Ezekiel 9:8)

____i____ 9. A Jewish place of worship (Luke 4:16)

a. balance

b. charge

c. diminish

d. mirth

e. pestilence

f. proclamation

g. residue

h. roll

i. synagogue

C. THINKING ABOUT BIBLE TRUTHS

God Controls History

God is in control of the events that make up history. The last several lessons have shown again how God sometimes uses sinful people to accomplish His plans. God's ability to control the events of history also makes it possible for Him to tell us about events before they happen.

1. Moses and other men had prophesied that the LORD would send the Israelites into captivity if they turned away from Him.

   a. How did Moses say the Israelites would feel in captivity? (Deuteronomy 28:65–67) _____

   They would fear and wish things were different.

   b. What did Solomon say the Israelites should do if they were taken captive? (2 Chronicles 6:37, 38)

   They should confess their sin and pray (toward the temple at Jerusalem).

2. Why might the Jews who lived in foreign lands have felt more need to meet in synagogues than the Jews who had lived in Judah and worshiped at Jerusalem? (Read Hosea 3:4 and think about what the Jews in captivity did not have.) _____

   The Jews in captivity no longer had their own leaders or their old forms of worship.

3. In one of Daniel's visions, the Medes and Persians were compared to a ram with two horns. The first horn to grow up represented the Medes, who became strong first. But Daniel's vision foretold that when the Persians (the second horn) gained power, they would become even stronger than the Medes. Copy the part of Daniel 8:3 that foretold that the Persians would be greater than the Medes. _____

   "One was higher than the other, and the higher came up last."

4. What did the ram in Daniel's vision do to the other beasts (kingdoms) of the world? (Daniel 8:4) ____

   He pushed them down and ruled over them according to his will.

D. LEARNING MORE ABOUT THE BIBLE

Babylonia and Persia: A New Home for the Jews

When the Jews were taken into captivity by the Babylonians, they left the hills and small towns of Judah behind them. They traveled eastward into what was then one of the most densely populated areas of the world. There they saw some of the world's largest cities. They also saw some of the world's most fertile farmland lying flat and green in the hot sunlight.

✎ *Write the names of these cities on the blanks below: Babylon, Achmetha, Nineveh, Persepolis, and Shushan. Use the clues and references given if you need help.*

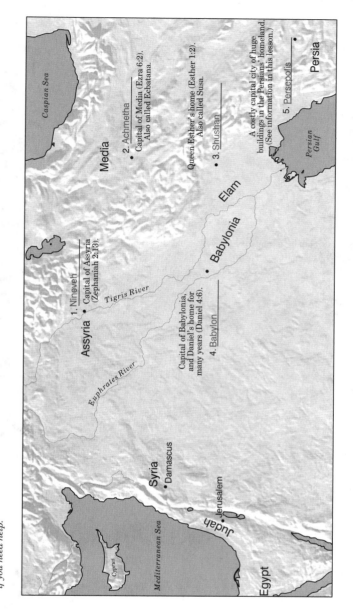

Map labels:

1. Nineveh — Capital of Assyria (Zephaniah 2:13).
2. Achmetha — Capital of Media (Ezra 6:2). Also called Ecbatana.
3. Shushan — Queen Esther's home (Esther 1:2). Also called Susa.
4. Babylon — Capital of Babylonia, and Daniel's home for many years (Daniel 4-6).
5. Persepolis — A costly capital city of huge buildings in the Persians' homeland. (See information in this lesson.)

Other labels: Caspian Sea, Media, Assyria, Tigris River, Euphrates River, Elam, Babylonia, Persia, Persian Gulf, Syria, Damascus, Jerusalem, Judah, Egypt, Mediterranean Sea, Cyprus

162

Chapter Five Review

A. ORAL REVIEW

✎ *Be sure you know the answers to these questions. Answer as many as you can from memory. If you need help, you may check the reference or lesson given in brackets.*

Why >>

1. Why could Jeremiah have hope for his people even after they were taken captive? [Lamentations 3:21–25]
2. Why did Daniel refuse to eat the king's meat? [Daniel 1:8]
3. Why did the princes want Daniel thrown to the lions? [Daniel 6:3]
4. Why did the Jews in Babylon sit and weep? [Psalm 137:1]

How >>

5. How long did Jehoahaz reign over Judah? [2 Kings 23:31]
6. How did God fulfill His promise that David's kingdom would be established forever? [Luke 1:30–33]
7. How long did Jeremiah say the Jews' captivity would last? [Jeremiah 29:10]
8. How many earthly empires did the image in Nebuchadnezzar's vision represent? [Daniel 2:38–40]
9. How did Ezekiel use his hair as a sign? [Ezekiel 5:1, 2]
10. How did the LORD use King Cyrus to help the Jews? [Ezra 1:1–3]

Who >>

11. Who removed Jehoahaz from his throne and made Jehoiakim king? [2 Kings 23:34]
12. Whom did Nebuchadnezzar take captive in the third year of Jehoiakim's reign? [Daniel 1:1–6]
13. Who were the last four kings of Judah? [Lesson 21]
14. Who wrote the words God gave to Jeremiah? [Jeremiah 36:4]
15. Who rescued Jeremiah from a dungeon? [Jeremiah 38:7–10]
16. Who will rule over all people and nations after all earthly kingdoms are overthrown? [Daniel 7:13, 14; Revelation 11:15]

Where >>

17. Where did God write a message for King Belshazzar? [Daniel 5:5]
18. Where did Ezekiel prophesy, in Judah or in Babylon? [Ezekiel 1:3]

1. The LORD is merciful; He is faithful, even when His people fail; He is good to them who wait for Him and seek Him.
2. He had purposed in his heart that he would not defile himself.
3. They were jealous of his high position.
4. They remembered Zion, their old home.
5. three months
6. Jesus, who will reign forever, was born into David's family.
7. seventy years
8. four
9. He cut it off, burned one-third, smote one-third with a knife, and scattered the other third; then he told the Jews that they would likewise be destroyed and scattered.
10. The LORD stirred him to make a decree allowing the Jews to rebuild the temple.
11. Pharaoh Necho
12. some of the king's children and princes, including Daniel and his three friends
13. Jehoahaz, Jehoiakim, Jehoiachin, and Zedekiah
14. Baruch
15. Ebed-melech and thirty other men
16. Jesus
17. on the wall of his palace
18. in Babylon

Chapter Five Review

This review is divided into two parts, an oral review and a written review. The oral review is intended for class discussion, but students could also use it for self-study.

B. WRITTEN REVIEW

✎ *Write the answers to these questions. Do as many as you can from memory. If you need help, you may check the reference or lesson given in brackets.*

What

1. What did the Babylonians do to Jerusalem? [Jeremiah 39:8] _____

   They burned it and broke down its walls.

2. What was used in Bible times to make a personal mark in soft clay? [Lesson 21]   a signet

3. What three things did God say Jeremiah would be as strong as? [Jeremiah 1:18] _____

   a defensed city, an iron pillar, and brazen walls

4. What encouraging promise did God give to Jeremiah when He called him? [Jeremiah 1:19] _____

   "I am with thee . . . to deliver thee."

5. What did Jeremiah do when God's people refused to repent? [Jeremiah 13:17] _____

   He wept.

6. What message did Jeremiah give to the remnant of the Jews when they wanted to go to Egypt?

   [Jeremiah 42:19]   "Go ye not into Egypt."

7. What does the word *remnant* mean? [Lesson 22] _____

   a small group of people who are left after the rest are destroyed

8. What did God want Nebuchadnezzar to recognize about the Most High? [Daniel 4:32] _____

   "The most High ruleth in the kingdom of men, and giveth it to whomsoever he will."

9. What was represented by the ram with two horns in Daniel's vision? [Daniel 8:20] _____

   the empire (kings) of Media and Persia

10. What did the Jews call the places of worship where they began meeting during the captivity? [Lesson 24]

    synagogues

11. What are the twelve Minor Prophets? (Be sure to use the correct order and spelling.) [Lessons 1, 21]

Hosea	Jonah	Zephaniah
Joel	Micah	Haggai
Amos	Nahum	Zechariah
Obadiah	Habakkuk	Malachi

Which

12. Which king of Judah was led captive to Babylon after reigning three months? [2 Kings 24:8, 12]

    Jehoiachin

164 Chapter Five Judah Taken Captive

13. Which king of Judah broke a covenant he had made with Nebuchadnezzar? [2 Chronicles 36:11–13]

_____ Zedekiah _____

14. Which king burned Jeremiah's scroll? [Jeremiah 36:9, 21–23] _____ Jehoiakim _____

15. Which prophet told the Jews in Babylon to build houses, plant gardens, raise families, and seek the peace of Babylon? [Jeremiah 29:5–7] _____ Jeremiah _____

16. Which king of Judah was released from prison by Evil-merodach? [2 Kings 25:27] _____ Jehoiachin _____

Where Is It Found?

_h_ 17. 2 Chronicles 36   a. Daniel and his friends are taken to Babylon.

_d_ 18. Jeremiah 1   b. Jeremiah is thrown into a dungeon.

_g_ 19. Jeremiah 36   c. God calls Ezekiel and shows him a vision of His glory.

_b_ 20. Jeremiah 38   d. God calls Jeremiah.

_c_ 21. Ezekiel 1   e. Daniel is saved from the hungry lions.

_f_ 22. Ezekiel 4, 5   f. Ezekiel uses signs to teach the Jews in Babylon.

_a_ 23. Daniel 1   g. Baruch writes the words of Jeremiah, but the king burns the scroll.

_i_ 24. Daniel 2, 4, 5   h. The last four kings of Judah reign; Nebuchadnezzar takes captives and destroys Jerusalem.

_e_ 25. Daniel 6   i. Daniel interprets dreams and visions.

Map Review

✎ *Fill in each blank on the map with the correct name from the list.*

Achmetha	Damascus	Nineveh	Euphrates River
Babylon	Jerusalem	Shushan	Tigris River

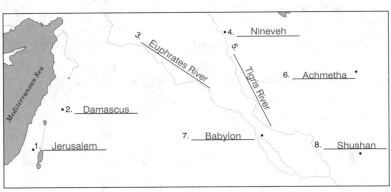

165

Lesson 25. Making a Living

Soon after Adam and Eve were driven from the Garden of Eden, their descendants began making their living in a variety of ways. Cain tilled the land, Abel herded sheep, Jabal raised cattle, and Tubal-cain worked with metal (Genesis 4). After the Flood, Noah planted a vineyard and became a husbandman (Genesis 9:20).

Abraham, Isaac, and Jacob were shepherds. Jacob and his sons took their herds with them when they moved to Egypt. After Joshua led the Israelites into Canaan, most of them raised sheep and cattle or farmed their land. Some who lived near the sea were fishermen, and a few worked in other trades.

Many Israelites learned carpentry, stonecutting, or masonry when Solomon built the temple and his palace. Solomon also needed sailors and merchants for his trade with other nations.

The Jews in captivity became less and less dependent on farming or herding. Many lived in cities and learned other trades. A few, such as Daniel and Nehemiah, worked for the king. As the Jews scattered to many countries of the world, they became known as craftsmen, merchants, and businessmen.

A. ANSWERS FROM THE BIBLE

Shepherds

The first Israelites were wandering shepherds. They led their flocks from pasture to pasture and from water hole to water hole. Because they lived in tents, they could take their wives and children with them wherever they went.

1. How did the Egyptians, who were farmers, feel about the Hebrews, who were shepherds? (Genesis 46:34)
   Shepherds were an abomination to the Egyptians.

Wild animals and robbers sometimes threatened the flocks.

2. What wild animals did David kill while caring for his father's sheep? (1 Samuel 17:34–36)
   a lion and a bear

3. What did Jesus say a good shepherd will do for his sheep? (John 10:11)
   A good shepherd will give his life for the sheep.

Shepherds often herded both sheep and goats. Certain differences set sheep and goats apart. Goats like to eat bushes and leaves; sheep prefer grass. Goats thrive in the hills; sheep thrive in lowland plains. Goats take risks and are aggressive; sheep are timid.

4. What did Jesus teach with a parable about separating sheep from goats? (Matthew 25:31–33)
   At the end of the world, Jesus will separate the righteous from the wicked as a shepherd divides
   his sheep from the goats.

Life in Bible Times

Lesson 25

Oral Review
1. What term was used to describe animals that the Israelites were forbidden to eat? [20] **unclean**
2. Which king of Judah was led captive to Babylon after reigning only three months? [21] **Jehoiachin**
3. What encouraging promise did God give to Jeremiah when He called him? [22] **"I am with thee . . . to deliver thee."**
4. How many earthly empires did the image in Nebuchadnezzar's vision represent? [23] **four**
5. What language besides Hebrew did Daniel use to write his book? [23] **Aramaic (Syriac)**
6. Who met at Ezekiel's house to inquire of the LORD? [24] **certain of the elders of Israel**
7. How did the LORD use King Cyrus to help the Jews? [24] **The LORD stirred him to make a decree allowing the Jews to rebuild the temple.**
8. What did the Jews call the places of worship where they began meeting during the captivity? [24] **synagogues**

166   Chapter Five   Judah Taken Captive

Sheep and goats served the Israelites in many ways. Meat, milk, and dairy products enriched the Israelites' diet. Leather and wool provided material for clothing. Sackcloth made from goats' hair covered their tents. Entire goatskins were sewed shut and used as containers for liquids.

5. What would a man have for taking good care of his flocks? (Proverbs 27:23–27) _____

   The lambs provided clothing (wool); the goats paid for the price of a field; goats' milk provided

   food for the household and maidens.

6. What event in the shepherd's work was a cause for celebrating? (2 Samuel 13:23, 24)

   sheepshearing

The Shepherd's Equipment

The shepherds of Bible times did not need much equipment.

7. The *sling* was a little pouch with two long cords attached. The shepherd swung it around and around, and then let go of one cord to send a stone flying toward a target. How skilled were seven hundred Benjamite with their slings? (Judges 20:16) _____

   They could sling stones and hit a target within a hair's

   breadth.

8. The *rod* was a wooden club used to control sheep or fight enemies. Some rods had stone or iron teeth. What shepherd was carrying a rod when the LORD appeared to him? (Exodus 4:1, 2)

   Moses

9. Shepherds carried their lunch and other small items in a *bag* (scrip) fastened to their belts. What did David put into his bag? (1 Samuel 17:40) ___

   five smooth stones

10. The shepherd's *staff* was a long stick, sometimes with a crook at one end. Shepherds used it to guide their sheep. What did David say God's rod and staff did for him? (Psalm 23:4) _____

    They comforted him.

Life in Bible Times

In This Lesson

Main Points
- People of Bible times made their living in a variety of ways.
- The early Israelites were shepherds. Many Israelites continued to raise sheep throughout Bible times.
- Good shepherds are willing to give their lives for their sheep.
- The 3,000-year-old Gezer calendar, found in modern times, tells when farmers planted and harvested their crops.
- Other occupations of Bible times included fishing, trading, and working at various skills.
- God expects us to labor in useful occupations to provide for our own needs and the needs of others.

Objectives
- The students should know
  —some of the main occupations of Bible times. (raising sheep and cattle, farming, and fishing)
  —that the Jews thought of the months in terms of planting and harvesting.
  —why God wants us to work. (to supply our own needs, and to have enough to give to others who are in need)

Farmers and the Gezer Calendar

In Old Testament times, the city of Gezer lay between Jerusalem and Joppa. About three thousand years ago, a schoolboy of Gezer wrote an exercise on a clay tablet. This tablet, discovered in modern times, tells how people farmed in Israel long ago.

Suggested extra activity. Have students use Bible dictionaries to learn more about the Hebrew calendar. Find information on the names of months, the observance of "moons," feasts and holy days, etc. Note that both a religious year (beginning in the spring) and a civil year (beginning in the fall) were used.

Speaking of the farmer, the Gezer calendar says:

His two months are (olive) harvest. ....(September/October)
His two months are wheat planting. ....(November/December)
His two months are (late) planting...(January/February)
His month is hoeing up of flax. ....(March)
His month is barley harvest. ....(April)
His month is wheat harvest and festivity.....................................(May)
His two months are vine tending. ....(June/July)
His month is summer fruit (figs, grapes, pomegranates, walnuts, and so forth)....(August)

The names of the months in parentheses are approximate. The Hebrew months did not match ours exactly.

✎ *Using the schoolboy's calendar as your guide, decide approximately which month of our year each event given below took place.*

11. The spies return to Moses (Numbers 13:23).
    August

13. Samuel calls for thunder and rain (1 Samuel 12:17).
    May

12. Ruth and Naomi arrive at Bethlehem (Ruth 1:22).
    April

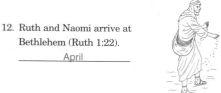

14. A man sows seeds in his field (Matthew 13:24, 25).
    November or December
    (January or February)

Point out that the months are approximate. Harvest was probably later in the highlands than at Gezer. Also, since Hebrew months were based on lunar cycles, the months varied slightly from year to year in relation to the seasons, just as Easter does on our calendar. The Jews added a thirteenth month about once every three years to keep the months in their proper seasons.

Life in Bible Times

Truths to Instill
- Jesus is the Good Shepherd, who gave His life for the sheep. He is also the Lamb of God, who takes away the sin of the world.
- At the end of the world, Jesus will separate the righteous from the wicked as a shepherd divides his sheep from the goats.
- God commands us to labor in useful occupations so that we can share with those in need (Ephesians 4:28).

168 Chapter Five Judah Taken Captive

B. BIBLE STUDY BOOKS

More Trades of Bible Times

✎ *Use a concordance to find a verse that mentions each worker by trade in the Bible book that is given. If the trade is mentioned more than once in the book, give the first reference. (In some cases, you will need to look up a slightly different form of the word.)*

1. Apothecary (2 Chronicles __16__ : __14__)
2. Baker (Jeremiah __37__ : __21__)
3. Carpenter (Mark __6__ : __3__)
4. Fisherman (Luke __5__ : __2__)
5. Fuller (Mark __9__ : __3__)
6. Mason (2 Chronicles __24__ : __12__)
7. Merchant (Matthew __13__ : __45__)
8. Potter (Romans __9__ : __21__)
9. Smith (1 Samuel __13__ : __19__)
10. Tanner (Acts __9__ : __43__)
11. Tentmaker (Acts __18__ : __3__)
12. Weaver (Job __7__ : __6__)

✎ *Use a Bible dictionary to learn more about the people in these trades. Describe each one briefly.*

13. Apothecary _____
    A person who prepared ointments, anointing oil, incense, and perfumes. These were used in religious ceremonies, for burials, or for personal use.

14. Fuller _____
    A person who washed and bleached clothes

15. Smith _____
    A person who worked with metal. Smiths made items of gold, silver, copper and bronze (brass), and iron.

16. Tanner _____
    A person who prepared animal skins for use by treating them with salt, lime, and the juices of certain plants

God notices not only what kind of work we do, but also how we work and why we work.

✎ *Use a concordance to find and complete this verse and reference. Then answer the questions in exercise 18.*

17. "Let him that stole steal no more: _____
    "but rather let him labour, working with his hands the thing which is good, that he may have to give to him that needeth" " (Ephesians __4__ : __28__).

18. a. What phrase in the verse you copied above tells what type of work we should do? _____
    "the thing which is good"

    b. Why should we work, even if we already have enough for our own needs? _____
    so that we have enough to give to those in need

Life in Bible Times

CHAPTER SIX

The Jews After the Captivity

Blessed are the undefiled in the way, who walk in the law of the LORD. Blessed are they that keep his testimonies, and that seek him with the whole heart.

Psalm 119:1, 2

TIME LINE—Chapter Six

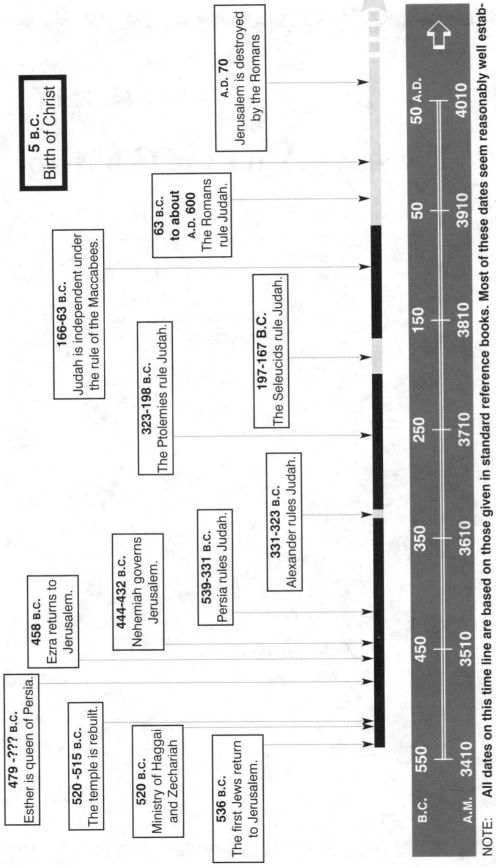

479 -??? B.C.
Esther is queen of Persia.

458 B.C.
Ezra returns to Jerusalem.

520 -515 B.C.
The temple is rebuilt.

444-432 B.C.
Nehemiah governs Jerusalem.

520 B.C.
Ministry of Haggai and Zechariah

539-331 B.C.
Persia rules Judah.

536 B.C.
The first Jews return to Jerusalem.

331-323 B.C.
Alexander rules Judah.

323-198 B.C.
The Ptolemies rule Judah.

166-63 B.C.
Judah is independent under the rule of the Maccabees.

197-167 B.C.
The Seleucids rule Judah.

63 B.C. to about A.D. 600
The Romans rule Judah.

5 B.C.
Birth of Christ

A.D. 70
Jerusalem is destroyed by the Romans

B.C.	550	450	350	250	150	50	50 A.D.
A.M.	3410	3510	3610	3710	3810	3910	4010

NOTE: All dates on this time line are based on those given in standard reference books. Most of these dates seem reasonably well established to within a year or two, but a few scholars have questioned the dates for the Persian period.

171

Lesson 26. The Jews Return Home

The Jews lived in captivity for many years. By the time of Belshazzar, king of Babylon, most of the original captives had died. Their children had settled down to a new life in Babylon and the surrounding lands. But some Jews still remembered God's promise to bring them back to Judah. Even though that seemed impossible, they clung to their hope of someday living in the land of their fathers.

Then suddenly events changed. The Babylonians, who had conquered the Jews, were conquered themselves by the Medes and Persians. In the first year of his reign, Cyrus, king of Persia, decreed that the Jews could return to Judah and rebuild the temple.

Zerubbabel and Jeshua were among the first to leave for their homeland. With them traveled a large company of Jews. Up the Euphrates River valley they traveled, leaving the flat, green lowlands of Babylonia behind them. Hundreds of miles further they turned south and passed the ancient city of Damascus, snow-crowned Mount Hermon, and the Sea of Galilee. They had a long journey back to Judah.

Many years later, Ezra and Nehemiah also traveled to Jerusalem. When Ezra arrived, he offered sacrifices to God. He fell down on his knees and wept for the sins of his people. He prayed, and the people followed his example. Hundreds of men and women changed their ways. They confessed their sins and put away their heathen wives and children. Nehemiah also helped the people return to God's Word. Such a return is called a revival.

God's people have needed many revivals. God uses faithful people, such as Ezra and Nehemiah, to revive what Satan has destroyed.

- The Bible dates events after the captivity by the reigns of heathen kings. The dates given in this chapter are based on the commonly accepted chronology for this period. Although exact dates are difficult to prove, this chronology provides a general framework for the sequence of these Biblical events.

A. ANSWERS FROM THE BIBLE

The Jews Return to Jerusalem

The Babylonians remained in power for seventy years after Daniel was taken captive. Then the LORD gave the Babylonian Empire into the hands of Cyrus, king of Persia. The LORD had foretold how He would use Cyrus: "He is my shepherd, and shall perform all my pleasure: even saying to Jerusalem, Thou shalt be built; and to the temple, Thy foundation shall be laid" (Isaiah 44:28).

Ezra 1

The Bible tells us that "the LORD stirred up the spirit of Cyrus king of Persia" to make a proclamation allowing the Jews to return to their homeland and build a temple there (Ezra 1:1, 3). God is able to direct a king's thoughts and to cause His will to be performed. "The king's heart is in the hand of the LORD, as the rivers of water: he turneth it whithersoever he will" (Proverbs 21:1).

1. King Cyrus asked for Jews who were willing
   a. to remain at Babylon and serve in his kingdom.
   (b.) to move to Judah and help build the temple.
   c. to help drive the rest of the Jews back to Jerusalem.

2. Cyrus told the Jews who wanted to remain at Babylon
   a. to build another temple of the LORD in Babylon.
   b. to sell their properties and move to Jerusalem immediately.
   (c.) to give gold, silver, and other goods to help build the temple.

Lesson 26

Oral Review

(The numbers in brackets tell which lessons are being reviewed.)

1. Why is David's family line important to us today? [3] **Jesus came through David's line.**
2. Which king of Judah caused his people to do worse than the heathen? [19] **Manasseh**
3. Who were the last four kings of Judah? [21] **Jehoahaz, Jehoiakim, Jehoiachin, and Zedekiah**
4. What did the Babylonians do to Jerusalem? [21] **They burned it and broke down its walls.**
5. How long did Jeremiah say the Jews' captivity would last? [23] **seventy years**
6. Why could Jeremiah have hope for his people even after they were taken captive? [22] **The LORD is merciful and good to those who seek Him.**
7. How did the LORD use King Cyrus to help the Jews? [24] **The LORD stirred him to make a decree allowing the Jews to rebuild the temple.**
8. What four tools did shepherds carry with them? [25] **a sling, a rod, a staff, and a shepherd's bag**

172 Chapter Six The Jews After the Captivity

Cyrus brought out the vessels that Nebuchadnezzar had taken from the temple and sent them back to Jerusalem with the Jews.

The leaders of the Jews were Zerubbabel, whom Cyrus appointed governor, and Jeshua the priest. *Sheshbazzar* (Ezra 1:8, 11; 5:14, 16) might have been another name for Zerubbabel. If not, Sheshbazzar was an additional leader. Zerubbabel was a descendant of David. He likely would have been heir to the throne of Judah if Cyrus had allowed the Israelites to have their own king. He is mentioned as an ancestor of Jesus in Matthew 1:12 and Luke 3:27.

The group that returned to Jerusalem with Zerubbabel and Jeshua included 42,360 Jews and 7,337 servants.

The Jews Rebuild the Temple

Ezra 3:10–13

When the Jews returned to Jerusalem, one of the first things they did was to set up an altar so that they could start offering the regular sacrifices again. They also kept the Feast of Tabernacles at this time. In the second year after they returned, they laid the foundation for a new temple to replace Solomon's temple, which the Babylonians had destroyed.

3. Why did the old men weep while the younger Jews were shouting for joy? (See also Haggai 2:3.) ____

   The old men had seen the first temple, which had been much greater than the second one they

   were building.

4. What did the enemies of Judah do when Zerubbabel refused to allow them to help build the temple?

   (Ezra 4:1–4) _____

   They weakened the hands of the Jews and troubled them.

The Jews' enemies caused so much trouble that the Jews became discouraged and stopped working on the temple for a number of years.

5. Who encouraged the Jews to begin building the temple again? (Ezra 5:1, 2) _____

   the prophets Haggai and Zechariah

6. In which year did the Jews finish building the temple? (Ezra 6:15) _____

   in the sixth year of Darius's reign

Note: The Darius mentioned in Ezra 6:15 is not Darius the Mede, who had Daniel thrown to the lions. The Darius in this verse is known as Darius the Great, who ruled over the Persian Empire from about 522–486 B.C.

Ezra Helps Bring Revival

Some of the Jews who remained in the lands of their captivity came into the special favor of the Persian kings. During this time King Ahasuerus chose Esther for his queen. About eighty years after the first Jews had returned to Judah, King Artaxerxes appointed Ezra to lead more Jews back to Jerusalem. The king told Ezra to establish worship according to the laws of the God of heaven.

7. In the seventh year of King Artaxerxes, Ezra the scribe gathered 1,754 men beside the Ahava River

   to fast and pray for safety on their journey to Jerusalem. Why was Ezra ashamed to ask the king for

   soldiers to protect them as they traveled? (Ezra 8:22) _____

   Ezra had told the king that God helps all those who seek Him.

In This Lesson

Scope: The books of Ezra and Nehemiah

Main Events
- Cyrus allows the Jews to return to Judah.
- Zerubbabel and Jeshua lead the first group of returning Jews and begin building the temple.
- After a time of discouragement, Haggai and Zechariah encourage the Jews to finish building the temple.
- Ezra travels to Judah with another group of returning exiles. He helps correct ungodly practices.
- Nehemiah hears that the walls of Jerusalem are still in ruins and receives permission from the king to rebuild them. While he is there, he helps to restore righteous practices among the Jews.

Objectives
- Students should know
  —how Cyrus helped the Jews. (He allowed the Jews to return to Judah and gave them the vessels Nebuchadnezzar had taken from the temple.)
  —who led the first group of Jews back to Jerusalem. (Zerubbabel and Jeshua)

8. What did Ezra's group take with them that made them especially concerned about the danger of robbers? (Ezra 8:24–29) _____

 <u>Ezra's group took back large amounts of gold, silver, and costly goods.</u>

9. The Jews arrived at Jerusalem safely because _____<u>God</u>_____ was with them, and He delivered them from their _____<u>enemies</u>_____ (Ezra 8:31).

At Jerusalem, Ezra and the Jews weighed the silver, the gold, and the vessels that they had brought. All the goods had arrived safely. Then they offered sacrifices to God. But Ezra soon discovered that not everything in Judah was as it should have been.

✎ *Write* true *or* false. *Correct each false statement on the lines after the sentence.*

Ezra 9:1–6

____<u>true</u>____ 10. The princes told Ezra that many Jews had married ungodly women. _____

_____

____<u>true</u>____ 11. What Ezra heard made him tear his clothes and pull out hair from his head and beard.

_____

____<u>false</u>____ 12. Ezra was very angry and commanded that the sinners be stoned. _____

 <u>Ezra *was astonished and prayed to God.*</u>

Ezra 10:10–12

Ezra sent out a message to all Judah, telling everyone to come to Jerusalem within three days. Even though it was a season of heavy rains, all the people gathered near the temple.

13. Ezra told the people to make _____<u>confession</u>_____ to the LORD and to separate themselves from the _____<u>people</u>_____ of the land and from their strange _____<u>wives</u>_____.

14. The people replied, " <u>As thou hast said, so must we do.</u> _____"

Nehemiah Restores the Walls of Jerusalem

Nehemiah was the king's cupbearer. About thirteen years after Ezra traveled to Jerusalem, Nehemiah heard that the walls of Jerusalem still lay in ruins.

✎ *Answer the questions or fill in the blanks. All references are from the Book of Nehemiah.*

15. Why was Nehemiah sad? (2:2, 3) _____

 <u>He had heard that Jerusalem lay in ruins.</u>

At Nehemiah's request, King Artaxerxes sent him to Jerusalem to rebuild the walls and to serve as governor. One night soon after he arrived, he went out to view the ruined walls. Then he set the Jews to work rebuilding them.

16. The walls were built rapidly because the people had a _____<u>mind</u>_____ to _____<u>work</u>_____ (4:6).

17. The walls were finished in ___<u>fifty-two</u>___ days (6:15).

In the rewritten sentence for number 12, the correction is in italics. The pupil's sentence may vary somewhat.

—why the old men wept when they saw the temple foundation. (They had seen the first temple, which had been much greater than the second one they were building.)

—which two prophets encouraged the Jews to finish building the temple. (Haggai and Zechariah)

—why Ezra did not ask the king for soldiers for protection. (Ezra had told the king that God helps all those who seek Him.)

—how Ezra responded when he heard of the Jews' sin. (See Part A, numbers 11–13.)

—who led the Jews in rebuilding the walls of Jerusalem. (Nehemiah)

—how Nehemiah overcame the opposition of his enemies. (See Part A, numbers 18–22.)

—what feast the Jews kept after Ezra read the Law. (the Feast of Booths, also called the Feast of Tabernacles)

—the meanings of *freewill offering* and *mingle*. (*freewill offering:* a gift given voluntarily; *mingle:* mix with)

174 Chapter Six   The Jews After the Captivity

Nehemiah Overcomes Opposition

The Jews' enemies were grieved when Nehemiah arrived. They wanted the Jews to remain weak and unprotected. Time after time they tried to stop the building of the wall and to hinder Nehemiah.

Even some of the Jews did not support Nehemiah. Twelve years after he first came to Jerusalem, Nehemiah returned to King Artaxerxes and gave a report of his work. He returned to Jerusalem to find more trouble. The Jews had begun marrying heathen wives again, and a priest had allowed Tobiah, one of Nehemiah's enemies, to live in a room in the temple. But Nehemiah met every challenge, and with God's help he overcame his enemies.

✎ *Match Nehemiah's actions with the challenges he faced.*

__d__ 18. Sanballat and Tobiah mock the wall builders (4:1–6).

__b__ 19. Sanballat and Tobiah plan to attack the builders (4:7–15).

__a__ 20. A priest prepares a chamber in the temple for Tobiah (13:4–9).

__e__ 21. Merchants sell goods in Jerusalem on the Sabbath (13:15–22).

__c__ 22. Some Jews have heathen wives (13:23–25).

a. Nehemiah throws out the goods and cleanses the rooms.

b. Nehemiah prays and arms the builders with weapons.

c. Nehemiah rebukes them, punishes them, and makes them promise to stop their evil practice.

d. Nehemiah prays and continues to build the wall.

e. Nehemiah rebukes them and shuts the city gates.

Nehemiah and Ezra Restore True Worship

Nehemiah wanted to do more than just rebuild the wall and restore good government. He and Ezra the priest also wanted the people to return to a true worship of the Lord.

23. The people gathered near the water gate to hear _____Ezra_____ read the Book of the _____Law_____ (8:1).

24. When the people heard the Law, they _____wept_____. But Nehemiah and Ezra told them not to weep, because "the _____joy_____ of the Lord is your _____strength_____" (8:9, 10).

25. After Ezra read about the Feast of Booths (also called the Feast of Tabernacles), the people decided to keep it. How did they feel when they obeyed the Law? (8:17) _____

_____They had very great gladness._____

Truths to Instill
- God moved Cyrus to let the Jews return to Jerusalem and rebuild the temple, just as He had foretold (Isaiah 44:28; Jeremiah 29:10). Cyrus even returned the vessels that Nebuchadnezzar had taken from the temple!
- Ezra displayed faith and courage in
  —not asking for soldiers to protect him.
  —remaining steadfast in the face of opposition.
  —taking a stand on the issue of ungodly wives.
  —restoring obedience to the Law.
- Nehemiah displayed zeal in his concern for Jerusalem and his people. He vigorously undertook the building of the wall, getting the people involved and overcoming opposition. He shared with the people the source of his enthusiasm: "The joy of the Lord is your strength" (Nehemiah 8:10).
- The Jews who had married ungodly wives paid a tremendous price to correct their error. How much better it is to avoid making such mistakes. (*Caution: Avoid encouraging a premature interest in marriage among your sixth graders. Rather, stress that marriage is a very serious matter.*)

B. BIBLE WORD STUDY

✎ *Match these definitions with the Bible words on the right.*

__e__ 1. A gift given voluntarily (Ezra 1:4)

__c__ 2. A large dish or platter (Ezra 1:9)

__h__ 3. Mixed with (Ezra 9:2)

__a__ 4. Filled with surprise or amazement; astonished (Ezra 9:3)

__d__ 5. Face; appearance (Nehemiah 2:2)

__g__ 6. Anger caused by something considered unjust or unworthy (Nehemiah 4:1)

__i__ 7. Worthless material; trash (Nehemiah 4:2)

__b__ 8. A gap or opening (Nehemiah 4:7)

__f__ 9. A coat of armor made of small, overlapping pieces of metal (Nehemiah 4:16)

__j__ 10. A title used for the Persian governor in Judea (Nehemiah 8:9)

a. astonied

b. breach

c. charger

d. countenance

e. freewill offering

f. habergeon

g. indignation

h. mingled

i. rubbish

j. Tirshatha

C. THINKING ABOUT BIBLE TRUTHS

God works through people. Often He uses godly people to do His will, but sometimes He also uses ungodly people. In this lesson He used an ungodly king to deliver His people from their captivity so that they could return to their homeland. Then He sent them godly leaders to help them obey His will.

Cyrus the King

Even though Cyrus was a heathen king, God used him. Cyrus conquered many countries in a short time. He even took the great capital city of Babylon without a fight! Soon Cyrus was more powerful than the Assyrian or Babylonian kings had been. But none of this happened by accident. God had a reason for giving Cyrus so much power.

1. Read Isaiah 44:28–45:6. God called Cyrus by name many years before Cyrus was even born. God gave at least three reasons for foretelling what Cyrus would do. One reason is given below. Find two more.

   a. *"That thou mayest know that I, the LORD, which call thee by thy name, am the God of Israel."*
   _____ (Isaiah 45:3)

   b. "For Jacob my servant's sake, and Israel mine elect, I have even called thee by thy name."
   _____ (Isaiah 45:4)

   c. "That they may know from the rising of the sun, and from the west, that there is none beside me."
   _____ (Isaiah 45:6)

2. Earlier in this workbook you studied how the Assyrians and the Babylonians treated the Israelites. In this lesson you saw how Cyrus treated them. Write *Assyrians, Babylonians,* and *Cyrus* in the correct blanks to tell how each treated the Israelites.

a. _____Babylonians_____ took Israelites captive, but allowed them to live together and keep some customs.

b. _____Cyrus_____ encouraged Israelites to return home and worship God.

c. _____Assyrians_____ took Israelites captive and scattered them among the heathen.

Ezra the Scribe

Besides being a priest, Ezra was a skillful scribe who understood and taught the Scriptures. Ezra's ability did not just happen. God blessed him because of his faithful preparation.

3. Find three things in Ezra 7:10 that Ezra had prepared his heart to do.

a. to seek the Law of the LORD

b. to do the Law of the LORD

c. to teach statutes and judgments (God's Law) in Israel

Nehemiah the Governor

Nehemiah was appointed governor of Jerusalem about ninety-five years after the first Israelites returned to their homeland. Like Ezra, he was very concerned about the spiritual welfare of his people.

4. Read Nehemiah 5:14, 15. Before Nehemiah came to Jerusalem, many of the rich Jews oppressed the poor. How did Nehemiah show that he did not want to burden his brethren? _____

Nehemiah did not take the bread and other goods that most governors charged.

What Do You Think?

5. Both Ezra and Nehemiah found Jews who had married heathen wives, whose children were half Jewish and half heathen. They took strong action to put away this wickedness. Why was marrying a heathen wife such a serious sin? (Ezra 9:10–12 and Nehemiah 13:23–26 may give you clues.) _____

(Answers may vary.) Heathen wives turned their husbands' hearts away from God. Also, their children could not speak Hebrew correctly and did not follow God's Law.

D. LEARNING MORE ABOUT THE BIBLE

Old Testament Books

✎ *Review the Old Testament books and their divisions. (See Lesson 1 if you need help.) You will need to know the names of the divisions and the number of books in each group for the Chapter 6 Test.*

Review the Old Testament books and their divisions as needed. For the Chapter 6 Test, the students will need to know the order and spelling of the five divisions, as well as the number of books in each division.

Zerubbabel's Temple

Zerubbabel built the second temple on the site where Solomon had built the first temple. Zerubbabel's temple was used for about five hundred years.

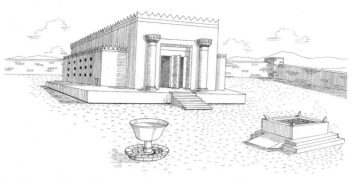

1. Zerubbabel's temple was not as beautiful as Solomon's (Haggai 2:3). But in Haggai 2:9, the LORD declared that the <u>glory</u>

of the latter house (Zerubbabel's temple) would be greater than that of the former (Solomon's temple).

2. Shortly before Christ's birth, Herod began a complete rebuilding of Zerubbabel's temple, making it larger and more magnificent.

   a. How did Jesus' disciples feel about Herod's temple? (Luke 21:5) <u>They admired it because it was adorned with goodly stones and gifts.</u>

   b. What did Jesus say about it? (Luke 21:6) <u>Jesus said it would be torn down and not one stone would be left upon another.</u>

The Feast of Tabernacles

The Feast of Tabernacles was one of the feasts and holy days that the LORD commanded the Israelites to keep each year. Other important holy days included the Passover, Pentecost, and the Day of Atonement.

On the first day of the Feast of Tabernacles, the Israelites made temporary shelters (called booths or tabernacles) with the branches of trees. They lived in these booths for seven days as a reminder of how their fathers had lived in the wilderness. This feast was a time of joy and gladness; a time of sharing with the poor, the widows, and the strangers.

Apparently the Israelites did not always take time to celebrate this joyous feast. The Feast of Tabernacles kept by the Jews of Nehemiah's time was the greatest since the time of Joshua.

3. What different kinds of tree branches did the Jews of Nehemiah's time gather to build their booths? (Nehemiah 8:15) <u>They gathered olive, pine (oil tree), myrtle, and palm branches, and the branches of thick (shady) trees.</u>

4. In what places did the Jews build their booths? (Nehemiah 8:16) <u>They made booths on the house roofs, in court(yard)s, in the temple courts, or in the streets.</u>

178

Lesson 27. Esther—the Jewish Queen

The events in this lesson took place during the time covered in Lesson 26, probably some time before Ezra returned to Jerusalem.

Esther was born after the first Jews returned to Jerusalem with Zerubbabel. Her parents had remained in the land of the Babylonians and Persians. When they died, her cousin Mordecai adopted and raised her.

No doubt Esther expected to live a quiet life as other Jewish girls did. She probably expected to marry a Jewish man and to keep house in Shushan until she grew old. But God had other plans for Esther. When He needed someone to deliver His people from a cruel law, He made a way for Esther to become the queen of Persia.

At first Esther and Mordecai did not realize how God planned to use her. But after Mordecai heard of Haman's wicked plan to destroy all the Jews, he told Esther, "Who knoweth whether thou art come to the kingdom for such a time as this?" (Esther 4:14).

The idea of a Jewish girl becoming the queen of Persia is so unusual that some people today do not believe the story. But it was not hard for God to make Esther a Persian queen. God is able to put a person in the right place at the right time even when it seems impossible.

Esther risked her life to save her people. Jesus said, "Greater love hath no man than this, that a man lay down his life for his friends" (John 15:13).

A. ANSWERS FROM THE BIBLE

Esther was chosen queen about sixty years after the first Jews returned to Jerusalem. By risking her life, she saved not only the Jews who were scattered among many foreign nations but also the Jews who were already living in Judah.

Esther Is Chosen Queen

✎ *Fill in the blanks. All references are from the Book of Esther.*

1. Ahasuerus, king of Persia, spent about a half year showing his treasures to the important leaders of his empire. After this he made a _____ seven _____-day feast for the people of Shushan (1:5).

2. Who else made a feast at the same time? (1:9) _Vashti the queen_

3. How did the king feel when Queen Vashti refused to come and be seen by all his guests? (1:12) _angry_

The king's counselors advised him to remove Vashti from being queen and to find a new queen. They were afraid that the other women of Persia would hear that the queen had refused to obey the king and would use that as an excuse to also disobey their husbands.

4. How did Ahasuerus find a new queen? (2:3, 4) _He told his officers to bring fair young virgins from all the provinces, and he would choose the one that pleased him._

5. What happened to Esther when she came before the king? (2:17) _The king loved her and made her queen._

6. Mordecai was Esther's cousin. What had he done for her? (2:7) _He had taken her as his own daughter after her parents had died._

- King Ahasuerus is usually identified as the Persian king known as *Xerxes* in secular history. According to the chronology generally accepted for this period, Xerxes reigned from about 485 to 465 B.C.

Lesson 27

Oral Review

1. Who remained loyal to Rehoboam after some of the tribes rebelled? [16] **the tribes of Judah and Benjamin, and many priests and Levites**

2. Who killed the idolatrous priests in Judah and Israel and burned their bones? [19] **Josiah**

3. How did God fulfill His promise that David's kingdom would be established forever? [21] **Jesus, who will reign forever, was born into David's family.**

4. Which month in our calendar is about the time of wheat harvest in Canaan? [25] **May**

5. Which king of Persia allowed the Jews to return to Jerusalem and rebuild the temple? [24, 26] **Cyrus**

6. Which two men were leaders of the first group of Jews who returned to Jerusalem? [26] **Zerubbabel and Jeshua (Sheshbazzar was an additional leader if he was not the same man as Zerubbabel.)**

7. What did Ezra tell the disobedient Jews to do with their heathen wives? [26] **He told them to separate themselves from their heathen wives.**

8. What feast did the Jews keep after Ezra read the Law? [26] **the Feast of Tabernacles**

7. How did Mordecai and Esther save the king's life? (2:21, 22) _____

   They warned the king that Bigthan and Teresh wanted to kill him. _____

Haman's Wicked Plan

Soon after the events in chapter 2, the king promoted Haman. He asked all the people to bow before Haman just as they did before the king himself. Haman was a very proud person.

8. When _____Mordecai_____ refused to bow to him, Haman was full of _____wrath_____ (3:2–5).

9. How did Haman plan to destroy Mordecai? (3:8, 9) _____

   by having all the Jews killed _____

10. To whom did Haman send letters in the king's name? (3:12) _____

    to the rulers of every province _____

Esther Pleads for Her People

Mordecai learned of Haman's plan before Esther did. He put on sackcloth and ashes and mourned in the middle of the city. When Esther learned of this, she sent messengers to him to find out what was wrong.

11. What did Mordecai ask Esther to do? (4:8) _____

    He asked her to go in unto the king and make supplication for her people. _____

12. Esther reminded Mordecai that whoever went into the king's inner court without being called would

    be _____put to death_____ unless the king held out his golden _____sceptre (scepter)_____ (4:11).

13. Mordecai knew that it was dangerous for Esther to go in to the king, but apparently he had great faith in God. Circle the letter of the statement that tells what his reply to Esther in 4:13, 14 shows about his faith.

    a. He believed that God would spare Esther and her father's house even if all the other Jews were killed.

    (b.) He believed that if Esther refused to help, she would be killed, but God would save the Jews another way.

    c. He believed that God would save Esther and all the Jews even if she did not go in to the king.

14. Mordecai believed that God could use Esther to save the Jews. He told her, "Who knoweth whether thou

    art come to the _____kingdom_____ for such a _____time_____ as _____this_____?" (4:14).

15. Esther asked Mordecai and the Jews to _____fast_____. She promised to "go in unto the

    _____king_____, which is not according to the _____law_____: and if I

    _____perish_____, I _____perish_____ " (4:16).

16. When Esther entered the inner court, the king held out his royal _____sceptre (scepter)_____, saving

    her from death (5:2).

17. Esther invited the _____king_____ and _____Haman_____ to a banquet (5:4).

• Haman was an Agagite (Esther 3:1). The Agagites may have been a family of the Amalekites: the Amalekite king whom Saul spared was named Agag (1 Samuel 15:8). The Agag mentioned in Numbers 24:7 may also have been an Amalekite.

In This Lesson

Scope: The Book of Esther

Main Events

- Ahasuerus decides he needs another queen. In his search, Esther is chosen.
- Because of his hatred of Mordecai, Haman schemes to destroy all the Jews.
- Queen Esther saves her people from the evil designs of Haman.

Objectives

- Students should know
  —why King Ahasuerus searched for a new queen. (Queen Vashti refused to obey him when he wanted her to come and be seen by all his guests.)
  —how Mordecai and Esther saved the king's life. (They warned the king that Bigthan and Teresh wanted to kill him.)
  —why Haman wanted to destroy all the Jews. (Mordecai refused to bow to him.)

180 Chapter Six The Jews After the Captivity

Haman's Downfall

At the banquet Esther invited the king and Haman to a second banquet the following day. Haman was very happy that he had been invited to the queen's banquets with the king. Perhaps this honor made him even more upset when he noticed that Mordecai still did not bow to him. He decided that he would not wait until all the Jews were destroyed to get rid of Mordecai.

18. What did Haman decide to do to Mordecai if the king would give him permission? (5:14) _____

    Haman decided to have Mordecai hanged on a gallows.

19. During that night, the king was informed that _____ Mordecai _____ had never been rewarded

    for warning him of a wicked plot against his life (6:3).

20. The next morning, before Esther's second banquet, the king told _____ Haman _____ to honor

    _____ Mordecai _____ by taking him through the streets on the king's horse and proclaiming

    before him: "_____

    Thus shall it be done unto the man whom the king delighteth to honour. _____ " (6:10, 11).

21. What did Ahasuerus do to Haman after he learned of Haman's wicked plot against the Jews and

    Mordecai? (7:9, 10) _____

    He commanded his servants to hang Haman on the gallows Haman had built for Mordecai.

Mordecai's Promotion

Esther told the king that Mordecai was her cousin and adoptive father. The king decided to promote Mordecai to Haman's former place. The law that Haman had passed against the Jews could not be changed, but the king allowed Esther and Mordecai to help the Jews protect themselves against their enemies.

22. Mordecai wrote letters in the king's name telling the _____ Jews _____ in every city to fight

    against their enemies on the day Haman had chosen for his evil plan (8:9–11).

23. Why did the rulers and officers of the provinces of Persia help the Jews to fight against their ene-

    mies? (9:3, 4) _____

    They were afraid of Mordecai.

24. What did Mordecai command the Jews to do every year on the fourteenth and fifteenth days of the

    month Adar? (9:20–22) He commanded them to celebrate those days with feasting and joy, and

    by sending gifts to one another and to the poor.

—how Queen Esther risked her life to save the Jews. (See Part A, numbers 11–16.)

—what happened to Haman after Esther revealed his wicked plan to the king. (He was hanged on the gallows that he had built for Mordecai.)

—how Haman's wicked plan was overthrown. (See Part A, numbers 22, 23.)

—why the Jews began keeping the feast of Purim. (They were delivered from destruction.)

—the meaning of *chamberlain.* (an important officer in a ruler's house)

Truths to Instill

• God's sovereignty is seen in this lesson. No matter how carefully Haman planned and schemed, God was in control.

• God has a work for each person. We can best prepare for that work by doing well whatever we have to do now. See Esther 4:13, 14.

• Mordecai's faith was a key factor in God's deliverance of the Jews through Esther. Because Mordecai was sure that God would somehow deliver the Jews (Esther 4:14), he could encourage Esther to go in to the king at the risk of her life.

B. BIBLE WORD STUDY

✎ *The meanings of these words from the Book of Esther become clearer when read in their context. Match them to their meanings.*

b	1. The responsibility to care for	a. chamberlain (1:12)
f	2. A special feast	b. custody (2:3)
d	3. An official messenger	c. pur (3:7)
c	4. A lot; a die (singular of *dice*) used to cast a lot	d. post (3:13)
g	5. A device for hanging criminals	e. sceptre (scepter) (4:11)
e	6. A ruler's staff	f. banquet (5:6)
a	7. An important officer in a ruler's house	g. gallows (5:14)
h	8. To attack violently	h. assault (8:11)

✎ *Use the tables of measure in the back of the book to complete this exercise.*

9. a. One talent equals about __75 (34 kg)__ pounds.

   b. Haman was willing to pay __10,000__ talents of silver to have the Jews destroyed (3:9). (Perhaps he planned to seize the money and goods of the Jews that he killed to recover his expenses.)

   c. This many talents of silver would equal about __750,000__ pounds.

   d. Challenge problem: Calculate how many tons this would be. __375__ tons (340,000 kg; 340 M.T.)

10. a. One cubit equals about __18__ inches (or __1½ (46 cm)__ feet).

    b. Haman's gallows was __50__ cubits high (5:14), which equals about __75 (23 m)__ feet.

Part B, numbers 9 and 10, and Part C may be difficult for some students. Discuss or complete these exercises in class if possible.

• Note the huge amount of silver Haman offered to pay. Also note the extreme height of his gallows—10 or 15 feet high would have been sufficient.

C. THINKING ABOUT BIBLE TRUTHS

God's Overruling Hand

The Book of Esther is the only book of the Bible that does not specifically mention God. In spite of this, the book clearly shows that God was directing events to save His people. Without God's overruling hand, many of these events would have been very unlikely to happen.

✎ *Explain how God used each of these events to preserve the Jews and to bring justice upon Haman. The first one is done for you.*

1. Out of all the young virgins in the vast Persian Empire, the king chooses Esther as his queen.

   God made sure that the king chose Esther as his queen so that she would be in a high position when His people needed help.

2. Mordecai learns of Bigthan and Teresh's plot against the king. _____

   When Mordecai learned of this wicked plot and told the king, he gained the king's favor.

Discuss in class if possible. Answers will vary.

• "Pride goeth before destruction, and an haughty spirit before a fall" (Proverbs 16:18). This lesson gives a real-life illustration of the course and result of pride.

3. The king holds out his scepter to Esther. <u>God moved the king to show mercy toward Esther.</u>

<u>(The king could have rejected Esther as he had Vashti.)</u>

4. When the king cannot sleep, his servant chooses to read about Mordecai's deed. <u>This reminded</u>

<u>the king of Mordecai's good deed, and Haman was humbled when he had to honor Mordecai.</u>

5. One of the king's servants learns that Haman had made a gallows on which to hang Mordecai, and

he tells the king about it while the king is very angry with Haman. <u> </u>

<u>Haman's plot to hang Mordecai was revealed to the king just when the king was pleased with</u>

<u>Mordecai and angry with Haman. The king immediately ordered that Haman be hanged.</u>

D. LEARNING MORE ABOUT THE BIBLE

Esther and Joseph

Like Joseph, Esther was separated from her family and lived in ungodly surroundings. Like Joseph, she was faithful. And like Joseph, she was in the right place at the right time to save her people.

The writer of the Book of Esther must have seen this likeness. He pointed out similar events in the two stories, and even used similar sentences at times.

✎ *Read the events in Joseph's life on the left. Find similar happenings in the Book of Esther and write them on the right.*

The Story of Joseph	**The Story of Esther**

"Let Pharaoh do this, and let him appoint officers over the land . . . and let them gather all the food of those good years" (Genesis 41:34, 35).

1. <u>"Let the king appoint officers . . . that they may gather</u>
<u>together all the fair young virgins unto Shushan."</u>

<u> </u>

<u> </u>

<u> </u> (Esther 2:3)

Two of the king's men, his butler and his baker, offend him. The king is angry with them (Genesis 40:1–3).

2. Two of the king's chamberlains seek to kill the king. The king commands them to be hanged.

(Esther 2:21–23)

Potiphar's wife speaks to Joseph day by day, but he does not listen to her (Genesis 39:10).

3. The king's servants speak to Mordecai day by day, but he does not listen to them.

(Esther 3:4)

Pharaoh has a bad night (Genesis 41:1–45).

4. "On that night could not the king sleep."

(Esther 6:1)

"Pharaoh took off his ring from his hand, and put it upon Joseph's hand, and arrayed him in vestures of fine linen, and . . . made him to ride in the second chariot . . . and they cried before him, Bow the knee" (Genesis 41:42, 43).

5. Haman puts royal apparel on Mordecai, leads him through the city on the king's horse, and proclaims that the king delights to honor him.

(Esther 6:11)

"How shall I go up to my father, and . . . see the evil that shall come on my father?" (Genesis 44:34).

6. "How can I endure to see the evil that shall come unto my people?"

(Esther 8:6)

The Feast of Purim

The holiday held in remembrance of the Jews' deliverance from Haman is called *Purim*, which means "lots." Haman had cast lots to determine which day he would set for the destruction of the Jews (Esther 3:7).

Purim was celebrated on the fourteenth and fifteenth days of the Jewish month of Adar (February or March). The Jews spent a day in fasting and prayer. Then they gathered to hear the whole Book of Esther read. After this they gathered in their homes for feasting and celebration.

7. What did they do for one another and for the poor? (Esther 9:22)

They sent portions to one another and sent gifts to the poor.

184

Lesson 28. The Last Prophets

The Old Testament Jews did not have the complete Bible that we have today. They did not even have all the Old Testament books until a few hundred years before Christ.

Because His Word was not complete, God sent messages to people through His prophets. The prophets were not chosen in the same way as priests and kings. Priests and kings usually inherited their offices from their fathers. This meant that an ungodly son sometimes became a king or a priest simply because his father had been a king or a priest.

God chose the prophets in a different way. When God wanted a new prophet, He called a faithful man, whether the man's father was a prophet or not. God sent prophets throughout much of Israel's history, but faithful prophets were especially important when the priests and the kings were turning away from God.

For about four hundred years before Jesus came, God sent no prophets. Perhaps He wanted His people to long for the Messiah. Before these four hundred years of "silence," God sent the last Old Testament prophets—Haggai, Zechariah, and Malachi.

Haggai and Zechariah prophesied during the same time. They urged Zerubbabel the governor and Jeshua the high priest to finish building the temple.

Malachi prophesied at about the time of Nehemiah. He rebuked the priests and the ungodly Jews for their insincere worship. He warned them that the Messiah whom they were looking for would judge their sins. But to those who feared the LORD, Malachi gave a message of hope. He told them that God would gather them as precious treasures and spare them from His wrath.

God blesses those who hear and obey His messages.

A. ANSWERS FROM THE BIBLE

After the Jews returned to Jerusalem and built the foundation of a new temple, their enemies raised threats. They frightened the Jews into stopping their work on the temple. They wrote letters to the king and turned him against the Jews' project.

Then God began to speak through two prophets, Haggai and Zechariah. Haggai may have been one of the old men who had seen Solomon's temple (Haggai 2:3). Zechariah was probably younger—his grandfather had been one of the priests who returned to Jerusalem with Zerubbabel (Zechariah 1:1; Nehemiah 12:4, 16). The two prophets brought messages of reproof and encouragement.

Haggai's Message to the Jews

Haggai 1

The Jews thought they should wait until later to build the temple. Notice God's answer and command to them in these verses.

✎ *Fill in the blanks.*

1. "Is it time for you, O ye, to dwell in your _____ cieled (ceiled) _____ _____ houses _____, and
    this _____ house _____ lie waste?"

2. "Go up to the _____ mountain _____, and bring _____ wood _____, and build the
    _____ house _____; and I will take pleasure in it."

Lesson 28

Oral Review

1. What are some kinds of tradesmen mentioned in the Bible? (Name at least seven.) [25] **Examples: shepherd, farmer, apothecary, baker, carpenter, fisherman, fuller, mason, merchant, potter, smith, tanner, tentmaker, weaver**

2. Which two prophets encouraged the Jews to finish rebuilding the temple? [26] **Haggai and Zechariah**

3. How did Nehemiah protect the wall builders from their enemies? [26] **He armed the builders with weapons.**

4. What feast did the Jews keep after Ezra read the Law? [26] **the Feast of Tabernacles**

5. How did Mordecai and Esther save the king's life? [27] **They told the king that two of his servants were planning to kill him.**

6. Why was Haman angry with Mordecai? [27] **Mordecai refused to bow to him.**

7. What did Queen Esther do to save the Jews? [27] **She went in to the king even though she had not been called.**

8. What did the king permit the Jews to do on the day Haman had planned to destroy them? [27] **He permitted them to fight against their enemies.**

God cannot bless those who consider their own work more important than His work. The Jews were suffering losses in their farms and businesses because of their neglect of spiritual things.

3. "Ye looked for _____much_____, and, lo, it came to _____little_____."

4. God asked them why they had experienced this trouble, and then He answered His own question: "Because of mine ____house____ that is ____waste____, and ye run every man unto his own ____house____."

5. After the Jews turned back to God, He was ready to bless them again. He said, "I am with ____you____, saith the LORD."

Haggai 2:1–9

The old men were grieved because the new temple was not as magnificent as the first one. But the LORD reminded them that having His glory within the temple was much more important than the outside adornment of the building.

6. God asked, "Who is left among you that saw this ____house____ in her first ____glory____? and how do ye see it now? is it not in your eyes in comparison of it as ____nothing____?"

7. God reminded them of the covenant He had made with their fathers many centuries before. He was still the same God, and they could trust Him to be faithful. "According to the word that I covenanted with you when ye came out of Egypt, so my ____spirit____ remaineth among you: ____fear____ ye not."

8. Circle the letter of the statement that tells why God did not mind having a temple that was not as great as Solomon's temple.

   a. God planned to shake money from the heathen nations and build a greater temple.

   b. Since God had plenty of silver and gold, He had no interest in the temple.

   (c.) God was more concerned that His glory fill the temple than that the temple be beautiful.

9. God said, "The ____glory____ of this latter house shall be ____greater____ than of the former."

Zechariah's Visions

Zechariah was a priest as well as a prophet. Like Haggai, he told the Jews to go to work and build the temple. God also gave Zechariah many visions and dreams concerning future events.

✎ *List the things Zechariah saw in these visions.* (Answers for numbers 10–15 may vary slightly.)

10. Zechariah 1:8 __a man on a red horse, myrtle trees, other (red, speckled, and white) horses__

11. Zechariah 2:1 __a man with a measuring line in his hand__

12. Zechariah 3:1 __Joshua the high priest, an angel, and Satan__

13. Zechariah 5:1 __a flying roll__

14. Zechariah 5:9 __two women with wings who flew with an ephah__

15. Zechariah 6:1 __four chariots that came out from between two brass mountains__

• Since we cannot read the mind of God, we do not know this for sure, but this is at least a possible reason. Both *a* and *b* are obviously not true. The students may have some other ideas they would like to discuss as possible answers.

In This Lesson

Scope: The books of Haggai, Zechariah, and Malachi

Main Events

• God sends His last Old Testament messages through Haggai, Zechariah, and Malachi.

• God's message through Haggai: If the Jews would put God's work first, God would bless them.

• God's message through Zechariah: There was a bright future for the Jews, if they would trust God.

• God's message through Malachi: The Jews should repent and serve God wholeheartedly.

Objectives

• Students should know

—why God withheld His blessings from the Jews of Haggai's time. (They were neglecting to build God's house.)

—how God said the second temple would be greater than the first. (God said His glory would be in the second temple.)

—some of Zechariah's prophecies concerning Jesus. (Jesus would come as the Branch from David's root, God would send a forerunner to prepare people for Christ's first coming, and Christ would be betrayed for thirty pieces of silver.)

Zechariah's Prophecies of the Messiah

God spoke many words of hope and comfort through Zechariah. This hope often pointed forward to the coming Messiah, Jesus Christ.

✎ *The references for four of Zechariah's prophecies are given on the left. Match them with their fulfillment in Jesus' life.*

__c__ 16. Zechariah 6:13

__d__ 17. Zechariah 9:9

__a__ 18. Zechariah 11:12, 13

__b__ 19. Zechariah 13:7

a. Jesus is betrayed for thirty pieces of silver.

b. Jesus' disciples all leave Him when He is arrested.

c. Jesus builds the church, and God glorifies Him. He rules on a throne in heaven and is a priest.

d. Jesus rides into Jerusalem on an ass's colt.

Malachi—the Last Old Testament Prophet

Malachi, who probably lived during Nehemiah's time, was likely the last prophet of Old Testament times. (Some people think that Joel might have prophesied after Malachi.) Malachi spoke against many of the same sins that Nehemiah dealt with, such as the Jews' oppression of the poor, their failure to pay tithes, and their marriages with the ungodly.

The Book of Malachi is interesting to read. The prophet often gave a statement or question from God, followed by a sarcastic statement or question from the people. God wanted the Jews to feel ashamed for asking such questions or saying such things. He wanted them to repent and live righteously. For every foolish question they asked, He gave them a wise answer.

20. The LORD rebuked the priests for despising His Name (Malachi 1:6).

    a. What did the priests ask? _____

      "Wherein have we despised thy name?"

    b. God replied that they had despised His Name by offering Him polluted ____bread____ and by

      sacrificing ____blind____, ____lame____, and ____sick____ animals (1:7, 8).

Malachi also used unforgettable figures of speech.

21. Malachi speaks of Jesus in Malachi 3:2. He likens Jesus to what two things? _____

    a refiner's fire, fullers' soap

22. The Jews were no longer paying their tithes. What did God say they were doing to Him? (3:8) ____

    robbing Him

23. From where did Malachi say God would pour out a blessing if the people brought their tithes to Him?

    (3:10) _____

    from the windows of heaven

—some of the sins Malachi spoke against. (the Jews' oppression of the poor, their failure to pay tithes, their marriages with the ungodly, and their despising of God's Name)

—that Malachi was probably the last Old Testament prophet.

Truths to Instill

• God cannot bless us if we put our work ahead of His. Are we building "ceiled houses" and seeking our own wealth while neglecting God's "house" and the spiritual ruins around us? How much time do we spend in the Lord's work? Jesus said, "But seek ye first the kingdom of God, and his righteousness; and all these things shall be added unto you" (Matthew 6:33).

B. BIBLE WORD STUDY

✎ *Match each italicized word with its meaning on the right.*

<u> d </u> 1. "Is it time for you, O ye, to dwell in your *cieled* [ceiled] houses?" (Haggai 1:4).

<u> c </u> 2. "They lifted up the *ephah* between the earth and the heaven" (Zechariah 5:9).

<u> g </u> 3. "O priests, that *despise* my name" (Malachi 1:6).

<u> b </u> 4. "Ye offer *polluted* bread upon mine altar" (Malachi 1:7).

<u> e </u> 5. "He is like a *refiner's* fire" (Malachi 3:2).

<u> f </u> 6. "He is like . . . *fullers'* soap" (Malachi 3:2).

<u> a </u> 7. "Bring ye all the *tithes*" (Malachi 3:10).

a. one tenth; the part that is due to God

b. defiled; impure

c. a measure equal to about ¾ bushel; a container that holds this amount

d. paneled; covered with tightly fitting boards

e. a person who removes impurities from metal

f. a person who washes or bleaches cloth

g. to think of with disrespect or hatred

The LORD of Hosts

The Old Testament writers used a number of titles for God. One of them is translated "LORD of hosts" in the King James Bible. This is a very reverent title that speaks of God's boundless power as LORD of all the hosts (armies) of heaven. Haggai, Zechariah, and Malachi used "LORD of hosts" in their writings more often than any other Old Testament writers except Isaiah and Jeremiah.

8. a. How many times is the title "LORD of hosts" used in Haggai 2:4–11? <u>   seven   </u>

   b. In Zechariah 8:1–9? <u>   nine   </u>

   c. In Malachi 1:6–14? <u>   seven   </u>

C. THINKING ABOUT BIBLE TRUTHS

Prophets and Prophecies

In Old Testament times, the prophets brought God's messages to the people. They spent much time teaching the people to follow God.

1. True prophets received their messages from the LORD. Copy the phrases from these verses that tell us God spoke through these prophets.

   a. Haggai 1:3 _____

   <u>"Then came the word of the LORD by Haggai the prophet."</u>

   b. Zechariah 1:1 _____

   <u>"came the word of the LORD unto Zechariah"</u>

   c. Malachi 1:1 _____

   <u>"The burden of the word of the LORD to Israel by Malachi."</u>

- God's promises are conditional. God, in His great love, longed to bless the Jews but was not able to because of their rejection of His Law. These prophets represented God's last call to a disobedient and stiff-necked people.

- Throughout these prophecies shines a positive note: God will send the Messiah and redeem His faithful people.

2. Haggai and Zechariah gave the exact dates that they received some of their messages from God.

  a. Haggai received his first recorded message from the LORD on the first day of the sixth month of the second year of Darius (Haggai 1:1). When did he receive his last recorded message? (Haggai 2:10) <u>on the twenty-fourth day of the ninth month of Darius's second year</u>

  b. When did Zechariah receive his first recorded message from God? (Zechariah 1:1)? <u>in the eighth month of Darius's second year</u>

3. Zechariah 3:8 and 6:12 speak of the Branch. Read these two verses, and then compare them with Jeremiah 33:14–17.

  a. Through what family line would the Branch come? <u>David's</u>

  b. Who is the Branch? <u>Jesus</u>

4. The Old Testament closes with a prophecy that God would send Elijah the prophet before the day of the LORD (Malachi 4:5, 6). Whom did God send in the spirit and power of Elijah to prepare people for Christ's first coming? (Matthew 17:10–13) <u>John the Baptist</u>

What Do You Think?

5. Circle the letter of the statement that gives a possible reason God stopped sending prophets to the Israelites about four hundred years before the time of Christ.

  a. They had become so wicked that He did not want to give them messages anymore.

  b. They had learned that sin does not pay, so they did not need prophets anymore to help them remain faithful.

  c. God wanted to show them that the Old Testament time was about over and a new time was coming.

God Spoke

God spoke, man wrote; the lines were penned
    By hands like yours and mine,
Yet every word of sacred writ
    Was formed by breath divine.

God did not place men in this world
    Without a guiding light;
He gave the blessed Book to be
    Our beacon in sin's night.

There is no doubt—the record is
    Exactly as He willed,
Nor shall one jot or tittle pass
    Till all has been fulfilled.

Within its pages man may find
    All that he needs to know:
His origin, his destiny,
    The way his feet should go.

How foolish, then, to turn aside,
    Or shun these holy lines,
When all who read and heed the Word
    May walk in light divine.
                    —Ada Wine

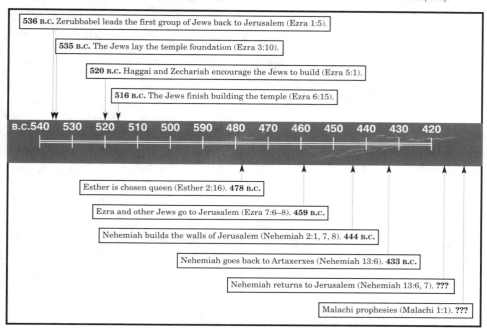

D. LEARNING MORE ABOUT THE BIBLE

The Return of the Jews

The Jews who returned to their homeland faced many challenges. Years passed before they finished building the temple and the wall of Jerusalem. But God faithfully sent leaders and prophets, even though the Jews were not always faithful to Him. The time line below gives approximate dates for some main events after the captivity.

536 B.C. Zerubbabel leads the first group of Jews back to Jerusalem (Ezra 1:5).

535 B.C. The Jews lay the temple foundation (Ezra 3:10).

520 B.C. Haggai and Zechariah encourage the Jews to build (Ezra 5:1).

516 B.C. The Jews finish building the temple (Ezra 6:15).

B.C. 540 530 520 510 500 590 480 470 460 450 440 430 420

Esther is chosen queen (Esther 2:16). **478 B.C.**

Ezra and other Jews go to Jerusalem (Ezra 7:6–8). **459 B.C.**

Nehemiah builds the walls of Jerusalem (Nehemiah 2:1, 7, 8). **444 B.C.**

Nehemiah goes back to Artaxerxes (Nehemiah 13:6). **433 B.C.**

Nehemiah returns to Jerusalem (Nehemiah 13:6, 7). **???**

Malachi prophesies (Malachi 1:1). **???**

✎ *Using the time line, give the approximate number of years between these pairs of events.*

1. From the return of the first Jews to Jerusalem until Ezra led a group back _____77_____

2. From the laying of the temple foundation to the completion of the temple _____19_____

3. From the return of the first Jews until Esther became queen _____58_____

4. From Haggai's and Zechariah's prophecies to the building of Jerusalem's walls by Nehemiah __76__

5. From Haggai's and Zechariah's prophecies to the birth of Christ _____520_____

- Malachi's prophecy is not dated, but clues in the book indicate that he was probably the last Old Testament prophet. A Persian governor ruled the land (Malachi 1:8). The temple had been rebuilt and the worship had become corrupt (1:7–10). As noted in the lesson, Malachi and Nehemiah rebuked some of the same sins. Some people think that the Book of Joel, which is also undated, could have been written as late as 400 B.C. It is also possible that, after Malachi, God sent prophets who left no writings.

Christ's birth is thought to have been about 4 or 5 B.C., so the answer to number 5 would be about 515 years. But since the dates are approximate, 520 years is close enough.

190

Lesson 29. Between the Old and New Testaments

We see God's works in nature, read about God in the Bible, and know that God hears our prayers. But some people do not want to acknowledge God's works. Instead of reading the Bible and praying to God, they try to forget that He exists. For such unbelievers, God has another way of revealing Himself. He shows Himself to them through His faithful people.

Ungodly men and women cannot forget God as long as they see God's people doing what is right. They cannot completely ignore God as long as God's people keep talking about Him. They cannot say that God is dead as long as God's people show by their lives that He lives.

The Jews who lived between the time of Malachi and the coming of Jesus had good opportunities and reasons to witness for God. They had moved to many countries of the world. They faced pressures to follow Greek customs that were against the Law of the LORD. Many of them failed to be good witnesses, but God always had a faithful remnant. God still needs faithful witnesses today!

Some people speak of the time between Malachi and the coming of Jesus as the four hundred silent years. It is true that God did not speak through prophets or inspire men to write additional Scripture passages during those years. But for people living then, those years were not at all silent. They were busy, tumultuous years during which God prepared the way for Jesus to come into the world.

Since much of the material in this lesson is probably new for your students, you may want to spend extra time discussing the lesson in class. A good understanding of this period will help students to see how God prepared the world for Christ's coming.

- Below are a few suggested background sources for the teacher for further study.
  —*Between the Testaments*, by Charles F. Pfeiffer, published by Baker Book House
  —*First Maccabees* (a historical book from the Apocrypha)
  —*The Complete Works of Josephus*
  —Encyclopedias and Bible dictionaries have articles on many specific subjects, such as empires, leaders, and sects. A number of sources, including the ones listed above, were consulted in preparing this lesson.

A. ANSWERS FROM THE BIBLE

The Persians Control Palestine: 539—332 B.C.

✎ *Read all the lesson comments carefully. You will find the answers to some questions in the comments rather than in the Bible.*

The kings of the great Persian Empire controlled Judah during Malachi's time and for a number of years following. The Persians taxed the Jews, but otherwise they usually allowed them to live and worship as they desired.

1. What had Cyrus, the first great king of Persia, allowed the Jews to do? (Ezra 1:1–3) _____

   <u>He allowed the Jews to return to Jerusalem and rebuild the temple.</u>

Alexander Overthrows the Persian Empire: 334—323 B.C.

Like the Assyrians and Babylonians before them, the Persians became wealthy, corrupt, and weak. In 334 B.C. they were attacked and began to fall before a new empire builder. This man was Alexander the Great. Alexander's Greek Empire became greater than any empire before it. His followers spread the Greek language and Greek ideas all the way from Europe to India and Africa.

Some of the Greek ideas caused the Jews much trouble, but God used the Greek language for His glory. By New Testament times, people in many lands knew Greek. When the early Christian missionaries preached the Gospel in Greek, most people understood their message. And since the Old Testament Scriptures had been translated into Greek, many Gentiles could read God's Word for themselves.

Alexander was kind to the Jews when he conquered Judah in 332 B.C. He invited many of them to live in Alexandria, a new city that he built on the northern coast of Egypt.

Lesson 29

Oral Review

1. What did King Manasseh do after he was taken captive and afflicted by the Assyrians? [19] **He humbled himself and prayed to God.**
2. How many earthly empires did the image in Nebuchadnezzar's vision represent? [23] **four**
3. Why was Ezra ashamed to ask the king for protection when he carried great riches back to Jerusalem? [26] **He had told the king that God helps all those who seek Him.**
4. What is a chamberlain? [27] **an important officer in a ruler's house**
5. Why did God withhold His blessings from the Jews of Haggai's time? [28] **They were letting His house lie waste while taking care of their own business.**
6. How many years did it take to rebuild the temple from start to finish? [28] **about nineteen**
7. Who prophesied that Jesus would be betrayed for thirty pieces of silver? [28] **Zechariah**
8. Who is the Branch of whom Zechariah spoke? [28] **Jesus**

2. Read Daniel 8:3–7, 20, 21. The ram in Daniel's vision represented the Medes and Persians. What animal, representing Alexander's Greek Empire, defeated the ram? <u>a goat</u>

3. Read John 19:19, 20. The Romans wrote the message on Jesus' cross in their own language (Latin) and in the Jews' language (Hebrew). Why did they also write it in Greek? <u>Many people who could not read Latin or Hebrew knew Greek.</u>

During the Persian reign, the Jews of Judah gradually began using Aramaic (ar uh MAY ihk), a language similar to Hebrew, for everyday speech. They continued to use the Hebrew Scriptures for worship services. Because Hebrew and Aramaic were closely related, the New Testament calls both languages Hebrew. The "Hebrew" language written on Jesus' cross was likely Aramaic.

4. How did the Greek language help the early Christians spread the Gospel? <u>People in many lands could understand Greek preaching and could read the Greek Scriptures for themselves.</u>

The Ptolemies and the Seleucids Control Palestine: 323–167 B.C.

Alexander reigned for only a few years. After his death, his vast empire was divided among four of his generals. For about one hundred years, Judah was governed by Alexander's Greek followers in Egypt (the Ptolemies). Later it came under the control of Alexander's Greek followers in Syria (the Seleucids).

The Ptolemies (TAHL uh meez) generally treated the Jews well, but the Seleucids (sih LOO sihds) were completely different. About 168 B.C. a Seleucid ruler, Antiochus Epiphanes (an TY uh kuhs ih PIHF uh neez), tried to completely stamp out the Jewish religion. He commanded all copies of the Hebrew Scriptures to be burned and all Jews who kept God's Law to be killed. He set up an image of the Greek god Zeus in the temple at Jerusalem, and he offered a pig in sacrifice before it.

The wealthy and powerful Jews helped the Seleucids and adopted Greek ways. In Jerusalem they built a gymnasium, where they taught young men to play Greek games. But some of the Jews wanted to be faithful to God and their old Jewish ways.

5. Read Daniel 8:8. In Daniel's vision, what took the place of the great horn of the goat (Alexander)? <u>four notable horns</u>

6. Why would sacrificing a pig in the temple have been extremely offensive to righteous Jews? (Leviticus 11:7) <u>Pigs (swine) were unclean animals for the Jews.</u>

The Maccabees Gain Jewish Independence: 167–63 B.C.

The Seleucid Greeks sent an officer to the Jewish village of Modin to force people to sacrifice to Zeus. But an elderly Jewish priest named Mattathias (mat uh THY uhs) objected. Mattathias and his five sons killed the officer and tore down the Greek altar. Then they fled to the hills.

This bold action set the Jews in open rebellion against the Greeks. Thousands of Jews sided with the sons of Mattathias, who were called the Maccabees (MAK uh beez). After three years of fighting, the Maccabees won control of the temple area. They cleansed the temple, rededicated it, and relit its lamps in the Name of the LORD.

The Jews still keep the Feast of Dedication, which they call Hanukkah (HAH nuh kuh), to remember the time when the Maccabees reestablished temple worship.

7. Mattathias lived under the Old Testament Law, which allowed the righteous to kill the wicked. Which of these Old Testament men was Mattathias most like: Cain (Genesis 4:8), Phinehas (Numbers 25:6–11), or Joab (2 Samuel 3:27–29)? <u>Phinehas</u>

In This Lesson

Main Events
• The Greeks conquer the Persian Empire. Soon their empire is divided, and the Jews find themselves caught between the Ptolemy Greeks of Egypt and the Seleucid Greeks of Syria.
• The Seleucids dominate Judea and defile the temple.
• The Jews free themselves from the Seleucids and remain independent until the Romans conquer them.

• The sects of the Sadducees and the Pharisees develop during this time.
• The Hebrew Old Testament is translated into Greek and becomes the Bible of the Greek-speaking world.

Objectives
• Students should know
—which empire controlled Palestine at the time of Malachi. (the Persian Empire)
—who conquered the Persian Empire. (the Greeks)

8. Where was Jesus during one Feast of Dedication? (John 10:22, 23) _____

   at Jerusalem (in the temple)

After twenty-four years of hit-and-run fighting, the Jews won complete independence from the Greeks. But their victory was a hollow one. After the death of Simon, the last son of Mattathias, Simon's son John Hyrcanus (hur KAY nuhs) took the office of high priest and leader of the Jews. He sided with the wealthy Jews who liked Greek ways. Before long the descendants of the Maccabees were little better than the Seleucid Greeks. They began to persecute the faithful Jews who criticized their worldly ways.

The Sadducees and the Pharisees

John Hyrcanus joined the Sadducees, a group of rich, worldly men who taught that the Books of Moses were the only portion of the Scriptures that needed to be obeyed. They accepted many Greek ways in order to gain favor with the Greek rulers. Many Sadducees were priests or other important leaders.

9. a. What three things did the Sadducees not believe in? (Acts 23:8) _____

      the resurrection, angels, and spirits

   _____

   b. The Sadducees claimed that Moses did not teach about the resurrection. Jesus quoted a verse

      from Exodus to show them that Moses indirectly referred to the resurrection (Mark 12:26). Copy

      the words that Jesus quoted. _____

      "I am the God of Abraham, and the God of Isaac, and the God of Jacob."

The Pharisees were a group of Jews who opposed the worldly ways of the Sadducees. The first Pharisees probably obeyed the Law because of their love for God and His Word. They knew God would be angry if they followed the ways of the heathen. But by Jesus' time, the Pharisees had made many additional rules to explain how they thought God's Law should be kept. These additional rules and traditions became more important to them than the actual Law of God. While keeping their traditions, they failed to obey the most important law: "Thou shalt love the LORD thy God with all thine heart, and with all thy soul, and with all thy might" (Deuteronomy 6:5).

10. a. What tradition did the Pharisees accuse Jesus and His disciples of breaking in Mark 7:5–8? ____

       the tradition of washing hands before eating.

    b. The Pharisees taught that a man could dedicate certain goods, which he should have used to help

       his parents, as a gift (Corban) to God instead. Which commandment of God did Jesus say they

       were disobeying? (Mark 7:9–13) _____

       "Honour thy father and thy mother."

11. To what did Jesus compare the Pharisees in Matthew 23:27? _____

    whited sepulchres (sepulchers) full of dead men's bones

The Apocrypha

Between the time of Malachi and the birth of Jesus, the Jews wrote a number of books that we call *the Apocrypha* (uh PAHK ruh fuh). The word *Apocrypha* means "hidden," or "concealed." These books contain wise sayings, stories, and some history. However, their wise sayings teach nothing of value that the Old Testament does not already teach, and not all the stories are true. Not all the history is completely based on facts either, although

—how the spread of the Greek language helped prepare the world for Christ's first coming. (When early Christian missionaries preached in Greek, most people understood. Also, since the Old Testament had been translated into Greek, the Gentiles could read God's Word.)

—why Mattathias and the Maccabees rose up against the Greeks. (See Part A, numbers 5–9.)

—which empire controlled Palestine at the time of Jesus. (the Roman Empire)

—which Jewish group did not believe in the resurrection. (the Sadducees)

—which Jewish group carefully kept their traditions, but lost their love for God. (the Pharisees)

—which Jewish writings we do not accept as part of the Scriptures. (the Apocrypha)

—what the word *hypocrite* means. (a person who pretends to be something that he is not)

—what the Greek translation of the Old Testament was called. (the Septuagint)

the history books do help us understand the period between Old and New Testament times.

We do not believe that the books of the Apocrypha are inspired by God. Jesus never quoted from them in the New Testament. The Jews never accepted them as part of the Scriptures, even though they were included with the Greek translation of the Old Testament. And some books of the Apocrypha teach doctrines or practices that are contrary to God's Word.

12. Until the 1500s, many Christians used the Apocrypha as part of the Bible. They did so because the books of the Apocrypha were included in the Greek translation of the Old Testament. List at least three reasons from the paragraphs above to explain why we do not believe they were inspired by God. (Answers may vary slightly.)

   a. _Jesus never quoted from them in the New Testament._

   b. _The Jews did not accept them as part of the Scriptures._

   c. _Some of their teachings are incorrect and contrary to God's Word._

Palestine Under the Romans: 63 B.C.–A.D. 614

In 63 B.C. two brothers (descendants of the Maccabees) fought each other for control of Jerusalem. While they fought, a new danger arose.

Like the empires before them, the Greek Empire had grown weak and corrupt with time. Now another power, Rome, was gaining strength. The Romans were building an empire even greater than that of Alexander the Great.

Pompey (PAHM pee), a Roman general, took advantage of the quarreling Jewish brothers. He surrounded Jerusalem, and after three months the city fell. Roman soldiers charged into the temple area and killed some of the priests. They looked into the holy of holies, which only the high priest was permitted to enter. Judah (which the Romans called *Judea*) became a Roman province.

Many Jews hated their Roman rulers. But God used the Romans to prepare the world for Jesus' coming. Since few nations dared to rise up against the powerful Roman armies, the world was in relative peace during Jesus' life and the beginning of the church. The good Roman roads made travel easier for the early Christian missionaries.

13. How did Caesar Augustus, a Roman emperor, help to fulfill Micah 5:2? (Also see Luke 2:1–6.) _____

   His decree that everyone should return to their hometown to be taxed brought Joseph and Mary to

   Bethlehem at the proper time.

14. Which apostle was a Roman citizen? (Acts 22:25–28) _____Paul_____

✎ *As a review of this lesson, match each description with the correct name. Some names are not needed. If you need help, reread the lesson text.*

  _c_   15. The empire that controlled Palestine in Malachi's time   a. Alexander

  _a_   16. The man who conquered the Persians   b. Mattathias

  _e_   17. The Greek rulers in Egypt   c. Persian

  _f_   18. The Greek rulers in Syria   d. Pompey

  _b_   19. A Jew who refused to worship Zeus   e. Ptolemies

                                                               f. Seleucids

*   *   *   *   *   *

Truths to Instill

• During these four hundred years, God was preparing for the coming Messiah.

  —The Jews in Judah longed for deliverance from foreign rule and for a message from God.

  —The scattered Jews and the Greek Old Testament spread a knowledge of God and the hope for the Messiah to many other lands.

  —God used the Greek and Roman Empires to help prepare the way for spreading the Gospel. "But when the fulness of the time was come, God sent forth his Son" (Galatians 4:4).

• While the Pharisees claimed to believe the Law of Moses, they actually were not keeping it. What they did keep were additional laws and rules they had developed, while they bypassed the true intent of Moses' Law. (See Mark 7:1–8.)

_____i_____ 20. The sons of Mattathias

_____l_____ 21. A group of worldly Jews who did not believe in the resurrection

_____j_____ 22. Strict Jews who kept many traditions, but who did not always love God

_____g_____ 23. Jewish books that we do not accept as part of the Scriptures

_____k_____ 24. The empire that controlled Palestine at the time of Christ's birth

g. Apocrypha

h. Greek

i. Maccabees

j. Pharisees

k. Roman

l. Sadducees

B. BIBLE WORD STUDY

✎ *Write a word from the verse given to fit each definition.*

_____swine_____	1. One or more pigs (Leviticus 11:7)
_____zealous_____	2. Showing an eager desire to accomplish something (Numbers 25:11)
_____choler_____	3. Anger (Daniel 8:7)
_____hypocrites_____	4. Persons who pretend to be something that they are not (Matthew 23:27)
_____tradition_____	5. A teaching handed down from one generation to another (Mark 7:8)
_____Corban_____	6. A gift dedicated to God (Mark 7:11)
_____scourge_____	7. To whip severely as a punishment (Acts 22:25)

C. THINKING ABOUT BIBLE TRUTHS

"Greek Jews" and "Hebrew Jews"

Alexander the Great died soon after he established his vast empire. But the Greek language and ideas that he had spread influenced the world for hundreds of years. By New Testament times, most of the Jews who were living outside Palestine spoke Greek. Even some Jews of Palestine spoke Greek instead of Hebrew (or Aramaic).

1. a. What were the Jews who spoke Greek called in the Bible? (Acts 6:1) _____Grecians_____

   b. What conflict arose in the early church between the Jews who spoke Greek and the Jews who

   spoke Hebrew? _____

   The Grecians complained that their widows were not being taken care of properly.

Greek-speaking Jews did not follow the Law as strictly as Hebrew Jews. Some Greek Jews forsook the faith of their fathers completely. But many of them still worshiped God in their synagogues and traveled to the temple at Jerusalem when they could. Some Gentiles (Greeks) learned about God from Greek Jews. By the time of the early church, the Greek Jews and their devout Greek neighbors were often more ready to receive the Gospel than the Hebrew Jews.

2. a. Which of Paul's helpers was the son of a Jewish mother and a Greek father? (Acts 16:1–3) _____

   Timothy (Timotheus)

   b. How does the Bible describe his mother and his grandmother? (2 Timothy 1:5) _____

   They had an unfeigned (genuine) faith.

3. How many devout Greeks of Thessalonica believed the Gospel? (Acts 17:4) _____

   a great multitude

4. During the period between the Old and New Testaments, God used both the Hebrew Jews and the Greek Jews to prepare the world for Jesus' coming.

   a. Which type of Jew preserved the worship at the temple and best kept the Law? _____

      the Hebrew Jews

   b. Which type of Jew helped spread the knowledge of God and the hope for the Messiah to many countries? _____

      the Greek Jews (the Grecians)

D. LEARNING MORE ABOUT THE BIBLE

Jews in a Greek World

✒ *During the time of the Greek Empire, Jews spread to many countries. A few of these places are marked on this map. Using the clues, label these places: Alexandria, Babylon, Ephesus, Jerusalem, Macedonia, and Shushan.*

1. Home of Alexander the Great. A man from here called Paul in a vision. (Acts 16:9).
2. An important city of Asia where Paul preached (Acts 18:19).
3. An Egyptian city named after Alexander. Apollos was born here (Acts 18:24).
4. Capital of Judah (Nehemiah 1:3)
5. Home of Ezra and many other Jews (Ezra 7:6)
6. Home of Queen Esther (Esther 2:5–7)

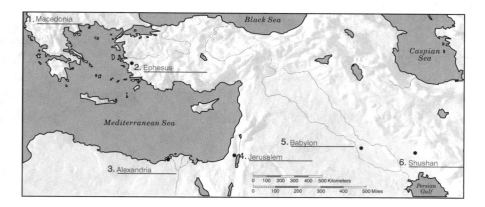

196   Chapter Six   The Jews After the Captivity

The Old Testament in Greek

After Alexander the Great brought the Middle East under Greek control, many Jews learned the Greek language and forgot Hebrew. These Greek-speaking Jews needed a Greek translation of the Old Testament to use in their synagogue services. By about 250 B.C., the Jews had translated the Books of Moses into Greek. Later they translated the rest of the Old Testament.

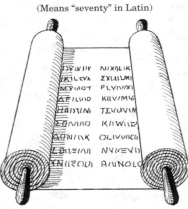

SEPTUAGINT
(Means "seventy" in Latin)

According to a legend, seventy-two Jews translated the Books of Moses into Greek in seventy-two days. Because of this, the version was called the *Septuagint* (SEHP too uh jihnt), which means "seventy" in Latin. We do not know how much, if any, of the legend is true. But we do know that the Greek translation of the Old Testament was widely used by the time of Christ. The early Christians used it regularly.

The verse below is Psalm 23:1 in Greek. The approximate pronunciation and literal English meaning are given below each Greek word.

ΚΎΡΙΟΣ	ΠΟΙΜΑΊΝΕΙ	ΜΕ,	ΚΑῚ	ΟΫΔΈΝ	ΜΕ	ΫΣΤΕΡΉΣΕΙ.
(KOO ree ahs)	(poy MAH ee neye)	(meh)	(kahee)	(oo DEHN)	(meh)	(hoos TEHR ay seye)
[The] LORD	tends like a shepherd	me,	and	nothing	I	shall want.

✎ *Using the information above, answer these questions.*

7. What does the word *Septuagint* mean? _____ "seventy" _____

8. The Septuagint was a translation of the Hebrew Scriptures into what language? _____ Greek _____

9. Besides the Jews, who used the Septuagint version for their worship services? _____

   the early Christians _____

• Some Jews and early Christians thought the translators of the Septuagint had been inspired by God just as the original Hebrew writers had been. We believe that God helps faithful translators, but God also expects men to carefully translate and preserve His Word. Like any other work of man, the translation of the Septuagint was not perfect. And because all books were written by hand at that time, additional errors were made as scribes copied the Septuagint repeatedly.

LXX
(The Roman numeral "seventy" is sometimes used as an abbreviation for the Septuagint.)

Because the early Christians used the Septuagint, the Jews who did not believe in Jesus began to find fault with it. They pointed out its errors and in time made new Greek translations for themselves. About two hundred years after Christ, a scholar named Origen tried to correct and standardize the Greek Old Testament.

197

Chapter Six Review

A. ORAL REVIEW

✎ *Be sure you know the answers to these questions. Answer as many as you can from memory. If you need help, you may check the reference or lesson given in brackets.*

Why >>

1. Why did the old men weep when they saw the foundation of Zerubbabel's temple? [Haggai 2:3]
2. Why did Mordecai raise his cousin Esther? [Esther 2:7]
3. Why was Haman angry with Mordecai? [Esther 3:5]
4. Why was Ezra ashamed to ask the king for protection when he carried great riches back to Jerusalem? [Ezra 8:22]
5. Why did God withhold His blessings from the Jews of Haggai's time? [Haggai 1:9]
6. Why did Mattathias kill a Greek officer and start a revolt? [Lesson 29]

How >>

7. How did Mordecai and Esther save the king's life? [Esther 2:21, 22]
8. How did Ezra show his grief when he heard of the Jews' sin? [Ezra 9:3]
9. How did Nehemiah protect the wall builders from their enemies? [Nehemiah 4:13]
10. How did Nehemiah keep merchants from selling their goods in Jerusalem on the Sabbath? [Nehemiah 13:19]
11. How did God say the temple built by Zerubbabel would be greater than the temple built by Solomon? [Haggai 2:9]
12. How many years did it take to rebuild the temple from start to finish? [Lesson 28]
13. How did the spread of the Greek language prepare the way for Christianity? [Lesson 29]

Who

14. Who refused to come when called by King Ahasuerus? [Esther 1:12] Vashti
15. Whom did King Ahasuerus promote after Haman was dead? [Esther 8:2] Mordecai
16. Who prophesied that Jesus would be betrayed for thirty pieces of silver? [Lesson 28] Zechariah
17. Who is the Branch of whom Zechariah prophesied? [Lesson 28] Jesus
18. Who was probably the last Old Testament prophet? [Lesson 28] Malachi

Where

19. Where did God say He would pour a blessing from if the Jews paid their tithes to Him? [Malachi 3:10] from the windows of heaven

B. WRITTEN REVIEW

✎ *Write the answers to these questions. Do as many as you can from memory. If you need help, you may check the reference or lesson given in brackets.*

What

1. What does the word *mingle* mean? [Lesson 26] "to mix with"

2. What did Queen Esther do to save the Jews? [Esther 4:16] She went in to the king even though she had not been called.

Answers column:

1. They had seen the first temple, which had been much greater.
2. Her parents had died.
3. Mordecai refused to bow to him.
4. He had told the king that God helps all those who seek Him.
5. They were letting His house lie waste while taking care of their own business.
6. He refused to worship an idol.
7. They told the king that two of his servants planned to kill him.
8. He tore his clothes and pulled out his hair.
9. He armed the builders with weapons.
10. He shut the gates on the Sabbath.
11. The glory of the latter house would be greater than the former.
12. about nineteen
13. People in many lands could understand Greek preaching and could read the Greek Scriptures for themselves.

Chapter Six Review

This review is divided into two parts, an oral review and a written review. The oral review is intended for class discussion, but students could also use it for self-study.

3. What did King Ahasuerus do when he heard that Haman had built a gallows for Mordecai? [Esther 7:9]

    He had Haman hanged on it.

4. What did the king permit the Jews to do on the day Haman had planned to destroy them? [Esther 8:11]

    He permitted them to fight against their enemies.

5. What event did the feast of Purim help the Jews remember? [Esther 9:22] _____

    their victory over their enemies

6. What is a chamberlain? [Lesson 27] an important officer in a ruler's house

7. What did Ezra tell the disobedient Jews to do with their heathen wives? [Ezra 10:11] _____

    He told them to separate themselves from their heathen wives.

8. What made Nehemiah sad while he was the king's cupbearer? [Nehemiah 2:3] _____

    He heard that Jerusalem lay in ruins.

9. What feast did the Jews keep after Ezra read the Law? [Nehemiah 8:13–17] _____

    the Feast of Tabernacles

10. What Jewish writings do we not accept as part of the Scriptures? [Lesson 29] _____

    the Apocrypha

11. What word describes a person who pretends to be something that he is not? [Lesson 29]

    _____ hypocrite _____

12. What was the Greek translation of the Old Testament called? [Lesson 29] _____ the Septuagint

Which

13. Which king allowed the Jews to return to Jerusalem and rebuild the temple? [Ezra 1:1] Cyrus

14. Which two men were leaders of the first group of Jews who returned to Jerusalem? [Ezra 3:2] _____

    Zerubbabel and Jeshua (Sheshbazzar was an additional leader if he was not the same man as
    Zerubbabel.)

15. Which two prophets encouraged the Jews to finish rebuilding the temple? [Ezra 5:1] _____

    Haggai and Zechariah

16. Which prophet rebuked the Jews for despising God's Name? [Lesson 28] Malachi

17. Which empire controlled Palestine in Nehemiah's time? [Lesson 29] Persia

18. Which group of Jews carefully kept their traditions, even when their hearts were not right? [Lesson 29]

    _____ the Pharisees _____

19. Which group of Jews refused to believe that the dead will rise again? [Lesson 29]

    _____ the Sadducees _____

20. Which empire controlled Palestine at the time of Jesus' birth? [Lesson 29] _____

    the Roman Empire

Where Is It Found?

✎ *Match the events on the right with the chapters that record them.*

_f_	21. Ezra 1, 2	a. The wall of Jerusalem is rebuilt in spite of threats and other problems.
_c_	22. Ezra 3–6	b. Esther invites the king and Haman to a banquet. Mordecai is honored and Haman is hanged.
_h_	23. Ezra 8–10	c. The Jews rebuild the temple at Jerusalem in spite of much opposition.
_d_	24. Nehemiah 1, 2	d. Nehemiah hears about the situation in Jerusalem and asks the king for permission to go there.
_a_	25. Nehemiah 3–6	e. Haman plans to destroy the Jews. Mordecai asks Esther to intercede with the king for them.
_g_	26. Nehemiah 13	f. Cyrus passes a decree allowing the Jews to return to their homeland.
_i_	27. Esther 1, 2	g. Nehemiah deals with those who do business on the Sabbath Day.
_e_	28. Esther 3, 4	h. Ezra takes another group to Jerusalem and leads a revival there.
_b_	29. Esther 5–7	i. Esther is made queen of Persia.
_j_	30. Esther 8–10	j. Mordecai is promoted and the Jews are delivered from their enemies.

Review of Old Testament Books

✎ *Write the names of the divisions and books of the Old Testament in the correct order. Be sure you know how to spell them correctly and how many books are found in each section.*

1. Books of _____Moses_____
- Genesis
- Exodus
- Leviticus
- Numbers
- Deuteronomy

2. Books of _____History_____
- Joshua
- Judges
- Ruth
- 1 & 2 Samuel
- 1 & 2 Kings
- 1 & 2 Chronicles
- Ezra
- Nehemiah
- Esther

3. Books of _____Poetry_____
- Job
- Psalms
- Proverbs
- Ecclesiastes
- Song of Solomon

4. Books of
- _____Major_____ _____Prophets_____
- Isaiah
- Jeremiah
- Lamentations
- Ezekiel
- Daniel

5. Books of
- _____Minor_____ _____Prophets_____
- Hosea
- Joel
- Amos
- Obadiah
- Jonah
- Micah
- Nahum
- Habakkuk
- Zephaniah
- Haggai
- Zechariah
- Malachi

200

Lesson 30. Old Testament Review

How well do you know the Old Testament? Even though we have the New Testament today, we can still learn valuable lessons from Old Testament examples and teachings. Are you like Timothy, whom the apostle Paul commended for knowing the Old Testament Scriptures from his childhood (2 Timothy 3:15)? Or are you like the Sadducees, to whom Jesus said: "Ye do err, not knowing the scriptures, nor the power of God" (Matthew 22:29)?

This lesson reviews a few Old Testament events, characters, covenants, and places. The real test of your Bible knowledge, however, is not how many Bible facts you remember, but whether you live according to God's Word. God wants you to read His Word, to understand His Word, and to humbly obey His Word.

"Blessed are the undefiled in the way, who walk in the law of the LORD" (Psalm 119:1).

A. ANSWERS FROM THE BIBLE

✎ *Most of these Old Testament events are listed under the books that record them. For each number, cross out the two events that are not under the correct heading. You may use your Bible, a concordance, or a Bible dictionary if you need help. The first one is done for you.*

1. Genesis
   a. God creates all things.
   b. Adam and Eve sin and are driven from Eden.
   c. God sends the Flood.
   d. God calls Abram.
   e. ~~The Israelites build the tabernacle.~~
   f. Abraham sacrifices Isaac.
   g. Joseph repays his brothers good for evil.
   h. ~~Moses is born.~~

   • God considered Abraham's offering complete (Hebrews 11:17), even though He stopped Abraham from killing his son.

2. Exodus, Leviticus, Numbers, and Deuteronomy
   a. ~~Jacob blesses his sons.~~
   b. God calls Moses.
   c. God sends the ten plagues.
   d. The Israelites escape from Egypt.
   e. God gives His laws on Mount Sinai.
   f. ~~Jephthah makes a rash vow.~~
   g. Moses numbers the Israelites.
   h. The Israelites wander in the wilderness forty years.

3. Joshua, Judges, and Ruth
   a. ~~Moses makes a brazen serpent.~~
   b. Rahab helps the two spies.
   c. The Israelites cross the Jordan River.
   d. Joshua divides Canaan among the twelve tribes.
   e. Gideon conquers the Midianites.
   f. Samson kills many Philistines.
   g. ~~David kills Goliath.~~
   h. Naomi's husband and sons die.
   i. Boaz marries Ruth.

4. 1 and 2 Samuel, 1 and 2 Kings, and 1 and 2 Chronicles
   a. Saul is anointed king.
   b. ~~Balaam tries to curse Israel.~~
   c. David reigns over all Israel.
   d. Solomon builds the temple.
   e. Jehu destroys the house of Ahab.
   f. God cures Naaman's leprosy.
   g. The Assyrians take Israel captive.
   h. ~~Haggai and Zechariah prophesy.~~
   i. Hezekiah helps bring a great revival.

Lesson 30

Oral Review

1. Why did the Jews in Babylon sit and weep? [24] **They remembered Zion, their old home.**
2. Why should we work, even if we have enough for our own needs? [25] **so that we have enough to give to those in need**
3. What event did the feast of Purim help the Jews remember? [27] **their victory over their enemies in Esther's time**
4. How did God say the temple built by Zerubbabel would be greater than the temple built by Solomon? [28] **The glory of the latter house would be greater than the former.**
5. Which empire controlled Palestine in Nehemiah's time? [29] **Persia**
6. How did the spread of the Greek language prepare the way for Christianity? [29] **People in many lands could understand Greek preaching and could read the Greek Scriptures for themselves.**
7. Why did Mattathias kill a Greek officer and start a revolt? [29] **He refused to worship an idol.**
8. What empire controlled Palestine when Jesus was born? [29] **the Roman Empire**

5. Ezra, Nehemiah, and Esther

a. Cyrus makes an important decree.

b. ~~The Babylonians conquer Judah.~~

c. Zerubbabel rebuilds the temple.

d. Esther risks her life to save her people.

e. Haman is hanged on his own gallows.

f. ~~Mattathias refuses to sacrifice to an idol.~~

g. Nehemiah rebuilds Jerusalem's walls.

h. Ezra reads the Book of the Law.

i. Mordecai establishes the feast of Purim.

✎ *Match the characters on the left with the Bible books on the right that tell about them. Some books tell about more than one of the characters. Use a concordance or a Bible dictionary if you need help.*

c	6.	Achan	a.	Genesis
f	7.	Elisha	b.	Numbers
e	8.	Hannah	c.	Joshua
h	9.	Mordecai	d.	Judges
f	10.	Naaman	e.	1 Samuel
i	11.	the people of Nineveh	f.	2 Kings
a	12.	Noah	g.	Ezra
a	13.	Rebekah	h.	Esther
f	14.	Uzziah	i.	Jonah
g	15.	Zerubbabel	j.	Malachi

✎ *Fill in the blanks.*

16. The Book of _____Psalms_____ is a collection of songs and prayers.

17. The trials of a faithful man who lost everything he owned are described in the Book of _____Job_____.

18. The Book of _____Daniel_____ contains a number of stories about four young men who were taken captive to Babylon.

19. The Book of _____Proverbs_____ is a collection of short, wise sayings.

20. The Major and Minor _____Prophets_____ contain many messages from the LORD.

21. The Old Testament foretold the coming of the Seed of Abraham, the Lawgiver of Judah, a Prophet like Moses, the Branch from the root of David, and the Messiah. Who fulfilled all these prophecies? _____Jesus_____

B. BIBLE STUDY BOOKS

✎ *The Old Testament records a number of special covenants God made with people. Use a concordance to find the references of these verses, and then write whom God made each covenant with.*

1. "I will establish my covenant with you; neither shall all flesh be cut off any more by the waters of a flood" (_____Genesis___9__:_11__). Noah and his sons_____

In This Lesson

Objectives

• Students should know

—how to find Bible verses or events when they do not know the references. (by using a concordance or a Bible dictionary)

—the location of important places on a map of Bible lands. (See Part B.)

—the order and spelling of the five divisions of the Old Testament and all the Old Testament books.

Truths to Instill

• Learning the Scriptures in childhood is a great blessing. A knowledge of the Scriptures can make us "wise unto salvation" (2 Timothy 3:15).

• A knowledge of Bible facts is of limited value unless we willingly obey God's Word because of our love for Him.

• An understanding of Old Testament covenants and prophecy helps us realize their perfect fulfillment in Christ.

202   Chapter Six   The Jews After the Captivity

2. "I will multiply thy seed as the stars of the heaven, and as the sand which is upon the sea shore; . . . and in thy seed shall all the nations of the earth be blessed" (_____ Genesis __22_:_17_, _18_).
_____ Abraham _____

3. "And he took the book of the covenant, and read in the audience of the people: and they said, All that the LORD hath said will we do, and be obedient. . . . And [he] said, Behold the blood of the covenant which the LORD hath made with you" (_____ Exodus __24_:_7_, _8_). _Moses and the Israelites_____

4. "Thine house and thy kingdom shall be established for ever before thee" (_____ 2 Samuel __7_:_16_).
_____ David _____

Map Review

✎ *Label the following places on Map A. (If you need help, use the maps in this workbook or in a Bible atlas.)*

Mediterranean Sea	Damascus	Nineveh
Euphrates River	Egypt	Shushan
Babylon	Jerusalem	

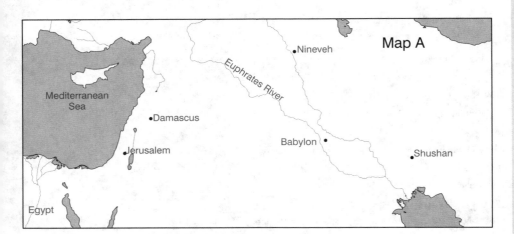

Map A

Lesson 30. Old Testament Review **203**

✎ *Label the following places on Map B. Mark the city locations with dots.*

Ammon	Judah	Phoenicia	Samaria (city)
Edom	Moab	Syria (Aram)	Dead Sea
Israel	Philistia	Jerusalem	Jordan River

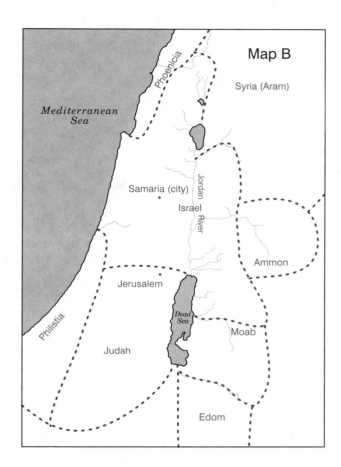

Answers for #10 on page 212

Books of Moses
  Genesis
  Exodus
  Leviticus
  Numbers
  Deuteronomy

Books of History
  Joshua
  Judges
  Ruth
  1 & 2 Samuel
  1 & 2 Kings
  1 & 2 Chronicles
  Ezra
  Nehemiah
  Esther

Books of Poetry
  Job
  Psalms
  Proverbs
  Ecclesiastes
  Song of Solomon

Books of the Major Prophets
  Isaiah
  Jeremiah
  Lamentations
  Ezekiel
  Daniel

Books of the Minor Prophets
  Hosea
  Joel
  Amos
  Obadiah
  Jonah
  Micah
  Nahum
  Habakkuk
  Zephaniah
  Haggai
  Zechariah
  Malachi

204

Reviewing What You Have Learned

✎ *This exercise reviews some of the important facts that you have studied this year. Be sure you know the answers to these questions before taking the final test. Try to answer as many as you can from memory. If you need help, you may check the Bible reference or the lesson given in brackets.*

Chapter One—Israel Becomes a Kingdom >>

1. What did Samuel say was more important than sacrifice? [1 Samuel 15:22]
2. What does the LORD look at rather than just the outward appearance of a person? [1 Samuel 16:7]
3. Why did Saul become angry with David? [1 Samuel 18:8]
4. What covenant did God make with David? [2 Samuel 7:16]
5. How clean did David want God to wash his heart from sin? [Psalm 51:7]
6. Why is David's family line important to us today? [Luke 2:4]
7. How did Solomon become the wisest man? [1 Kings 4:29]
8. What did Solomon realize about riches by the end of his life? [Ecclesiastes 5:10]
9. What is the meaning of *covenant*? of *talent*? [Lessons 1, 4]
10. Name the thirty-nine books of the Old Testament and their five divisions. (Be sure you know the correct order and spelling.) [Lesson 1]

Chapter Two—The Northern Tribes Set Up a Separate Kingdom >>

11. What did the ten northern tribes ask Rehoboam to do? [1 Kings 12:2–4]
12. Why did Jeroboam make golden calves at Bethel and Dan? [1 Kings 12:27, 28]
13. What words does the Bible use repeatedly to describe Jeroboam? [1 Kings 16:19, 26]
14. What two dynasties in Israel lasted for more than two generations? [Lesson 7]
15. Who married Jezebel and worshiped Baal? [1 Kings 16:31]
16. What did Elijah prophesy about Ahab and Jezebel's deaths? [1 Kings 21:19, 23]
17. In what two places did Elijah stay during the years of drought? [1 Kings 17:5, 9]
18. Where did Elijah hear the still, small voice? [1 Kings 19:8, 12]
19. How did Elijah go to heaven? [2 Kings 2:11]
20. What is the meaning of *blaspheme*? of *mantle*? of *morsel*? [Lessons 8, 9]

Chapter Three—Israel's Downfall >>

21. What request did Elisha make before Elijah was taken up to heaven? [2 Kings 2:9]
22. Who told Naaman where to go for healing? [2 Kings 5:2, 3]
23. How was Gehazi punished for his covetousness? [2 Kings 5:20–27]
24. What did Elisha's servant see on the hills when God opened his eyes? [2 Kings 6:17]
25. Where were lepers required to live? [Leviticus 13:46]
26. How was Elijah's prophecy concerning Jezebel fulfilled? [2 Kings 9:32–37]
27. How did the LORD reward Jehu for destroying Ahab's house and the Baal worshipers? [2 Kings 10:30]
28. What idols did Jehu leave in Israel? [2 Kings 10:29]
29. How many times did Joash, the grandson of Jehu, smite the Syrians? [2 Kings 13:25]
30. What nation conquered Samaria and scattered the Israelites into foreign lands? [2 Kings 17:6]

Final Review

This review is intended for class discussion or as a self-study review before the final test. It could also be used for extra review throughout the school year.

1. to obey the voice of the LORD
2. the person's heart
3. Saul was jealous that David was more popular than he was.
4. God promised to establish David's kingdom forever.
5. whiter than snow
6. Jesus came through David's line.
7. He depended on God to give him true wisdom.
8. Riches do not satisfy.
9. *covenant:* a binding agreement
   talent: a Bible weight equal to about 75 pounds (34 kg)
10. (See answers on page 211.)
11. to make their burdens lighter
12. He wanted to keep the northern tribes from returning to Jerusalem.
13. "He made Israel to sin."
14. Omri's and Jehu's
15. Ahab
16. The dogs would lick Ahab's blood and eat Jezebel.
17. near the Brook Cherith, and with a widow at Zarephath
18. on Mount Horeb
19. He went up by a whirlwind.
20. *blaspheme:* to curse or speak evil of; *mantle:* a cloak or robe; *morsel:* a piece of food
21. "Let a double portion of thy spirit be upon me."
22. an Israelite maid
23. He was smitten with leprosy.
24. horses and chariots of fire
25. outside the camp
26. The dogs ate most of her body.
27. He promised that four generations of Jehu's descendants would reign.
28. the golden calves that Jeroboam had made at Bethel and Dan
29. three
30. Assyria

Chapter Four—David's Family Reigns Over Judah >>

31. Who remained loyal to Rehoboam after some of the tribes rebelled? [2 Chronicles 11:5, 12, 13]
32. What good king was a friend to Ahab? [2 Chronicles 18:1]
33. What were some results of Jehoram's marriage to Athaliah? [Lesson 17]
34. What mistake did good King Uzziah make? [2 Chronicles 26:16]
35. How can we know that the people enjoyed Hezekiah's Passover feast? [2 Chronicles 30:23]
36. How many Assyrians were killed by the angel of the LORD? [Isaiah 37:36]
37. What king caused the people of Judah to do worse than the heathen? [2 Chronicles 33:9]
38. What did Manasseh do when he was taken captive and afflicted by the Assyrians? [2 Chronicles 33:12, 13]
39. Who killed the idolatrous priests in Judah and Israel and burned their bones? [2 Kings 23:19, 20]
40. Which six kings in the following list were mostly good? Which six are remembered for their wickedness? [Lesson 19 chart]

Asa	Ahaziah	Ahaz	Amon
Jehoshaphat	Uzziah	Hezekiah	Josiah
Jehoram	Jotham	Manasseh	Jehoiakim

Chapter Five—Judah Taken Captive >>

41. Whom did Nebuchadnezzar take captive in the third year of Jehoiakim's reign? [Daniel 1:1–6]
42. What did the Babylonians do to Jerusalem? [Jeremiah 39:8]
43. How did God fulfill His promise that David's kingdom would be established forever? [Luke 1:30–33]
44. Which king burned Jeremiah's scroll? [Jeremiah 36:9, 21–23]
45. Who wrote the words that God gave to Jeremiah? [Jeremiah 36:4]
46. Why did Daniel refuse to eat the king's meat? [Daniel 1:8]
47. What did God want Nebuchadnezzar to recognize about the Most High? [Daniel 4:32]
48. How long did Jeremiah say the captivity would last? [Jeremiah 29:10]
49. Why did the Jews in Babylon sit and weep? [Psalm 137:1]
50. How did the LORD use King Cyrus to help the Jews? [Ezra 1:1–3]

Chapter Six—The Jews After the Captivity >>

51. Which two men were leaders of the first group of Jews who returned to Jerusalem? [Ezra 3:2]
52. What did Ezra tell the disobedient Jews to do with their heathen wives? [Ezra 10:11]
53. What made Nehemiah sad while he was the king's cupbearer? [Nehemiah 2:3]
54. Why was Haman angry with Mordecai? [Esther 3:5]
55. What did Queen Esther do to save the Jews? [Esther 4:16]
56. What event did the feast of Purim help the Jews remember? [Esther 9:22]
57. Why did God withhold His blessings from the Jews of Haggai's time? [Haggai 1:9]
58. Who prophesied that Jesus would be betrayed for thirty pieces of silver? [Lesson 28]
59. Who is the Branch of whom Zechariah spoke? [Lesson 28]
60. How did the spread of the Greek language prepare the way for Christianity? [Lesson 29]

31. the tribes of Judah and Benjamin, and many priests and Levites
32. Jehoshaphat
33. (Sample answers) Jehoram did evil like Ahab's house; Athaliah was Ahaziah's wicked counselor; Athaliah killed most of the royal descendants and reigned wickedly.
34. He went into the temple to burn incense.
35. They decided to keep the feast for an extra week.
36. 185,000
37. Manasseh
38. He humbled himself and prayed to God.
39. Josiah
40. *mostly good:* Asa, Jehoshaphat, Uzziah, Jotham, Hezekiah, Josiah
remembered for their wickedness: Jehoram, Ahaziah, Ahaz, Manasseh, Amon, Jehoiakim
41. some of the king's children and princes, including Daniel and his three friends
42. They burned it and broke down its walls.
43. Jesus, who will reign forever, was born into David's family.
44. Jehoiakim
45. Baruch
46. He had purposed in his heart that he would not defile himself.
47. "The most High ruleth in the kingdom of men, and giveth it to whomsoever he will."
48. seventy years
49. They remembered Zion, their old home.
50. The LORD stirred him to make a decree allowing the Jews to rebuild the temple.

51. Zerubbabel and Jeshua (Sheshbazzar was an additional leader if he was not the same man as Zerubbabel.)
52. He told them to separate themselves from their heathen wives.
53. He heard that Jerusalem lay in ruins.
54. Mordecai refused to bow to him.
55. She went in to the king even though she had not been called.
56. their victory over their enemies in Esther's time
57. They were letting His house lie waste while taking care of their own business.
58. Zechariah
59. Jesus
60. People in many lands could understand Greek preaching and could read the Greek Scriptures for themselves.

Life in Bible Times >>

61. What was a tunic? a cloak? an ephod? [Lesson 5]
62. With what ornament does the New Testament tell godly women to adorn themselves? [1 Peter 3:4]
63. What two practices did the Old Testament Law permit that were not according to God's original plan for marriage? [Lesson 10]
64. Who was the ancestor of the Israelites, the Ishmaelites, the Edomites, and the Midianites? [Lesson 15]
65. Who was the ancestor of the Moabites and the Ammonites? [Lesson 15]
66. What was the most important food in Bible times? [Genesis 3:19]
67. What kind of animals did the Law forbid the Israelites to eat? [Leviticus 11:8]
68. Name at least two tools used by shepherds of Bible times. [Lesson 25]
69. Name at least five kinds of tradesmen mentioned in the Bible. [Lesson 25]
70. Why should we work, even if we have enough for our own needs? [Ephesians 4:28]

61. *tunic*: an inner, sacklike garment
    cloak: a heavy outer coat
    ephod: a special coat worn by priests
62. a meek and quiet spirit
63. having more than one wife, divorce
64. Abraham
65. Lot
66. bread
67. unclean
68. a sling, a rod, a staff, and a shepherd's bag
69. (Sample answers) shepherd, farmer, apothecary, baker, carpenter, fisherman, fuller, mason, merchant, potter, smith, tanner, tentmaker, weaver
70. so that we have enough to give to those in need

God's Chosen Family as a Nation
Chapter One Test

Name _____ Date _____ Score _____

A. *Match. Names may be used more than once or not at all.*   *(10 points)*

__e__	1. Gave his robe to David	a. Absalom
__h__	2. Asked a witch about the future	b. David
__b__	3. Brought the ark of the LORD to Jerusalem	c. Hiram
__d__	4. Reigned over Israel while David reigned in Hebron	d. Ishbosheth
__b__	5. Captured Jerusalem from the Jebusites	e. Jonathan
__c__	6. Sold cedar and fir trees to Solomon to build a temple	f. Queen of Sheba
__i__	7. Asked God for wisdom	g. Samuel
__a__	8. Tried to take the kingdom away from David	h. Saul
__f__	9. Came to ask Solomon questions	i. Solomon
__i__	10. Spoke 3,000 proverbs and wrote 1,005 songs	

B. *Write* true *or* false *in each blank.*   *(9 points)*

_____true_____ 11. Saul was humble when he was first anointed king.

_____true_____ 12. Saul waited for Samuel seven days before offering the sacrifice himself.

_____false_____ 13. David hid when Samuel came to anoint him.

_____false_____ 14. Saul became angry when David offered to fight Goliath.

_____false_____ 15. David faced Goliath with confidence because he knew slings were better weapons than swords and spears.

_____true_____ 16. One talent equals about 75 pounds.

_____false_____ 17. God promised to establish Saul's kingdom forever.

_____true_____ 18. David suffered much because of his sin, even though he sincerely repented.

_____false_____ 19. The reign of Saul is recorded in 1 Kings.

C. *Fill in the blanks or underline the correct words.*   *(10 points)*

20. The first enemies Saul led the Israelites to battle against were the (Amalekites, <u>Ammonites</u>, Philistines).

21. "To _____obey_____ is better than sacrifice."

22. "Man looketh on the outward appearance, but the LORD looketh on the _____heart_____."

23. David mourned and fasted when he heard that _____Saul_____ and _____Jonathan_____ were dead.

24. A (covenant, respite, supplication) is a binding agreement.

25. Altogether, David reigned ___forty___ years at Hebron and Jerusalem.

26. After David repented, he wanted God to wash his heart _____whiter_____ than _____snow_____.

27. By the end of his life, Solomon realized that riches do not bring (worldly fame, discontentment, real satisfaction).

D. *Write answers for these questions.*   *(8 points)*

28. What excuse did Saul give for not completely destroying the Amalekites' sheep and oxen? _____
   He said that the people had spared the best sheep and oxen to sacrifice to the LORD.

29. How did David show that he had great respect for God's chosen leaders? _____
   David spared Saul's life when he could have killed him.

30. Why is David's family line important to us? _____
   Jesus came through David's line.

31. What did Solomon allow his wives to do when he was old? _____
   Solomon allowed his wives to turn his heart away from the LORD to serve other gods.

E. *Write the names of the Books of Moses. Be sure to use the correct order and spelling.*   *(5 points)*

32. _____Genesis_____
33. _____Exodus_____
34. _____Leviticus_____
35. _____Numbers_____
36. _____Deuteronomy_____

Total Points: 42

God's Chosen Family as a Nation
Chapter Two Test

Name _____ Date _____ Score _____

A. *Match. Names may be used more than once or not at all.*   *(10 points)*

___f___ 1. Built Samaria for his capital

___h___ 2. Conspired against Elah's and Baasha's house

___d___ 3. Fled for his life after a great victory

___e___ 4. Fled to Egypt to escape from Solomon

___g___ 5. Fled to Jerusalem after his tax collector was killed

___e___ 6. Known as the king who made Israel to sin

___c___ 7. Prophesied that Jeroboam would be king of ten tribes

___d___ 8. Met Ahab in Naboth's vineyard with a prophecy of judgment

___b___ 9. Sent groups of soldiers to capture Elijah

___a___ 10. "[Sold] himself to work wickedness in the sight of the Lord"

a. Ahab

b. Ahaziah

c. Ahijah

d. Elijah

e. Jeroboam

f. Omri

g. Rehoboam

h. Zimri

B. *Write* true *or* false *in each blank.*   *(5 points)*

_____false_____ 11. The five kings that followed Jeroboam were all his descendants.

_____true_____ 12. The Bible says that Omri did worse than all the kings before him.

_____true_____ 13. Ahab died after he was wounded in a battle against the Syrians.

_____false_____ 14. Elijah killed the prophets of Baal after Ahab died.

_____false_____ 15. Elisha was taken up into heaven by a whirlwind.

C. *Fill in the blanks or underline the correct words.*   *(6 points)*

16. Jeroboam was a mighty man of (God, wisdom, <u>valor</u>).

17. The prophet (<u>Ahijah</u>, Elijah, Micaiah) told Jeroboam's wife that her son would die.

18. Zimri reigned over Israel for only _____seven_____ days.

19. During a drought, Elijah stayed near a brook and with a widow of (Samaria, Tirzah, <u>Zarephath</u>).

20. _____Jezebel_____ fed 850 false prophets at her table.

21. Elijah and the false prophets met on Mount _____Carmel_____.

D. *Write complete answers for these questions.*   *(10 points)*

22. What advice did the old men give to Rehoboam? _____
   They advised him to be a servant to the people and to speak good words to them.
   _____

23. Why did Jeroboam make altars and golden calves at Bethel and Dan?_____
   He wanted to keep the northern tribes from returning to Jerusalem.
   _____

24. Why were both Ahab and Jezebel guilty of killing Naboth and taking his vineyard?_____
   Jezebel planned and commanded the killing of Naboth. Ahab did not stop her wicked plans, and
   he went to take possession of the vineyard after Naboth was killed.

25. When did Ahab put on sackcloth and fast? _____
   Ahab put on sackcloth and fasted after he heard of God's coming judgments on him and his family.
   _____

26. When did the LORD speak to Elijah in a still, small voice? _____
   The LORD spoke to Elijah in a still, small voice while he was at Mount Horeb.
   _____

E. *Write the names of the Books of History. Be sure to use the correct order and spelling.*   *(12 points)*

27. _____Joshua_____   33. _____2 Kings_____
28. _____Judges_____   34. _____1 Chronicles_____
29. _____Ruth_____   35. _____2 Chronicles_____
30. _____1 Samuel_____   36. _____Ezra_____
31. _____2 Samuel_____   37. _____Nehemiah_____
32. _____1 Kings_____   38. _____Esther_____

F. *Match the letters on the map with the cities listed below.*   *(7 points)*

___F___ 39. Bethel

___B___ 40. Dan

___G___ 41. Jerusalem

___C___ 42. Jezreel

___D___ 43. Ramoth-gilead

___E___ 44. Samaria

___A___ 45. Zarephath

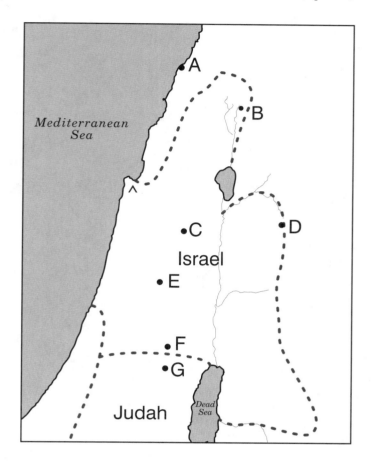

Total Points: 50

God's Chosen Family as a Nation
Chapter Three Test

Name _____ **Date** _____ **Score** _____

A. *Match. Names may be used more than once or not at all.*   *(7 points)*

  _b_   1. Smitten with leprosy as a punishment   a. Ahab's seventy sons

  _e_   2. Learned about Elisha through an Israelite girl   b. Gehazi

  _a_   3. Killed by the men of Samaria   c. king of Israel

  _f_   4. Recognized that the spirit of Elijah had come upon Elisha   d. king of Moab

  _c_   5. Made a feast for enemy soldiers   e. Naaman

  _d_   6. Sacrificed his son to an idol   f. sons of the prophets

  _e_   7. Cured of his leprosy   g. Zachariah

B. *Write* true *or* false *in each blank.*   *(5 points)*

_____false_____ 8. The Shunammite woman's son came back to life when Gehazi placed Elisha's staff on him.

_____false_____ 9. One seah equals about five bushels.

_____true_____ 10. *Avenge* means "to punish in return for a wrong."

_____true_____ 11. Jehu was less wicked than the kings who ruled Israel before him.

_____false_____ 12. Jehu destroyed the two golden calves that Jeroboam had made.

C. *Fill in the blanks.*   *(7 points)*

13. Elisha used twenty loaves of barley bread and some ears of grain to feed _____one hundred_____ men.

14. Elisha threw _____salt_____ into the water of Jericho to heal it.

15. King _____Jehu_____ was very zealous in some ways, but he failed to follow the LORD with all his heart.

16. King Joash smote the Syrians _____three_____ times.

17. The prophet _____Hosea_____ brought God's message of love to Israel.

18. Jeremiah said that God's _____Word_____ is like a hammer.

19. King _____Zachariah_____ was the last descendant of Jehu to reign.

D. *Write answers for these questions.*   *(10 points)*

20. What request did Elisha make before Elijah was taken up into heaven? _____
    <u>"Let a double portion of thy spirit be upon me."</u> _____
    _____

21. How did God break the siege of Samaria? _____
    <u>God made the Syrians hear the noise of a great army.</u> _____
    _____

22. When was Elijah's prophecy concerning God's judgment on Jezebel fulfilled? _____
    <u>It was fulfilled when the dogs ate most of her body after she was thrown down from a window.</u>
    _____

23. Why did God promise to allow four of Jehu's descendants to reign over Israel? _____
    <u>Jehu destroyed Ahab's wicked house and killed the Baal worshipers.</u> _____
    _____

24. How did the kingdom of Israel come to an end? _____
    <u>The Assyrians came and carried the Israelites away to distant lands.</u> _____
    _____

E. *Write the names of the Books of Poetry in order.* Be sure to use the correct spelling.   *(5 points)*

25. _____ <u>Job</u> _____
26. _____ <u>Psalms</u> _____
27. _____ <u>Proverbs</u> _____
28. _____ <u>Ecclesiastes</u> _____
29. _____ <u>Song of Solomon</u> _____

Total Points: 34

God's Chosen Family as a Nation
Chapter Four Test

Name _____ **Date** _____ **Score** _____

A. *Match. Use each name only once.*   *(8 points)*

   a   1. Sought healing from physicians instead of from the Lord   a. Asa

   d   2. Helped Ahab in battle   b. Athaliah

   b   3. Tried to kill all the royal descendants of David   c. Hezekiah

   e   4. Was rescued from death by his aunt   d. Jehoshaphat

   h   5. Tried to offer incense in the temple   e. Joash

   c   6. Asked that the shadow on the sundial move back ten degrees   f. Josiah

   g   7. Sacrificed his children to a false god   g. Manasseh

   f   8. Kept the greatest Passover since Samuel   h. Uzziah

B. *Write* true *or* false *in each blank.*   *(7 points)*

_____false_____ 9. Asa's counselor was Maacah, his wicked grandmother.

_____true_____ 10. Jehoram married wicked Athaliah.

_____true_____ 11. Amaziah sent the Israelite army back home after a man of God told him the
LORD was not with Israel.

_____false_____ 12. *Consecrate* means "a humble prayer or request."

_____true_____ 13. The LORD did not want His people to marry people from other nations.

_____true_____ 14. Micah prophesied about the same time as Isaiah.

_____false_____ 15. The LORD wanted His people to worship Him at high places.

C. *Fill in the blanks.*   *(5 points)*

16. Abijah walked in the sins of his _____father_____.

17. After Amaziah defeated the Edomites, he began worshiping the gods of the
_____Edomites_____.

18. When King _____Hezekiah_____ kept a great Passover, the people wanted to keep the feast for
seven extra days.

19. King _____Manasseh_____ caused his people to do worse than the heathen.

20. King _____Josiah_____ killed the idolatrous priests and burned their bones. He also defiled the high places and destroyed the idols.

D. *Place a check (✓) before the names of five kings who were mostly good.* (5 points)

21. __✓__ Jehoshaphat   _____ Ahaz

    _____ Jehoram   __✓__ Hezekiah

    _____ Ahaziah   _____ Manasseh

    __✓__ Uzziah   _____ Amon

    __✓__ Jotham   __✓__ Josiah

E. *Write answers for these questions.* (10 points)

22. Who remained loyal to Rehoboam when some of the tribes rebelled? _____
    Those who remained loyal to Rehoboam included the tribes of Judah and Benjamin, and many
    priests and Levites.

23. When did Joash stop serving the LORD? _____
    Joash stopped serving the LORD after Jehoiada died.

24. What did Hezekiah do when the Assyrians came up against Judah? _____
    Hezekiah prayed to the LORD.

25. When did Manasseh humble himself and pray to the LORD? _____
    Manasseh humbled himself and prayed when he was carried away captive and afflicted by the
    Assyrians.

26. What did Josiah do when the Book of the Law was read to him? _____
    Josiah humbled himself, rent his clothes, and wept. (Count the answer correct if at least one or two
    of these is given.)

F. *Write the names of the Major Prophets in order.* Be sure to use the correct spelling. (5 points)

27. _____Isaiah_____

28. _____Jeremiah_____

29. _____Lamentations_____

30. _____Ezekiel_____

31. _____Daniel_____

Total points: 40

God's Chosen Family as a Nation
Chapter Five Test

Name _____ **Date** _____ **Score** _____

A. *Match. Names may be used more than once.*   *(10 points)*

  d   1. Was taken captive the third year of Jehoiakim's reign   a. Baruch

  f   2. Burned Jeremiah's scroll   b. Belshazzar

  g   3. Prophesied to the Jews at Jerusalem   c. Cyrus

  a   4. Wrote Jeremiah's words in a scroll   d. Daniel

  h   5. Became angry when three Jews refused to worship his image   e. Ezekiel

  g   6. Told the remnant of the Jews not to go to Egypt   f. Jehoiakim

  d   7. Purposed not to defile himself   g. Jeremiah

  e   8. Cut off his hair as a sign   h. Nebuchadnezzar

  b   9. Saw a hand writing on the wall

  c   10. Allowed the Jews to rebuild the temple

B. *Write* true *or* false *in each blank.*   *(7 points)*

    false   11. Jehoiachin reigned for eleven years.

    false   12. Daniel prophesied that the Roman Empire would last forever.

    false   13. The Jews in Babylon sang songs of joy when they remembered Zion.

    true   14. Ezekiel prophesied in Babylon.

    true   15. Jehoiachin was released from prison by Evil-merodach.

    false   16. The Book of Daniel was originally written entirely in Hebrew.

    true   17. Jeremiah wept when his people refused to listen to his warnings from God.

C. *Fill in the blanks or underline the correct words.*   *(8 points)*

18. God said He would make Jeremiah strong like a defensed city, an (<u>iron</u>, ivory) pillar, and brazen (spears, <u>walls</u>).

19. King _____Zedekiah_____ broke a covenant he had made with Nebuchadnezzar.

20. Jeremiah prophesied that the captivity would last _____seventy_____ years.

21. Jeremiah told the Jews in Babylon to build _____houses_____, plant _____gardens_____, and raise families in their land of captivity.

22. People in Bible times used a (remnant, <u>signet</u>) to make a personal mark in clay.

23. The image in Nebuchadnezzar's vision represented (<u>four</u>, six, seven) earthly empires.

D. *Write answers for these questions.*   *(8 points)*

24. What happened to Jerusalem at the end of Zedekiah's reign? _____

   <u>The Babylonians burned it and broke down its walls.</u>_____

   _____

25. How did God fulfill His promise that David's kingdom would last forever? _____

   <u>God sent Jesus, who will reign forever, through David's family.</u>_____

   _____

26. How did Ebed-melech help Jeremiah? _____

   <u>He rescued Jeremiah from a dungeon.</u>_____

   _____

27. What did God want Nebuchadnezzar to recognize about the Most High? _____

   <u>(Wording may vary slightly.) "That the most High ruleth in the kingdom of men, and giveth it to</u>

   <u>whomsoever he will."</u>_____

E. *Write the names of the Minor Prophets in order.* Be sure to use the correct spelling.   *(12 points)*

28. _____Hosea_____   34. _____Nahum_____

29. _____Joel_____   35. _____Habakkuk_____

30. _____Amos_____   36. _____Zephaniah_____

31. _____Obadiah_____   37. _____Haggai_____

32. _____Jonah_____   38. _____Zechariah_____

33. _____Micah_____   39. _____Malachi_____

F. *Match the letters on the map with the names of the cities.*   *(5 points)*

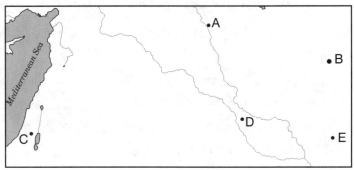

__B__ 40. Achmetha

__D__ 41. Babylon

__C__ 42. Jerusalem

__A__ 43. Nineveh

__E__ 44. Shushan

Total Points: 50

God's Chosen Family as a Nation
Chapter Six Test

Name _____ **Date** _____ **Score** _____

A. *Match. You will not need all the words on the right.*   *(12 points)*

__g__	1. Helped lead the first group of Jews back to Jerusalem	a. Ezra
__f__	2. Foretold that Jesus would be betrayed for thirty pieces of silver	b. Malachi
__e__	3. Rebuilt the walls of Jerusalem	c. Mattathias
		d. Mordecai
__d__	4. Had faith that God would deliver the Jews from Haman's wicked plan	e. Nehemiah
__c__	5. Refused to sacrifice to a Greek idol	f. Zechariah
__b__	6. Rebuked the Jews for despising God's Name	g. Zerubbabel

    *   *   *   *   *   *

__h__	7. A person who pretends to be something that he is not	h. hypocrite
__n__	8. Greek translation of the Old Testament	i. Persian
__k__	9. A holiday observing the Jews' victory over Haman's wicked plan	j. Pharisees
		k. Purim
__i__	10. The empire that ruled Palestine at the time of Malachi	l. Roman
__l__	11. The empire that ruled Palestine when Jesus was born	m. Sadducees
__m__	12. A group of Jews who did not believe in the resurrection	n. Septuagint

B. *Write* true *or* false *in each blank.*   *(7 points)*

_____false_____ 13. King Cyrus of Persia tried to completely stamp out the Jews' religion.

_____true_____ 14. Zechariah recorded a number of visions in his book.

_____false_____ 15. Haman's hatred for Mordecai began after he learned that Mordecai was Esther's cousin.

_____true_____ 16. Haman was hanged on the gallows that he had made for Mordecai.

_____true_____ 17. The king gave the Jews permission to fight against their enemies on the day that Haman had planned to destroy the Jews.

_____true_____ 18. Ezra told the Jews to separate themselves from their heathen wives.

_____false_____ 19. Nehemiah shut the gates of Jerusalem on the Sabbath to keep Tobiah from moving back into the temple.

C. *Fill in the blanks or underline the correct words.* *(6 points)*

20. God said that the (beauty, <u>glory</u>, wealth) of the second temple would be greater than that of the first temple.

21. Zechariah and (<u>Haggai</u>, Nehemiah, Malachi) encouraged the Jews to finish building the temple.

22. The Branch of whom Zechariah spoke is _____Jesus_____.

23. Mordecai saved King (Cyrus's, Alexander's, <u>Ahasuerus's</u>) life by warning him of his servants' plot.

24. After Ezra read the Law, the Jews joyfully kept the Feast of (<u>Tabernacles</u>, Purim, Dedication).

25. _____Malachi_____ was probably the last Old Testament prophet.

D. *Write answers for these questions.* *(10 points)*

26. Why did the old men weep when the foundation for the second temple was laid, even though most of the Jews shouted for joy? _____
   The old men had seen the first temple, which had been much greater.

27. Why did God withhold His blessing from the Jews of Haggai's time? _____
   They were letting His house lie waste while taking care of their own business.

28. Why was it a great risk for Esther to enter the king's inner court without being called? _____
   Anyone who entered the inner court was killed unless the king held out his golden scepter.

29. Why was Ezra ashamed to ask the king for soldiers to protect his group as they traveled to Jerusalem? _____
   Ezra had told the king that God helps those who seek Him.

30. How did the spread of the Greek language help prepare the way for Christ's coming? _____
   People in many lands could understand Greek preaching and could read the Greek Scriptures for themselves.

E. *Write the names of the five Old Testament divisions in order and give the number of books in each group.* Be sure to use the correct spelling.

(10 points)

Names of Old Testament Divisions	Number of Books
31. Books of _____Moses_____	5
32. _____Books of History_____	12
33. _____Books of Poetry_____	5
34. _____Books of Major Prophets_____	5
35. _____Books of Minor Prophets_____	12

Total Points: 45

God's Chosen Family as a Nation
Final Test

Name _____   Date _____   Score _____

A. *Match. Names may be used more than once or not at all.*   *(16 points)*

__h__   1. Was jealous of David

__i__   2. Learned that riches and many wives do not satisfy

__e__   3. Known as the king who made Israel to sin

__a__   4. Heard God's still, small voice on Mount Horeb

__d__   5. Destroyed Baal worship, but continued to worship the golden calves

__c__   6. Kept a great Passover feast that lasted for an extra week

__g__   7. Caused Judah to do worse than the heathen

__f__   8. Fulfilled a prophecy by burning the bones of the idolatrous priests
        on the altar at Bethel

a. Elijah

b. Elisha

c. Hezekiah

d. Jehu

e. Jeroboam

f. Josiah

g. Manasseh

h. Saul

i. Solomon

*   *   *   *   *   *

__o__   9. Prophesied to Jehoiakim and other kings of Judah

__j__   10. Scattered the Israelites of the Northern Kingdom to many lands

__k__   11. Burned Jerusalem and broke down its walls

__l__   12. Made a decree allowing the Jews to return to Jerusalem

__q__   13. Helped lead the first group of Jews back to Judah

__p__   14. Rebuilt the wall of Jerusalem

__m__   15. Went in to a Persian king to save the Jews

__p__   16. Was King Artaxerxes' cupbearer

j. Assyrians

k. Babylonians

l. Cyrus

m. Esther

n. Ezekiel

o. Jeremiah

p. Nehemiah

q. Zerubbabel

B. *Fill in the blanks or underline the correct words.*   *(10 points)*

17. Samuel said that to _____obey_____ is better than sacrifice.

18. The word (*blaspheme*, *covenant*, *supplication*) means "a binding agreement."

19. In fulfillment of Elijah's prophecy, dogs ate most of _____Jezebel_____'s body.

20. Jeremiah foretold that the Jews' captivity in Babylon would last _____seventy_____ years.

21. The Jews at Babylon sat down and _____wept_____ when they remembered Zion.

22. Daniel refused to eat the _____king_____'s _____meat (food)_____.

23. _____Jesus_____ is the Branch of whom Jeremiah and Zechariah prophesied.

24. The feast of (Booths, Dedication, Passover, <u>Purim</u>) was held in remembrance of the Jews' deliverance from Haman's wicked plot.

25. Ezra told the disobedient Jews to (<u>separate from</u>, remain with, try to change) their heathen wives.

26. The widespread use of the (Aramaic, <u>Greek</u>, Hebrew, Latin) language helped the early Christians to spread the Gospel.

C. *Place a check (✓) by the names of kings who were mostly good.*   *(12 points)*

27. _✓_ Asa   _✓_ Uzziah   _____ Manasseh
    _✓_ Jehoshaphat   _✓_ Jotham   _____ Amon
    _____ Jehoram   _____ Ahaz   _✓_ Josiah
    _____ Ahaziah   _✓_ Hezekiah   _____ Jehoiakim

D. *Write answers for the following questions.*   *(12 points)*

28. What covenant did God make with David? _____
    God promised to establish David's kingdom forever. _____
    _____

29. Why did Jeroboam make golden calves at Bethel and Dan? _____
    He wanted to keep the northern tribes from returning to Jerusalem. _____
    _____

30. What request did Elisha make before Elijah was taken up to heaven? _____
    He asked that a double portion of Elijah's spirit would be upon him. _____
    _____

31. How did God fulfill His covenant with David, even though Judah was taken captive? _____
    Jesus was born into David's family, and He will reign forever. _____
    _____

32. What did God want Nebuchadnezzar to recognize about the Most High? _____
    "The most High ruleth in the kingdom of men, and giveth it to whomsoever he will." ___
    _____

33. Why did God withhold His blessings from the Jews of Haggai's time? _____
    The Jews were letting God's house lie waste while taking care of their own business. ___
    _____

E. *Write the names of the Old Testament books and divisions in the correct order.* Be sure to use the correct spelling. *(40 points)*

34. **Books of Moses**

Genesis

Exodus

Leviticus

Numbers

Deuteronomy

Books of History

Joshua

Judges

Ruth

1 & 2 Samuel

1 & 2 Kings

1 & 2 Chronicles

Ezra

Nehemiah

Esther

Books of Poetry

Job

Psalms

Proverbs

Ecclesiastes

Song of Solomon

Books of the

Major Prophets

Isaiah

Jeremiah

Lamentations

Ezekiel

Daniel

Books of the

Minor Prophets

Hosea

Joel

Amos

Obadiah

Jonah

Micah

Nahum

Habakkuk

Zephaniah

Haggai

Zechariah

Malachi

Exercises From "Life in Bible Times" Lessons

F. *Write* true *or* false *in each blank.* *(6 points)*

false 35. A tunic was a special outer coat worn by priests.

true 36. The New Testament instructs women to adorn themselves with a meek and quiet spirit.

true 37. The Old Testament Law permitted divorce.

false 38. Abraham was an ancestor of the Moabites and the Ammonites.

true 39. Bread was the most common food in Bible times.

true 40. The Bible instructs us to work so that we have enough to share with those in need.

G. *Name four kinds of tradesmen mentioned in the Bible.* *(4 points)*

41. (Sample answers) shepherd, farmer, apothecary, baker, carpenter, fisherman, fuller, mason, merchant, potter, smith, tanner, tentmaker, weaver

Total Points: 100

Index of Special Features

Life in Bible Times

Miscellaneous Special Features